Modern
Biblical Scholarship:
Its Impact
on
Theology
and
Proclamation

Modern Biblical Scholarship: Its Impact on Theology and Proclamation

Francis A. Eigo, O.S.A.
Editor

The Villanova University Press

iii

Copyright© 1984 by Francis A. Eigo, O.S.A.
The Villanova University Press
Villanova, Pennsylvania 19085
All rights reserved
Library of Congress Cataloging in Publication Data
Main entry under title:
Modern Biblical scholarship.

Includes index.
1. Bible—Criticism, interpretation, etc.—History—20th
century—Addresses, essays, lectures.
I. Eigo, Francis A.
BS500.M58   1984   220.6'09'04   84-3634
ISBN 0-87723-038-2

À

Marc-Patrice:

"Je rends grâces à mon Dieu

chaque fois que je fais mémoire de vous,

en tout temps dans toutes mes prières

pour vous . . .,

prières que je fais avec joie . . ."

(Épître aux Philippiens 1:3–4).

Contents

Contributors

JOHN R. DONAHUE, S.J., who teaches New Testament Studies at the Jesuit School of Theology and the Graduate Theological Union (Berkeley, California), is the author of a number of articles, essays, book reviews, and books, including *Are You the Christ? The Trial Narrative in the Gospel of Mark.*

ELISABETH SCHÜSSLER FIORENZA is a teacher, an editor *(Aspects of Religious Propaganda in Judaism and Early Christianity)*, and the author of numerous articles on exegetical-theological issues and of such books as *Invitation to Revelation* and *In Memory of Her: A Feminist Theological Reconstruction of Christian Origins.*

ROBERT NORTH, S.J., an archeologist and a teacher at the Pontifical Biblical Institute (Rome), has authored a number of books: *Guide to Biblical Iran, Archeo-Biblical Egypt, Teilhard and the Creation of the Soul, Stratigraphia Geobiblica, In Search of the Human Jesus,* and *Elenchus bibliographicus biblicus* (1979, 1982-).

PETER SCHINELLER, S.J., teaches dogmatic theology at the Catholic Institute of West Africa and has written a number of articles, book reviews, and essays.

W. SIBLEY TOWNER, professor of Biblical Interpretation at the Union Theological Seminary in Virginia, has written articles for scholarly journals and books as well as a book entitled, *How God Deals with Evil.*

BRUCE VAWTER, C.M., on the faculty of DePaul University where he chairs the Department of Theology, is an editor, a consultant, and the author of pamphlets, articles, and books, including *A Path through Genesis, The Bible in the Church, The Conscience of Israel, New Paths through the Bible, Biblical Inspiration, This Man Jesus,* and *On Genesis: A New Reading.*

Introduction

After Elisabeth Schüssler Fiorenza's introductory essay, which gives an overview of contemporary biblical scholarship, this sixteenth volume of the *Proceedings of the Theology Institute of Villanova University* focuses on the various areas of Theology and Proclamation on which Modern Biblical Scholarship has impacted: Creation (Bruce Vawter's essay), the Fall (W. Sibley Towner's), the Economy of Salvation (Robert North's), Christology (Peter Schineller's), and, finally, Revelation (John Donahue's).

At this time an expression of my gratitude to those who have figured in the Theology Institute and the production of this volume is in order: John M. Driscoll, O.S.A., Emily Binns, Bernard A. Lazor, O.S.A., Bernard Prusak, Patricia Fry, and, of course, the essayists—John R. Donahue, S.J., Elisabeth Schüssler Fiorenza, Robert North, S.J., Peter Schineller, S.J., W. Sibley Towner, and Bruce Vawter, C.M.

Francis A. Eigo, O.S.A.,
Editor

Contemporary Biblical Scholarship: Its Roots, Present Understandings, and Future Directions

Elisabeth Schüssler Fiorenza

There is a story about a priest and his very economical housekeeper who used to combine all the leftovers of the week for a Sunday night dinner. Once the priest forgot to say grace, and she reprimanded him: "A priest shouldn't forget to say grace before dinner." "Oh, that's not necessary," was Father's retort: "The food is already blessed six times."[1] There may be the danger that it looks like a warmed up dinner when one addresses so broad a topic as "Contemporary Biblical Scholarship: Its Roots and Present Understandings."[2] All of you are probably familiar with the sentiment that contemporary historical-critical scholarship has its roots in the Enlightenment, that its pathos is anti-doctrinal, rationalistic, and academic-Germanic, but that "modern man" cannot exist without it. This is one of the reasons the Roman Catholic church rejected it for such a long time as "modernism," but finally accepted it wholeheartedly at the Second Vatican Council.

1

I realize that as a representative of contemporary Biblical scholarship I got off to a wrong start. Rather than be somewhat flippant, I should have followed *NCR,* noting in its February 1980 *Forum on Scripture for Today:* "In the world of biblical studies U.S. Catholic Scholars have moved to the front rank." And, the interviewers quote the eminent Roman Catholic Scriptures scholar Raymond Brown as saying: "We are probably the strongest group of biblical scholars in the world in Catholicism right now. Maybe it's chauvinism, but I think we have moved ahead even of Germany."[3] And, he is doubtless correct. Every time I return from a visit to Germany I am impressed by how versatile, open, ecumenical, and engaged American Catholic scholarship is. No inquiry is tabu, no method ruled out from the start, no doctrinal *caveat* enforced.

I.   Roots and Present Self-understanding of Biblical Scholarship.

A.   The Present Crisis of Biblical Scholarship

And yet . . . If one faithfully reads the *Catholic Biblical Quarterly*—as I do—one finds neither here nor in its counterpart, the *Journal of Biblical Literature,* a self-critical evaluation and serious discussion of the methods, goals, and research of Biblical scholarship nor a candid investigation of areas in which Biblical scholarship and traditional teachings are in tension today. The limits of established historical-critical methods, the challenge of Latin American liberation theology, materialist or psychoanalytic exegesis, feminist interpretations, or the ideological implications of Biblical scholarship are rarely discussed or even mentioned. Is Catholic Biblical Scholarship still too insecure in its academic self-identity to raise such basic hermeneutical and theological questions and to critically evaluate its own intellectual enterprise?

First: Some of my colleagues might interject that it is not the task of Biblical scholarship to raise such philosophical and theological questions. The Biblical scholar is an exegete and historian, but not a theologian or preacher. He—and many would still say "he"—must work out what the text meant to the author and original readers and find out what happened and how it happened in Biblical history, but then leave it to the preacher or the teaching authority of the church to say what the text *means* for us today. Disciplined historical-critical scholarship thus restricts itself to the task of philological, historical, and literary analysis. The Biblical scholar addresses the issues and questions raised by the community of historical-literary critical scholars, while the theologian and preacher address the questions of the faith-community today.[4] This argument for the division of labor between historical-critical Biblical scholarship and theology overlooks, however, that Biblical scholarship, insofar as it calls itself *Biblical,* announces not just a historical-literary claim but also expresses a

theological self-understanding insofar as the Bible is the Holy Scripture of Christian communities today. Inasmuch as, e.g., New Testament Studies do not define themselves as explorations of Christian
literature, history and religion of the first century but as *New Testament Studies,* they are not only canonical studies but also related to
the contemporary Christian community which reads the New Testament as Holy Scripture.[5]

However, the questions explored by historical-literary Biblical
scholarship and those raised by believers and churches today are often
so disparate that it is often impossible to "apply" a historical-critical
interpretation, addressing questions of scholarship, to a pastoral situation. The proliferation of commentaries to the lectionary testifies to
this predicament of Biblical scholarship and Biblical preaching. No
wonder that readers of the Bible continue to adhere to a literalist
reading that promises "instant" pietism and that ministers skip
historical-critical exegesis for the sake of actualizing rhetorics. This
dilemma between Biblical scholarship and Biblical preaching is aptly
expressed in the following conversation of two ministers: "When I have
found a text," says the first, "I always begin by studying the context in
order to make sure of its original setting and meaning." "After I have
found a text," replies his colleague, "I never will look up the context
for fear it will spoil the sermon."[6]

Second: A second group of my colleagues might argue that the
established Biblical journals cannot engage in such a discussion of
their scholarly methodological self-understandings because the very
basis of Biblical scholarship as *historical*-theological scholarship is
challenged today. To engage in such a self-critical discussion would
mean to jeopardize all the critical gains that Biblical scholarship has
made in the past two hundred years or so. At Biblical conferences and
in publications there seems to be a war being waged presently, a war
similar to that fought among literary critics for several decades since
the advent and decline of the New Criticism.[7]

For instance, in a recent issue of the *Biblical Theology Bulletin*
Augustine Stock, O.S.B., argues for a replacement of the historical-
critical method through the synchronic approach of the New Criticism
or of structuralism.[8] Whereas the diachronic method of historical-
critical exegesis seeks to reconstruct the historical context of the
Biblical text, to find the original text to reconstruct "what actually
happened" by means of textual and historical criticism, and to narrow
down the diverse meanings of the text to the one "meaning intended by
the author," linguistic structuralism elaborates the "meanings perceived by the readers," and the New Criticism insists that the text
receives its meaning, not from outside itself, but that the text means
what it says and says what it means. Therefore, he argues, we must
work with the text as we have it, rather than postulate antecedent
sources, traditions, or external social-historical "influences."

While Leland White's theological appraisal of historical-critical exegesis is positive, stressing that it has generated historical consciousness and pluralistic understandings in contemporary theology and church,[9] Charles Davis declares categorically: "Historical criticism of the Bible, while it may still have a glorious future as a branch of history, would seem to be near the end of its career in theology."[10] Moreover, "Since theology is concerned with the meanings of Biblical texts themselves and not with their use as clues in an investigation alien to their original intention, it is now time for theology to bow historical criticism out and bow literary criticism in."[11] However, the discussions on the New Criticism and the "New, New Criticism" among American literary critics and among Biblical scholars have progressed beyond this either/or stance proposed by Charles Davis.

Third: A third group of colleagues might argue that historical-critical scholarship has to render a useful service to church and theology by restricting itself to the scientific discussion of what "the text meant" and to the historical reconstruction of what actually happened in the life of Jesus or the early churches, because the present day danger is not too much historical critique but rather literalist pietism and rightist dogmatism. Although literalist biblicism and traditionalist fundamentalism are not restricted to Roman Catholicism, Raymond Brown addresses specifically the Roman Catholic situation. He proposes that Roman Catholic scholarship has moved through three distinct periods in this century.

The first period was plagued by the official Catholic rejection of Biblical criticism (1900-1940). The second period began in the 1940s and climaxed in the acceptance of Biblical Studies with Vatican II and in the church after Vatican II. This period is characterized by a gradual acceptance of historical-biblical scholarship by Roman Catholicism, although the wide-ranging implications of such scholarship are still not quite clearly perceived today. The present period of Biblical criticism, beginning in the 1970s, will have to deal with these ramifications for Catholic ecclesial self-understandings, doctrine, theology, and practice. Brown fears that Biblical criticism could be suffocated by pietism and exaggerated traditionalism as was the case at three other crucial moments in church history—he mentions Jerome, St. Victor in Paris, and Richard Simon—when biblical criticism began to make an impact on Roman Catholic theology.[12]

In order to safeguard the impact of biblical criticism on the church, R.E. Brown suggests a division of labor between the biblical scholar and the teaching authority of the church. Biblical scholarship has the task to say what a text *meant* in its own time and thereby to enable Catholics to see why, e.g., other Christian churches have a different church order or doctrinal position. The teaching office of the church, however, has not to decide what the text *meant* but what it *means* today. Therefore, the meaning of a passage in the literal-historical sense, as worked out by exegesis, might be something quite different from what the official church interpretation of that passage for today teaches. For instance, he argues that the understanding of what Matthew or Luke *meant* in telling us about the origins of Jesus in the infancy narratives can be the same among Catholic and Protestant scholars approaching the texts with the same methods, while the present-day *meaning* of these texts is quite different for a Catholic and Protestant Christian to the extent that the Catholic tradition and doctrine on the Virginal Conception of Jesus inform the understanding of a Catholic today.[13] What the text *meant* for its authors and what it has come to *mean* in the church, therefore, can stand in creative tension.

It seems that the argument in favor of historical-critical exegesis has come full circle here. While historical criticism was developed in confrontation with the dogmatic understandings and doctrinal authority of the institutional church, R.E. Brown stresses the fact that it has remained relatively independent and restricted to Biblical scholars in order to avoid a conflict with the teaching authority of the church. Yet, only time can tell whether the argument will protect Roman Catholicism from a spiritualistic pietism and exaggerated traditionalism emerging within the official church that is intolerant of historical distance and pluralism. Meanwhile, in order to understand this emphasis and clear distinction of what the Bible meant and what it means as the central point in the present crisis of historical-critical Biblical scholarship one has to uncover the roots of this present self-understanding, especially of American Biblical scholarship.

B. . The Immediate Roots of American Biblical Scholarship: Historical-Critical Exegesis and the Biblical Theology Movement

James Barr[14] has pointed out that American Biblical scholarship has restricted the task of the exegete to working out what the text *meant* in response to the so-called Biblical theology movement that flourished after World War II until the early sixties.[15] Common to the entire program was a strong reaction against the ways in which the Bible had been studied under the aegis of "liberal" theology. Analytic philological and often rather dry historical exegesis, with its great reliance on grammar, style, and source-criticism, its rationalism and evolutionism as well as its tendency to understand Biblical materials in terms of its cultural environment and surrounding religions, had lacked for many an explicitly theological and existential concern.[16]

Vis-à-vis such a dry philological-historical exegesis and history of religions approach in historical-critical scholarship as well as over and against dogmatic-systematic strictures, the Biblical theology movement asserted the uniqueness of Biblical thought and theology by emphasizing the following aspects:[17]

1) It stressed its opposition to philosophy and universalizing-systematizing philosophical theology. Biblical thought was contrasted with philosophical modes of thinking. Therefore, it opposed the systematizing tendencies of dogmatic theology. Biblical thought could not be reduced to a dogmatic system since it was a living organism. As such, this movement was parallel to the neo-orthodox movement in general theology. At the same time, it identified Biblical thought as Hebrew thought which was distinctly different from the Greek thought that dominated dogmatic thinking. Systematic theology, in turn, had been distorted by its adoption of Greek categories.

2) This movement stressed the unity of the Bible and maintained that the New Testament had to be understood solely in terms of Old Testament-Hebrew thought. This emphasis on the Hebrew thought-character of the Old Testament, however, entailed at the same time a very negative understanding of early Judaism, the dominant environment in which the New Testament originated because intertestamental Judaism was influenced by Greek thought. Correlative with the stress on the unity of the Bible was its emphasis on the distinctiveness of the Bible over and against its environment. The cultural-religious parallels that existed were only partial and isolated phenomena.

3) The theological basis for this emphasis on unity and distinctiveness of the Bible was understanding God's revelation in history. The whole of history was conceived as *Heilsgeschichte* — salvation history. Revelation in and through history was assumed to be typically for Hebrew thought, unknown to the extrabiblical world but characteristic for the entire Bible.

Although the Biblical theology movement appears not to have developed its own particular methods, two emphases seem to have been characteristic for its way of doing exegesis: It stressed, on the one hand, the "word-study" method and, on the other hand, engendered a division of labor within theology because it was not able to integrate theological claims and historical method.

✓ *First:* Word-Study-Method was advocated in the hope that it was possible to trace the outlines of Biblical Hebrew thought in and through the words of the Hebrew language. Greek words, when they came to be used in Christian writings, were assumed to take on Hebraic content and to mirror the Jewish-Christian-Hebrew thought pattern.[18] To interlink the New Testament even closer with Hebrew thought it was often assumed that its writings were either translations from a Hebrew or Aramaic source or that their forms and outlines were patterned after forms and books of the Hebrew Bible. One of the major tools for Biblical theology was Kittel's *Dictionary of the New Testament*,[19] which traces words of the New Testament back to their Hebrew roots. Although this method has been thoroughly debunked by modern semantics and structuralism, it is still widely in use, probably because it allows for an easy extraction of "theological thought" from Biblical texts without having to enter into the literary-historical complexities raised by historical-critical exegesis. Moreover, although modern linguistics has rejected the evolutionism of the word-study method, its emphasis on the "text" and its anthropological essential substructures to the detriment of its historical context allows for a similar easy access to the Biblical texts and their religious constructs without the encumbrances of historical-sociological reconstructions.

Second: In contrast to the history of religions approach, the Biblical theology movement insisted that the Bible should be interpreted for believing communities today, and not simply to be explained with a dry philological or historical statement about the past. Yet, at the same time, this movement maintained that Biblical theology must not simply work with modern categories and reconstructive models, but must submit itself to those of the Bible and Hebrew thought. Against theology it maintained that only a theocentric method, concentrating on the kerygma, is appropriate for biblical interpretation. In Old Testament Studies Eissfeldt and Sellin, e.g., urged a twofold method: historical investigation of Hebrew religion and systematic presentation of the timeless truth of Old Testament revelation in classical theological categories.[20] In New Testament studies O. Cullmann[21] found the key to New Testament theology in time, maintaining that the categories of time and history rather than of essence, eternal or existential truth and normative principles are decisive for Biblical theology. As O. Betz summed up: "The difficulty with Biblical theology lies in the fact that it comprises a diversity of witness interrelated with history rather than a theological system. Yet Biblical theology should take its principle of exposition from the Bible itself. It is not possible to grasp the Hebrew way of thought in the Bible with the systematic principle which came from Greek thought and wove itself into Christian dogma" and ethics.[22]

Writing in 1960 and 1968 review articles on American New Testament Scholarship[23] in the past fifty years, Henry J. Cadbury and R.M. Grant respectively defend and exalt historical-critical inquiry but mention Biblical theology only in passing. Ironically, Cadbury characterizes the Biblical theology movement as focusing on the Gospel *about* Jesus and on the unity of New Testament and Old Testament, but he does not mention a single one of its proponents by name. The quest for the historical Jesus has, according to him, been supplanted by concern for interpretation on a different plane. "Not what Jesus did and said but what his figure meant or means is nowadays to the fore. History is still used of him—but it is the cosmic fact of history—of *Heilsgeschichte* that many are concerned with, not with the minor features of his life and teaching."[24]

Even more sweeping is the comment of R.M. Grant:

The basic method among my teachers, I believe, can be put very simply.

> It was to try to find out what writings meant to their authors and first readers and to find out, as far as history was concerned, what happened and how it happened. . . . It is true that during the quarter of a century since then there has been a tremendous emphasis upon the theological meaning of the NT and of early Christian literature in general. This emphasis now reminds me of the Augustan propaganda literature determined to exalt the empire at the expense of the republic. [25]

After having described American scholarship as characterized by "common sense" combined with a daring "to damn the torpedos" and "steam ahead," he suggests that the American motto might well be expressed as "Investigate, then invest," since Americans not only like to keep their feet on the ground but "in the ground," as their concern with archeology and paleography rather than philosophical theology indicates. He concludes his article by stating that the work and permanent achievement of the period were done by those whose "goal was understanding rather than proclamation. They did not sell their birthright as critics and historians for what has been called 'a pot of message'." [26]

Ernest Cadman Colwell is more constructive in his assessment of New Testament theological scholarship since, as a member of the "Chicago school," he is more open to form criticism. Yet, he bemoans the fact that Biblical theology is too strongly influenced by philosophy and systematic theology. He, therefore, suggests that it should be called Systematic-Biblical theology in order to distinguish it from a future Historical-Biblical theology which he saw emerging from the "post-Bultmannian" discussions of the "new quest for the historical Jesus." While Systematic-Biblical theology, in his opinion, has only unsatisfactorily dealt with the problems arising from the historical nature of Christian faith, Historical-Biblical theology will be—so he hopes—"more sophisticated in theology and philosophy than some of our past studies, and it will be historically more comprehensively-rigorous than much of our contemporary study." [27]

In his influential article on Biblical theology which appeared in 1962 in the *Interpreter's Dictionary of the Bible,* Krister Stendahl sought to do justice to the historical-critical as well as theological-contemporary concerns of Biblical scholarship. He proposed two distinct tasks and three stages for doing Biblical theology. The first was a descriptive task. [28] The exegete must give an objective historical analysis and description of the "data" of the Bible. Stendahl stresses objective analysis and scientific description of "what the text meant" in its historical context as the primary task of the exegete. The task of the theologian, on the other hand, is, according to him, the hermeneutical task through which a "translation" or application of Biblical statements and thoughts into modern situation and thought horizon was to be attempted. These two tasks, the exegetical working out what the Bible meant and the hermeneutic-theological stating of what the Bible means today, must be strictly kept apart in order to do justice to the historical-critical task of the exegete as well as to the theological-interpretive task of the contemporary Biblical theologian.

This distinction was widely accepted and — as we have seen — is still operative in Biblical scholarship today. Stendahl proposes a three stage method[29] for Biblical theology:

> With the original in hand, and after due clarification of the hermeneutic principles involved, we may proceed toward tentative answers to the question of the meaning here and now . . . How much of the two last stages should belong to the discipline of Biblical studies or to what extent they call for teamwork with the disciplines of theology and philosophy is a practical question which in itself indicates the nature of the problem. If the three stages are carelessly intermingled, the theology as well as the preaching in our churches becomes a mixed or even an inarticulate language.[30]

However, it must not be overlooked that Stendahl stresses the distinction between "what the text meant" and "what it means" in tween Old Testament and New Testament, as well as a common basis for today, the "sacred history" of the people of God.[31] Descriptive Biblical theology thus seems to give him the hermeneutical key that allows for a common hermeneutical bond between the contemporary church and that of the New Testament era. Consequently, he maintains that the pulpit is the place or "life situation" where "the meaning of the original meets with the meaning for today."[32]

However, it must not be overlooked that Stendahl stresses the distinction between "what the text meant" and "what it means" in order to emphasize that "the descriptive task has no claim or intention toward the normative. This is of utmost importance, since anything called 'biblical' has a tendency to participate in the authority assigned to the Bible in Christian churches."[33] In other words, Stendahl maintains that the biblical exegete and historian does not seek to answer the normative question of what, e.g., Paul's theological statements "*mean*" in a timeless and absolute manner. Insofar as Stendahl defines the problem of what the "text means" in a normative manner and ascribes to it an ahistorical or transhistorical character, which must be elaborated by the systematic theologian and preacher, his proposal anticipates that of Raymond E. Brown who, however, ascribes the normative task to the teaching office of the church. Stendahl's theological *interest* points, of course, in the opposite direction from that of Brown. As H. Boers has stressed, the Reformation maintained that the Bible was not part of the contemporary life of the church but belonged to the historical past in order "to establish the Bible as the sole base and norm over against the contemporary church by means of which to judge and renew it." Yet, in doing so, the Reformers "set a process in

motion which made it increasingly questionable how a collection of
documents from the past could be normative for the present."[34]

In his response to Stendahl, A. Dulles recognizes this and therefore
stresses continuity:

> What the text meant to the inspired author and as taken up in the in-
> spired tradition, is still normative. While the church's understanding of
> Scripture is far from static, it is not so fluid that the meaning in biblical
> times has lost all binding force. If the original meaning is in any sense
> normative, the basis of Stendahl's dichotomy is seriously impaired.[35]

At the same time, he concedes that such a claim to the normative
value of "what the Bible meant" would mean a "confessional" approach in biblical theology. However, he also maintains a descriptive
objective, scientific, non-committed approach on the level of factual
biblical history and the description of the religious history of the Bible.
He is able to do so because he takes over R. de Vaux's[36] distinctions of
three levels of biblical work: the level of the historical, of the history of
religions, and that of theological inquiry. Yet, contemporary discussions on biblical method and hermeneutics throw into question such
dichotomies in the self-understanding of biblical scholarship as
historical-textual interpretation.

C. Method and Hermeneutics

Biblical scholarship agrees widely on what kind of methods[37] and
procedures are involved in working out an "objective" description of
what the text meant within its socio-historical context. Critical Biblical
scholarship demands that we give adequate reasons for the assertions
we make, that we are cognizant of the research pertaining to the interpretation of a certain Biblical text, and that the various disciplines involved in the historical-critical method must control our analysis,
scholarly argument, and historical reconstruction. The "external"
disciplines of the historical-critical method[38] are philology, archeology, and ancient history which correlate the Biblical text with
evidence from independent sources. Textual, source, form, tradition,
and redaction history and criticism deal with the "internal" analysis of
the text.

Linguistic, rhetorical, architectonic, literary, genre, structuralist or
deconstructionist analyses[39] have been added in recent years for enabling the interpreter to understand the text as text and to chart the
literary dynamics of a biblical book more fully. Thus, the historical-
critical method has become a historical-literary critical method that
defines the enterprise of contemporary Biblical studies. While at the
beginning literary critics absolutized the synchronic reading of the
biblical text over and against the diachronic readings of traditional
historical-critical studies, an equilibrium in methods seems gradually

to be accepted today. Insofar as many historical texts, and especially Biblical texts, have predominantly social communicative and not primarily aesthetic functions, their social-historical setting needs to be explored in order to understand their meanings. [40]

While the New Criticism and certain directions in Structuralism deny any scientific-theoretical possibility for a diachronic reading of texts, epistemological discussions among literary critics and historians have highlighted that such an abstractionist-positivist understanding of language and texts is not justified. [41] Any literary theory must place the literary work at "the meeting point of two 'axes' of literature: the rhetorical axis of communication connecting author and reader and the mimetic axis of representation connecting language and information." [42] By extending the horizontal rhetorical axis beyond implied author and reader, one can see the actual author and reader against their "world" as a source of motivation or a field for action. By extending the vertical-mimetic axis, one can understand language systems as different ways of utilizing the world as reservoir of signs, while "world-views" emerge as results of employing signs to represent them. In other words, the critical study of a Biblical text begins with language and literary analysis but cannot eschew social-historical analysis if it intends methodically to elaborate and scientifically to describe "what the text meant" in its social-ecclesial-historical situation.

First: Such a "scientific" reading of the Bible makes the text the object of its attention. It places "distance" between the text and the interpreter, the world of the text and that of the exegete, the worldview of the text and that of the contemporary believer. This "distancing" effect is part of a "historical consciousness" that allows the community of faith "to disengage itself" from its past as well as from its present socio-cultural embeddedness and mistakes.

Leander E. Keck has, therefore, argued that historical analysis and reconstruction is a "major factor in the community's capacity to come to terms with its own past—precisely in relation to its canon." [43] It is historical-critical analysis that allows the Christian church, e.g., to recognize its Jewish roots and therefore to reject antisemitism in its teachings and practice as well as in past and present biblical interpretations of exegetical commentators. In short, the methods of historical-critical scholarship and its diachronic reconstructions "distance" us in such a way from the Biblical communities, writers, and texts that they critically-theologically relativize not only them but also us by elucidating their and our own culture- and time-boundedness. Thus, historical-criticism enables contemporary Christian communities as well as scholars to be self-critical.

Biblical texts have a long history of reception, interpretation, and use. In the process they have been understood in terms of certain dogmatic assumptions, cultural ideologies or church practices. Contemporary believers approach them with their own dogmatic questions

and spiritual interests. Certain biblical texts are quoted over and over
again so that they have lost their meaning and have become
stereotypical injunctions. By "distancing" the text, historical-critical
interpretation seeks to make it "alien" to our own experiences, expec-
tations, and interests. This is an important *theological* function of
historical-critical scholarship insofar as Christian faith and community
are bound back to the historical person Jesus of Nazareth and to the
witness of his first followers and believers.[44]

Thus, historical-critical interpretation of the Bible can function as a
theological corrective in the process of the reception of Biblical texts by
the Christian community.

1. It asserts the meaning of the original witness over and against
later dogmatic and societal usurpations, for different purposes.

2. It makes the assimilation of the text to our own experience,
parochial pietism, and church-interests, more difficult.

3. It keeps alive the "irritation" of the original text by challenging
our own assumptions, worldview, and practice.

4. It limits the number of interpretations which can be given to a
text. The "spiritual" meanings of a biblical text are limited by its
literal-historical meanings.

Second: The goal and paradigm of historical-critical method has
changed in the past fifty years. While in the last century Biblical exegesis sought to determine with scientific exactitude what actually
happened in the life of Jesus or Paul, source-, form-, and redaction-
criticism shifted the focus on the early Christian communities and
writers who produced the New Testament texts. Their needs, interests
and debates play a major role in the reasoning and reconstructions by
historical biblical scholars.

Form- and redaction-criticism have demonstrated that[45] the biblical
tradition is not a doctrinal or a exegetical tradition, but a living tradition of the community of faith. In order to understand biblical texts, it
is important not just to analyze and understand the context of a given
text but also to know and determine the situation and community to
which this text is addressed. This is obvious when we study the Pauline
letters. Whereas the Pauline literature has long been seen as a com-
pendium of the theological teaching and principles of Paul, scholars
today understand them as letters and not as dogmatic handbooks. The
letter of Paul to the Galatians could not have been written to the
Corinthians and vice versa. Similarly, the Gospels were written for concrete communities with specific problems and theological understandings. It is therefore necessary not only to study the content of the
biblical writings but also to determine the situation and type of community to which they were written.[46]

Form-, source-, and redaction-criticism have shown that the material that the "biblical" writers transmit was collected and selected and
formulated in such a way that it could speak to the needs and situation

of the community of faith. The materials and traditions about Jesus, for instance, were selected and reformulated so that they would have meaning for the Christian community that transmitted them. It can be seen that the early Christians were true in their usage of the Jesus-traditions. They changed or reformulated them and reinterpreted them by bringing them into a different context and framework. Not only does Matthew change the form of Mark's text on the great commandment from a scholarly dialogue to a controversy dialogue, but he also reformulates the question. Whereas in Mark the lawyer asks which commandment is the chief or first commandment, Matthew changes the question into one concerning the "key" to the Law, in order to adapt the question to the Jewish discussion, where it was most important to know how one could do justice to the six hundred thirteen commandments. Luke, on the other hand, connects the controversy dialogue with the story of the Good Samaritan and shifts the emphasis from knowing the commandments to doing them.[47] Thus, the Gospel writers were not content to repeat formulas and stories just because they belonged to the tradition, but they reformulated them in order to respond to the needs of the Christians of their own day.

However form- and redaction-critical studies can be criticized for focusing too narrowly on the community and for conceptualizing the situation of the early Christian communities too much in terms of a confessional struggle between different theologies and church groups. Such a reconstruction often reads like the history of the European Reformation in the sixteenth century or a description of a small town in America where five or six churches of different Christian groups are built within walking distance of one another. We must, therefore, recognize that the early Christian writers responded not only to inner-theological or inner-church problems, but that the early Christian communities were missionary communities,[48] deeply embedded in their own culture or critically distancing themselves from it. The biblical writers transmit their faith response to the cultural and religious problems of their own time. They indicate that Christian faith can be acculturated or countercultural.

The studies of the social world of early Christianity underline that Christian faith and revelation are always intertwined with their cultural, political, and societal contexts, so that we no longer are able neatly to separate biblical revelation from its cultural expression. It does not suffice to understand texts just as religio-theological texts. What is necessary also is to analyze their socio-political contexts and expression. While, for instance, the historicist approach to the miracles of the New Testament discusses whether or not they actually could have happened or whether they happened as they are told, the historical-theological approach debates whether miracle-faith is a genuine Christian expression of faith or whether it shares too much in the magic beliefs of the times when it understands Jesus in analogy to the miracle-workers of antiquity.

While the historical-theological understanding emphasizes a "heretical" Christian group as the proponent of such crude miracle-faith, the societal interpretation of miracle points out that miracle-faith was wide-spread in lower classes who were uneducated and did not have money for medical treatment. The miracle stories, therefore, strengthen the hope of those who were exploited and oppressed. For instance, the demon in MK 5:1-13 is called Legion, with the same name as the Roman soldiers who occupied Palestine. The story presents an irony of the Roman exploitation when it has the demon expelled into a herd of pigs, animals that were, for Jewish sensitivities, the paradigm of ritual impurity. Miracle-faith is here protest against bodily and political suffering. It gives courage to resist all the life-destroying power of one's society.

In sum: In reinterpreting their traditions, the biblical writers do not follow the doctrinal or historicist paradigm but the paradigm of pastoral or practical theology, insofar as the concrete pastoral situation of the community is determinative for the selection, transmission, and creation of biblical traditions.[49] The New Testament authors rewrote their traditions in the form of letters, gospels, or apocalypses, because they felt theologically compelled to illuminate or to censure the beliefs and praxis of their communities. The biblical books are thus written with the intention of serving the needs of the community of faith and not of revealing timeless principles or transmitting historically accurate records. They, therefore, do not locate revelation just in the past but also in their own present, thereby revealing a dialectical understanding between present and past. The past, on the one hand, is significant because revelation happened decisively in Jesus of Nazareth. On the other hand, the writers of the New Testament can exercise freedom with respect to the Jesus traditions because they believe that the Jesus who spoke speaks now to his followers through the Holy Spirit.

The relevance of this understanding of tradition is obvious for the Scriptures. We have to learn that not all texts speak to all situations and to everyone. It is therefore necessary for the minister to learn how to determine the situation and needs of his or her congregation with the same sophistication with which he/she studies the biblical texts. A repetition of biblical texts does not suffice. For example, if a minister preached about the theology of grace expressed in Rom 9-11 during the time of the Nazis but did not say something about the gas chambers of Auschwitz and the annihilation of the Jewish people, s/he did not preach the gospel but perverted the biblical message. The "pastoral-theological" paradigm does not permit a mere repetition or application of biblical texts, but demands a translation of their meaning and context into our own situation.

Third: Biblical hermeneutics[50] seeks to explore the dialectic among past and present, biblical texts and our own contemporary understandings operative in the process of interpretation. It seeks to illuminate *how* "translation" of "what the text meant" to "what the text means" today takes place in the act of interpretation and proclamation. While Stendahl proposed that exegesis and normative interpretation are the two poles of the hermeneutical dialogue, Ricoeur distinguishes explanation and understanding as the two poles of the hermeneutical arc. While explanation is truly methodical, understanding is the first step toward bringing back to life a particular text.[51] As we have seen, in historical-critical description interpreters must seek to silence their own subjectivity and strive for a detached objectivity which excludes the existential-religious questions which the Bible addresses. Such historical inquiry is necessary because of its distancing function so that the text can speak for itself and not merely mirror the ideas of the interpreter. Yet, such historical-critical exegesis is either only preliminary to the interpretive act or it it restricted to the historico-critical exegete in distinction to the systematic theologian or the ecclesial teaching office.

Hermeneutical theory rejects this dichotomy in the process of understanding and questions the subject-object relationship between the interpreter and the text. It conceives of the interpretive task as a continuous dialogue between the interpreter and the text or the "world" of the text that has as its goal a fusion of horizons. While so-called descriptive exegesis seeks to eliminate the subjectivity of the interpreter in order to produce an objective description of "what the text meant," the hermeneutical circle situates interpreter and biblical text within an ongoing and corrective dialogue.[52] To understand what the "text means" is to understand "what the text meant" and vice-versa. Therefore, no division of labor between the descriptive biblical exegete and the interpreting systematic theologian is possible.

R. Bultmann[53] has already argued that understanding is possible only because we share certain existential concerns and anthropological presuppositions with the authors of biblical texts. The interpreter's mind is not a *tabula rasa,* but before we attempt to understand how an author deals with a certain subject-matter or before we can get interested in a text, we have to have a certain common experience, understanding or life-relation to the issues and "world" which the text expresses. Just as we must have an appreciation of music in order to understand a text-book on musicology, so must the biblical interpreter have a certain relationship to the intentionality and subject matter of Biblical texts. Therefore, "presuppositionless" exegesis is not only not possible but also not desirable.

Moreover, as Gadamer has pointed out, every interpreter stands within a historical tradition of interpretation which provides her/him with certain preunderstandings and prejudgments.[54] It is necessary to

bring these presuppositions and prejudgments to consciousness so that
the temporal and cultural distance between the interpreter and the
text comes to the fore.[55] Only the awareness of the differences between
their respective horizons allows the distinctive message of the text to
reshape the questions, concepts, values, and horizon of the interpreter.
In the process of interpretation "the rights of the text" must be
guarded, acceptance or consent to the text sought if a "fusion" or
"communion" of horizons is to be achieved. However, to enter the
hermeneutical circle with a prejudice forecloses the dialogue with the
text and makes an encounter with it impossible.

In short, understanding takes place in a circular manner: interpretation and answer are to a certain extent determined by our
presuppositions, prejudgments as well as by the questions we ask and
how we ask them. Our questions and readings, in turn, are confirmed,
extended, or corrected by the text. A new question then grows out of
this understanding, so that the hermeneutical circle continues to
develop in a never ending spiral of deeper and deeper understanding.
However, illegitimate prejudice refuses to alter its preconceived questions and judgments when new insights and understandings are derived from the text. Such a refusal to be challenged by the text reduces
the hermeneutical spiraling process of interpretation to a repetitive
circle. Nevertheless, P. Stuhlmacher insists:

> Historical-critical exegesis is not in and of itself theological interpreta-
> tion of scripture. But it can be such when it is hermeneutically reasoned
> out as an interpretation of consent to the biblical texts, and when it is
> carried on theologically in regard for the enduring hermeneutical
> relevance for the Third Article of the Apostles' Creed.[56]

Since the New Hermeneutic has links with the thought of R.
Bultmann, it is also concerned with the relevance and effectiveness of
Christian preaching. However, it is more concerned with the
linguisticality and the "rights of the text" as text so that the text can
become not only an illumination of, but also a challenge to, present
experience. "The preacher 'translates' the text by placing it at the
point of encounter with the hearer from which it speaks anew into
his(*sic*) own world in his (*sic*) own language."[57]

However, hermeneutical theory does not stress critical consciousness
as much as it emphasizes surrender and fidelity to the Biblical text.
This comes to the fore, e.g., in Sandra Schneiders' proposal that seeks
to utilize especially Gadamer's hermeneutical theory for Roman
Catholic biblical interpretation. She argues that exegesis is not a
science but an art. Just as there are techniques for playing a musical
instrument, so there are techniques for analyzing a text. But, such
techniques must be integrated into and must serve the artistic process
of interpretation:

> Just as the score remains normative for the musician, and the rendition is always judged by the score and by the history of interpretation of the piece, so the interpretation of the exegete remains always under the judgment of the text and of the faith tradition of the church.[58]

She argues that philosophical hermeneutical theory also enables us to relate the Biblical interpretation of the "ordinary" Christian with that of the exegete. She likens the interpretation of the believing community to the enjoyment of listening to a symphony and that of the exegete to the musicians who reenact the musical score of the symphony. "Unless *someone* can play Chopin the ordinary person will never have the chance to appreciate his music"[59] In a similar fashion, it is the exegete who makes the meaning of the text available to the community. Finally, she identifies biblical interpretation with the "excess of religious meaning," because the biblical text is "a mediation of meaning about the relation of God and the human race."[60]

However, this delineation of the relationship between exegete/preacher and the "ordinary" believer seems to expect at the same time too much and too little from biblical scholarship. It ascribes too much to biblical scholars/preachers insofar it likens their work to that of artists reenacting a symphony. Yet, insofar as "ordinary" members of the community have the skill of reading, they are able to understand and interpret a text.[61] Insofar as they are able to read the text itself, not only the "score" of a work is accessible to them, but also the "making of music" in the sense that the technique of reading is equivalent to the technique of playing the violin. "Ordinary" believers may not be accomplished as "artists," but exegete/preachers are also not yet "artists" in interpretation just because they have the techniques and knowledge of historico-critical interpretation. Insofar as "ordinary" Christians do not have sufficient philological, historical, archeological, theological or literary skills of interpretation, their "readings" are necessarily limited or distorted. However, their "readings" might often be more accurate and expressive than that of exegetes because they share the religious experience or the social "Sitz im Leben" of a text.

In short, I would maintain that the "ordinary" believer and the professional biblical interpreter or preacher should not be related to each other as non-expert and expert, or as consumer and producer of meaning. Rather than understand biblical scholars in analogy to artists making present the meaning of biblical texts for today, I would suggest that they are more like cultural critics who subject historico-critical interpretations of their colleagues as well as those of "ordinary" believers and preachers to a critical evaluative process and hermeneutics of liberation.[62]

The consensual-hermeneutical self-understanding of biblical scholarship seems, therefore, too restrictive insofar as it eliminates the critical task of biblical interpretation or relegates it to historical-critical method, defined as description or explanation, but excludes it from the "artistic re-enactment" of biblical texts and meanings. Yet, such a critical aspect of biblical scholarship must be maintained, not just with respect to what the text "meant," but also to "what it means today," since we are never able to say what the text means without saying what it meant and vice-versa. Rather than eliminating preliminary assumptions and presuppositions, they have to become conscious in a public critical discussion and interpretation.

Biblical students, therefore, should not be trained just in historical critical analysis but also learn to reflect methodologically on their own presuppositions, interests, prejudices, commitments as well as on those of scholarly commentators or theological writers. They must learn to analyze critically the presupposed frameworks and implicit interests of scholarly as well as of pietistic and ecclesiastical interpretations of the Bible. Historical-criticism becomes theological-criticism whenever this task of the biblical scholar is taken seriously. This is also stressed by Paul Hanson:

> Throughout the world, in bodies large and small, similar retrenchment and declaration of immunity to criticism are occurring. More emphatically in the present moment than in any time in the recent past, professors of the Bible and biblically-trained pastors and church leaders are called back to one of their responsibilities that has slipped into neglect. They must subject to ongoing criticism the ways in which Scripture is being used and the sources of the presuppositions guiding both the scholarly and the popular use of the Bible, whether they are derived from dogma, cultural fads, national ideologies, or philosophical assumptions. In holding biblical theologians to account, we can measure their activities against the two qualities required of all professions, moral responsibility and self-criticism of guiding principles and presuppositions.[63]

At the same time, such critical-theological interpretation of Scripture must not just evaluate the contemporary interpretations of biblical texts but also move from "a hermeneutics of consent" to a "hermeneutics of suspicion" with regard to the Bible itself in order not only to understand biblical texts and their worlds of meaning but also to evaluate them in terms of a critical theology of liberation. Already A. Schlatter has called for such a critical biblical theology:

> We can never give past occurrence absolute power to shape us so that the telling of what was could render our judgment superfluous, or tradition replace our own reflection . . . We are always called to an act of reflection, in which our own personality forms its judgment.[64]

Such a self-understanding of biblical scholarship as the critical-theological evaluation of present as well as past interpretations and articulations of the religious experiences of biblical people is increasingly developed today by liberation theology, and especially in the context of a critical feminist theology of liberation.[65]

II.   *Toward a New Critical Self-understanding of Biblical Scholarship.*

In contradistinction to hermeneutical theology, liberation theologies in all different forms maintain that the goal of biblical interpretation is not only understanding but also, ultimately, a new, different praxis.[66] Biblical interpretation must not just aim at the understanding of biblical texts and their meanings; it does not merely ask for a "hermeneutics of consent," but seeks to foster a new liberation praxis in the community of believers. Thus, "the meaning of a text is disclosed not only in reflection upon it but also in concrete social action based on it."[67] Moreover, a critical-theological evaluation, not only of contemporary biblical interpretations and their interests but also of those of biblical traditions and writers, derives its criteria of evaluation from its theoretical and practical commitment to the contemporary struggle for liberation.

A.   *The Challenge of Liberation Theology*

Liberation theologies, then, do not only call for a critical-theological analysis and evaluation of contemporary biblical interpretations as well as of biblical texts, but also challenge biblical scholars, preachers, and the whole Christian community to articulate their theological commitment and engagement in the liberation struggle of those who suffer from patriarchal oppressions: from racial, sexual, colonial, as well as economic and technological exploitation. The basic methodological starting-point of liberation theologies is the insight that all theology, knowingly or not, is by definition always engaged for or against the oppressed.[68] Intellectual neutrality is not possible in a historical world of exploitation and oppression. If this is the case, then theology cannot talk about human existence in general, or about biblical theology in particular, without identifying whose human existence is meant and about whose God the biblical symbols and texts speak. This avowed "advocacy" stance of all liberation theologies seems to be the major point of contention between academic historical-critical or liberal-systematic theology on the one side and liberation theology on the other.[69]

Insofar as a detached self-understanding of Biblical scholarship prides itself on being impartial, value-neutral, objective-descriptive, scientific-antiquarian, it must reject any feminist reconstruction of early Christian history or liberation-theological interpretation of the Bible as "ideological" and "unscientific" because it is influenced by present-day concerns. A feminist or liberationist interpretation, in turn, cannot acknowledge the claims and assumptions made by such biblical scholars as valid if it does not want to relinquish its own interests in women's Biblical past and heritage. While a value-neutral, detached, scientific Biblical scholarship, e.g., can collect the Biblical passages on "women," it cannot conceive of women as equally involved in shaping early Christian origins and articulating its religious vision. It cannot do so because it understands androcentric Biblical sources as "data" and "evidence" as well as its own androcentric linguistic interpretative models and narrative as totally divorced from contemporary concerns.[70] Such scholarship, claiming to be "objective" and "neutral," is, however, not more value-free and less ideological because it hides its subjectivity, culture-boundedness and contemporary interests from itself.[71]

Over and against the objectivist-reified or hermeneutical-dialogic understanding of the Bible, liberation theologians maintain that theology as well as biblical interpretation are never done in an institutional and personal vacuum but, consciously or not, are always "interpretation for." In order to be able to sustain the "advocacy stance," the interpreter of the Bible must first understand her own experience, adopt a clear political-social-theological analysis, and act upon her commitment to the oppressed and marginalized.

Segundo has outlined four decisive factors in the liberation-theological hermeneutic of the Bible. Our experience of reality leads us to ideological suspicion(1), which applies itself to the whole ideological superstructure in general and to theology in particular(2). This new way of experiencing theological reality leads us to "exegetical" suspicion that the prevailing interpretations of Scripture have not done justice to all biblical texts and to the reality about which they speak or are silent(3). Finally, we interpret Scripture within our new theological perspective(4) that sheds fresh light on all previous readings of the text.[72] For instance, women who have become consciousness-raised and self-identified as women will experience a tension between their own self-understanding and the position of women in the church(1) which leads them to scrutinize prevailing androcentric theological systems(2). This new insight, that theology was formulated by men and in the interest of patriarchal male structures, will lead them to question the prevailing androcentric interpretations of Scripture(3). Now reading Scripture from a feminist theological perspective will result in a new interpretation of Scripture which will take into account not only androcentric language but also patriarchal tendencies that have already informed the biblical writers(4).

In addition, liberation theologians maintain that their preunderstanding—the option for the poor—is not eisegesis but exegesis, insofar as this message is already found in the text: the God of the Bible is the God of the poor and oppressed.[73] At this point it becomes apparent that the critical hermeneutical task of feminist theology is more complicated since it cannot state without qualification that the "God of the Bible is the God of women," [74] because there is considerable evidence that the Bible was not only used against women's liberation but also seems to have no clear "option" for women's liberation. [75]

Segundo is aware that some biblical texts are oppressive formulations, but argues that they must be understood as faith-responses in certain historical situations. Therefore, he maintains that biblical interpretations must reconstruct the "second-level learning process" of biblical faith. Faith is identical with the total process of learning in and through ideologies; it is an educational process throughout biblical and Christian history. This second-level educational process expresses the continuity and permanency of biblical revelation, whereas ideologies document the first-level, historical character of biblical revelation. "In the case of . . . . the Bible we learn to learn by entrusting our life and its meaning to the historical process that is reflected in the expressions embodied in that particular tradition." [76]

It is obvious that Segundo's interpretative model stands within the hermeneutic-dialogical paradigm. He shares with Neo-Orthodoxy the hermeneutical presupposition that Scriptural traditions are meaningful, that the process engendered by the Scriptural traditions are meaningful, that the process engendered by the Bible can be trusted, and that it can, therefore, claim our "empathy" and "consent." Yet, in contradistinction to neo-orthodox theology, Segundo does not claim that the content of biblical texts is *eo ipso* meaningful and liberative, but maintains that only the educational faith process engendered by them is meaningful and liberative.

However, by separating content and process to such a degree, the "advocacy stance" for the oppressed cannot develop its full critical potential. Feminist theology, therefore, insists that we have to bring to bear a critical evaluation and "hermeneutics of suspicion," not only upon the content, but also upon the process of biblical tradition as well as upon biblical texts themselves. The critical evaluation of literary works demanded by feminist literary critics must also be carried out by a critical-theological feminist interpretation of biblical texts and their historical impacts and effects:

> The traditional formalist assumption has been that the reader should 'give in' to the vision imposed by the work . . . I believe that rather than suspending disbelief and allowing the ethics of the text to be imposed upon one by the form, one should enter into the fictional world . . . only if it seems that the characters and situations depicted therein are authentic and just. Whenever one cannot accept the ethics of the text, one cannot accept the aesthetics. [77]

To paraphrase and restate this statement theologically: whenever one cannot accept the religious, political, personal ethos and ethics of a biblical text, one cannot accept its authority as revealed and as Holy

Scripture; that is, if one does not want to turn the biblical God into a God of oppression. Such a critical evaluation of biblical texts cannot locate inspiration in the text, even not in its "surplus" or polyvalence of meaning. Instead, it must place it in biblical people and their contexts. As J. Barr has proposed, inspiration must be understood "as the inspiration of the people from whom the books came."[78] Inspiration cannot be located in texts or books, but its process is found in the believing community and its history as God's people. The feminist liberation theologian would qualify this statement further by insisting that the process of inspiration must be seen as the inspiration of people, especially poor women, struggling for human dignity and liberation from oppressive powers because they believe in the biblical God of creation and salvation despite all experiences to the contrary.

Therefore, feminist biblical hermeneutics stands in conflict with the dialogical-hermeneutical model developed by Bultmann, Gadamer and the New Hermeneutic, because it cannot respect the "rights" of the androcentric *text* and seek for a "fusion" with the patriarchal-biblical horizon. Its goal is not "identification" with or "consent to" the androcentric text or Biblical traditioning process, but faithful remembrance and critical solidarity with women in biblical history. In other words, it does not focus on *text* as revelatory word, but on the story of women as the people of God. Its "canonical" hermeneutics insists that the people of God are not restricted to Israel and the Christian Church, but include all of humanity, because the Bible begins with creation and ends with the vision of a new creation.[79] This challenge of feminist theology to hermeneutical theology is well expressed in John Cobb's review of David Tracy's position:

> Hermeneutical theology makes sense as long as we believe that our classics are essentially adequate to our needs. But what if they are not? What if our need is for really new thinking and practice? Our classics point ahead to such newness, and in that very important sense they are adequate. But the new thinking we need about Jews and women breaks the boundaries of what is appropriately called hermeneutics.[80]

B.   Toward a Biblical, Historical, Literary, and Critical Interpretation

However, this feminist and liberation theological challenge to the hermeneutical paradigm in biblical and theological interpretation does not mean that "historical criticism has come to the end of its theological career," as, we have seen, Charles Davis argues. The opposite seems to me the case. Rather than make historical-criticism obsolete, it forces theologians, on the one hand, to relinquish their understanding of the Bible as a "classic" and to develop a critical hermeneutics rather than a "hermeneutics of consent." It forces historical-critical biblical scholars, on the other hand, to sharpen their critical acumen by utilizing the epistemological insights of historical and literary criticism.

Since I have elsewhere addressed the question of a critical feminist hermeneutics of the Bible more fully,[81] I would like to argue here that the feminist liberation-theological challenge to an objectivist-factual as well as a hermeneutical-textual-consensual model of biblical scholarship provokes also a more critical understanding of the historical and literary task of biblical interpretation. The following insights of theoretical discussions among historians and literary critics appear to me crucial: 1) the rhetorical character of historiography as "history for," 2) the definition of literary criticism as "criticism for," and 3) the understanding of history not only as "what happened" but also as "what shall be remembered."

First: The debate between an "objectivist" and a "constructionist" historical epistemology highlights two different perceptions of what we can know historically.[82] The "objectivist" direction holds to the Rankean view that the past can be known scientifically as "it actually was." In this understanding, historical facticity and theological meaning and truth are interchangeable. A "constructionist" epistemology stresses, in turn, the "time-boundedness" and "linguisticality" of historical knowledge. Statements of "historical facts" do not emerge of themselves as ready-made mirrors of past events. In order to make statements of "historical fact" scholars have to make inferences based in part upon their sources and "evidence" and based in part on their general understanding of human behavior, nature and world. Historians, however, not only deal selectively with their "data" in order to present a "coherent" narrative account, but also ascribe historical significance to them in accordance with the theoretical model or perception that orders their information.[83]

Reconstructive inferences, selection of data, and ascription of historical significance do not only depend on the choice of explanatory models but also on the rhetorical aims of the work. Historians "shape" their materials, not just in accordance with a narrative framework of preconceived ideas, but also in response to the narrative discourse in general which is rhetorical in nature. History is never just *history of* but always also *history for,* not only in the sense of being told with some ideological goal in mind, but also in the sense of being *written for* a certain group of people.[84]

History and Biblical interpretation are not written today for people of past times, but for people of our own time. The antiquarian, objectivist understanding of biblical texts and history is not only epistemologically incorrect but also historically undesirable. What needs to be recovered is the understanding of history, not as artifact, but as historical consciousness for people of the present.

American historians have shown that historiography in this country was from its inception occupied with questions of public policy and sought to imbue Americans with a sense of national pride and unity.[85] Feminist historians, in turn, have pointed out that most historical accounts are written as if women did not exist or as if we were some rare creatures on the fringes of social life. The reason for such an anomalous impression was that history was not only written by men but also written about the dominant class. The portrayal of Indians or Blacks in history was similarly written from the perspective and for the readership of white middle class men. Similarly, church history was written primarily as "clerical" history, because clerics were not only writing but also reading these historical accounts.

In short, the insistence of liberation theology on an explicit "advocacy stance" brings into the open what is always operative in historical interpretation. A critical feminist liberation theology, therefore, does not obstruct but enhances the self-understandings of critical biblical scholarship when it insists that all theological and biblical scholarship begin with an analysis of its own historical-political situation and with an articulation of its own "hermeneutical option," rather than with the deceptive posture of representing detached, value-neutral, scientific and unbiased scholarship.

Since the Bible is not only a document of biblical communities of the past but also of those of the present, Biblical scholarship must not only respond to academic standards but must also become accountable again to biblical communities and be done *for* biblical communities today.[86] The intellectual freedom from doctrinal control is to be used as creative freedom *for* nurturing the faith and vision of contemporary biblical communities struggling for liberation. While the historical-factual self-understanding of biblical scholarship ascribed the central role in interpretation to the detached and scientifically trained historian, the paradigm of Hermeneutics accorded the primary role in biblical interpretation to the preacher and pastor. Yet, it appears that a new model of biblical interpretation is emerging in which the members of believing communities have a central role. This is the case in the Christian base-communities of Latin America as well as in the feminist biblical communities of women in North America. This new direction in biblical interpretation is oriented, not so much to scientific validation and stature in the academy,[87] nor to authoritative proclamation in the church. As interpretation *for,* it seeks to formulate a new liberating-biblical vision that can sustain, encourage, and challenge biblical communities of faith. The authority of the Bible is not that of control but that of enabling power:

> Salvation as the possibility of freedom and peace has not only to be acknowledged, it also has to be grasped and practiced by the reader. The text only helps to create possibilities; it is for the reader to realize them in life.[88]

Second: If historical interpretation is not just descriptive but always also rhetorical, then we cannot simply strive for "identification" or "empathy" with the text in order to understand it, but we must also seek to evaluate its meanings and significance. Since biblical texts do not claim just the authority of meaning but also that of Holy Scripture, biblical exegetes have to pay special attention not only to the rhetorical aims of the text but also to those of its subsequent interpretations in the history of the church. While form, redaction, and literary criticism analyze the theological dynamics and aims of a story, author, or text, such an interpretation must move to a critical evaluation of its own theological rhetoric at the same time. It also must evaluate the "rhetorical" aims of past as well as contemporary interpretations.

Wayne Booth[89] has recently argued that the literary critic must not only interpret but also evaluate a classic work of art in terms of justice. Thereby he seeks to revive a responsible ethical and political criticism that recognizes the ideological limitations of a great work of art. Such a criticism does not simply evaluate the ideas or propositions of a work, but seeks to determine whether the very language and composition of a work portray persons stereotypically and thus unjustly, without itself criticizing such a literary portrayal. What does the language and text do to the reader who submits to its world of vision? Does it promote dehumanization and injustice or does it enhance our freedom to become more fully human? Similarly, biblical interpreters, especially those who teach and preach today, must critically evaluate in terms of a Christian scale of values, not only the rhetorical aims of biblical texts, but also the rhetorical interests coming to the fore in the history of interpretation as well as in contemporary exegesis. Historical-critical interpretation needs to be complemented by a controlled and disciplined theological-critical evaluation in order to become *biblical-critical* interpretation. Biblical scholarship has fought hard for, and therefore always prized, its freedom *from* dogmatic and ecclesiastical control or pietistic bias. Liberation theology now challenges biblical scholarship to articulate its own self-understanding more fully, not only as freedom *from* but also as freedom *for* critical evaluation.[90]

Such a *freedom for* would presuppose a public discussion of the interests, theological commitments, and theological assumptions of Biblical scholars. It would mean, moreover, that there is a need to develop a scale of values for judging which theological texts may be preached or accepted today as "Word of God" and which should not. For example, I have argued elsewhere that no biblical patriarchal text that perpetuates violence against women, children or "slaves" should be accorded the status of divine revelation if we do not want to turn the God of the Bible into a God of violence.[91] That does not mean that we can not preach, for instance, on the household-code-texts of the New Testament. It means only that we must preach them critically in order to unmask them as texts perpetrating violence today. Naturally, such an evaluation would presuppose that biblical students not only learn to discuss the interpretations of biblical scholars but also become skilled in the analysis of contemporary situations and ideologies.

Finally, liberation theology challenges biblical scholarship to complement its Rankean understanding of history as "what actually happened" with an understanding of history as "what shall be remembered." This notion was expressed by Friedrich Schlegel who characterized the historian as "rückwarts gekehrten Prophet," as "prophet turned backwards." Paul Hernadi[92] has pointed out that such an understanding of interpretation and historiography is based on an understanding of history as "continual translation." All original sources and documents at the disposal of historians as well as the work in which they are engaged are *verbal* accounts of the non-verbal fabric of historical events. To the extent that historians "communicate," they translate the idiom of events past into the idioms and perspectives of present discourse. They continually translate the sealed book of "How it Really Was" into interpretation after interpretation, disclosing "how it shall be remembered." In other words, historians and interpreters narrate past events as envisioned by a present critical consciousness.

History as "what shall be remembered" does not operate so much in terms of logical operations of cause and effect, but seeks to make us comprehend and choose between different types of theological goals and purposes, in order to lead us to a historical praxis. "While conservative science claims, 'All things are determined' and radical myth insists, 'All things are purposeful'," the art of scientific historical interpretation suggests that "causality and teleology are complementary idioms."[93] While factual historical criticism seeks to trace lines of causal determination in the past, teleological-historical criticism views the past with the prospective orientation of contemporary participants facing the future.[94] Liberation movements have pointed out that it is a sign of oppression not to have a written history and historical self-identity. History and historiography are not just a collection of facts or a meaningless chronicle, but either a means of domination or the heritage of a people that looks to the past for its vision of the future. If, therefore, oppressed peoples should have a future, freedom, and autonomy, they must recover their historical roots and root their solidarity in a common historical self-understanding.[95]

Such an understanding of history as the memory of a believing community comes close to the remembrance of the Exodus and the Lord's supper enjoined to the Jewish and Christian communities, respectively, and celebrated in ever new ritual actualizations. However, as James Sanders has pointed out, such a reactualization of the central remembrances of the biblical communities depends on once "taking sides." In a "constitutive reading," e.g., of Lk 4:16–30, one takes automatically the side of Jesus and is thus, as a Christian, bound to read the story in an anti-Jewish sense. In a "prophetic reading" of the same text, one takes the side of and identifies with the people of Nazareth and thus is challenged by the word of Jesus:

> The two basic modes are the constitutive and the prophetic, according to context. The crucial distinction between them is theological, the freedom of God on the one hand, and his *(sic)* generosity and grace on the other; and his *(sic)* apparent bias for the powerless, those who have not yet confused his *(sic)* power with theirs. [96]

Such biblical remembrance has not antiquarian interests, but is oriented toward the future, as J. Barr has suggested:

> A story of Abraham, for instance, may have been told originally not in order to give exact information about situations of the second millenium BC, but to convey patterns of hope borne by the figure of the man who had received the promise of God . . . The narratives of Jesus are not there only to tell what he historically said and did. They are there also to furnish visions of the present and future life of the one who lives after death and who will come in the end as judge. [97]

III. *Conclusion*

I have argued here that the challenge of liberation theologies to the self-understanding of biblical scholarship can be buttressed with reference to recent epistemological discussions among historians and literary critics. A critical feminist biblical interpretation, therefore, enhances rather than obstructs historical-critical scholarship. In my recent book, *In Memory of Her: A Feminist Theological Reconstruction of Christian Origins,* I have sought to demonstrate how this is the case. Insofar as androcentric—male centered—scholarship does not sufficiently take seriously the ideological character of androcentric texts and language, it cannot do justice to its sources. Insofar as it presupposes an androcentric-patriarchal model for reconstructing early Christian origins without critically reflecting upon it, it cannot do justice to those texts which mention the leadership of women. More importantly, such androcentric scholarship obscures the early Christian vision of the discipleship of equals and of the community embodying the new creation. Finally, insofar as it does not reflect critically on its own societal situatedness and ecclesial commitments, it cannot evaluate the significance and validity of biblical texts for women who constitute, usually, the majority of biblical faith-communities today.

Such a new critical self-understanding of biblical scholarship must lead to a new hermeneutic, not a hermeneutic of consent, but a hermeneutic of critical solidarity that can preserve the historical distance between the present and the past and at the same time share the faithful "memory" and the liberating visions of the past for the future. Such a new critical hermeneutics does not center on the text but on the people whose story with God is remembered in the texts of the Bible. Or, as James Barr has so succinctly stated: "The true believer is a believer in God and in Christ, not in the first place a believer in the Bible."[98] In such a theological hermeneutics, the biblical canon becomes the "prime paradigm" (J. Barr), the "paradigm of the verbs of God's activity" (J. Sanders), the "root-model" of Christian faith and practice (E. Schüssler Fiorenza), rather than the unchangeable "archetype" or the "magic Word" (A.C. Thiselton). If the process of inspiration is located in the history of God's people, then it is historical in character. But, this history is not closed, it is ongoing, and it looks to the future of liberation and salvation for all of humanity. I also agree with Barr that this "future direction of Scripture" is of fundamental importance for the believing community on its way with God through history. The story of Sarah or the story of the Syrophoenician woman were not so much told in order to record what "actually happened," but much more in order to encourage us in the present and to furnish visions of an open future.

Because of the critical and future oriented dimensions of biblical scholarship as *interpretation for* the church of women, I have argued elsewhere that a critical feminist hermeneutics of liberation must have a fourfold dimension: It must be a *hermeneutics of suspicion,* critically entering the biblical worlds and the works of scholars in order to detect their ideological deformations; a *hermeneutics of remembrance,* facilitated by literary- and historical-critical reconstructions; a *hermeneutics of proclamation,* critically evaluating what can be proclaimed and taught as an inspired vision for a more human life and future; and, finally, a *hermeneutics of actualization* that celebrates its critical solidarity in story and song, in ritual and meditation as a people of the "God with us," who was the God of Judith as well as of Jesus.[99]

We find signs today that biblical scholarship takes the challenge of liberation theologians seriously and that it is in the process of reconceptualizing its own understanding of history and interpretation. It no longer can articulate as its unqualified goal the intention to declare with scientific certainty what the text *meant*—because this is virtually an epistemological impossibility. Rather, it must seek to subject prevalent interpretations and dominant understandings of "what the text meant" to a critical analysis, thereby testing for theological validity the self-understanding that social-ecclesial groups have of themselves. Historical biblical consciousness is valuable, not just as an "anti-dogmatic weapon," but also as "a critical theological instrument for inquiring into the historical dimensions and social political ramifications of contemporary religious value-systems"[100] as well as for challenging the theological self-understandings of contemporary Christians and church communities.

Such a renewed historical-critical self-understanding of biblical scholarship does not invite simply to hermeneutical identification with biblical texts and historical practice—identification that obliterates the historical strangeness of the text—but to historical solidarity[101] with the people of God in biblical history. It does not unreflectively reconstruct biblical history as mirror images of our society and church, but seeks to become a critical memory and theological-prophetic challenge to establishment society and church. Studying the biblical past for recovering its unfulfilled historical possibilities and mandates becomes thus a primary task for biblical scholarship. It enables us to keep our futures "open" in light of our biblical heritage and communal identity. It allows us to integrate biblical history and theology as a historical-theological biblical rhetoric for the future of the world and, thereby, also for the future of the church. Such a new self-understanding of biblical scholarship as a critical historical-theological undertaking would not require detachment and neutrality, but conversion and commitment to the biblical vision of humanity as the people of God. The common hermeneutical ground between the past and the present as well as the future would not be "sacred history" or "sacred-text," but commitment to the biblical vision of God's new creation.

NOTES

[1] Cf. E. Schweizer, *Luke: A Challenge to Present Theology* (Atlanta: J. Knox Press, 1982), p. 56.

[2] For a review and description of the historical development of biblical historical-critical scholarship, see, e.g., R.E. Clements, *One Hundred Years of Old Testament Interpretation* (Philadelphia: The Westminster Press, 1976); R.M. Grant, *A Short History of the Interpretation of the Bible* (rev. ed.; New York: Macmillan, 1963); H.F. Hahn, *The Old Testament in Modern Research* (2nd ed.; Philadelphia: Fortress, 1966); P. Henry, *New Directions in New Testament Study* (Philadelphia: Westminster, 1979); W.G. Kümmel, *The New Testament: The History of the Investigation of Its Problems* (Nashville: Abingdon, 1972); S. Neill, *The Interpretation of the New Testament 1861–1961* (London: Oxford University Press, 1964); J. Weingreen *et al.*, "Interpretation, History of," in *Interpreter's Dictionary of the Bible, Suppl. Vol* (Nashville: Abingdon, 1976), 436–56; W.G. Doty, *Contemporary New Testament Interpretation* (Englewood Cliffs: Prentice Hall, 1972), and the contributions in the *Jerome Biblical Commentary* (Englewood Cliffs: Prentice Hall, 1968): Alexa Suelzer, "Modern Old Testament Criticism," *ibid.*, vol. II, 590–604, and John S. Kselman, "Modern New Testament Criticism," *ibid.*, vol. II, 7–20.

[3] Joan Turner Beifuss, "It's not chauvinistic to note US Catholic Biblical Scholarship," *National Catholic Reporter,* 22 February 1980, p. 10. However, for a more cautious assessment, cf. R.E. Brown, "Difficulties in Using the New Testament in American Catholic Discussions," *Louvain Studies* 6(1976): 144–58. See also D.J. Harrington, "The Ecumenical Importance of New Testament Research," *BTB* 12(1982): p. 23: "It would not be unfair to say that North America is now the center of New Testament research."

[4] For a spirited critique of this dichotomy in biblical studies, see W. Wink, *The Bible in Human Transformation: Toward a New Paradigm for Biblical Study* (Philadelphia: Fortress, 1973), and his *Transforming Bible Study: A Leader's Guide* (Nashville: Abington, 1980).

[5] See especially Phyllis A. Bird, *The Bible as the Church's Book* (Philadelphia: Westminster, 1982).

[6] See C.K. Barrett, *Biblical Problems and Biblical Preaching* (Bibl. Ser. 6; Philadelphia: Fortress, 1964). p. 37.

[7] For a review, see R. Detweiler, "After the New Criticism: Contemporary Methods of Literary Interpretation," in R.A. Spencer, ed., *Orientation by Disorientation. Studies in Literary Criticism and Biblical Literary Criticism*, presented in Honor of W.A. Beardslee (Pittsburgh Theological Mon. Ser. #35; Pittsburgh: The Pickwick Press, 1980), pp. 3–23; N.R. Peterson, "Literary Criticism in Biblical Studies," *ibid.*, pp. 25–50; E.V. McKnight, "The Contours and Methods of Literary Criticism," *ibid.*, pp. 53–69.

[8] Augustine A. Stock, "The Limits of Historical-Critical Exegesis," *BTB* 13(1983): 28–31.

[9] Leland J. White, "Historical and Literary Criticism: A Theological Response," *BTB* 13 (1983): 32–34.

[10] Charles Davis, "The Theological Career of Historical Criticism of the Bible," *Cross Currents* 32 (1982): 267.

[11] *Ibid.*, p. 279.

[12] See his *Virginal Conception and Bodily Resurrection of Jesus* (New York: Paulist Press, 1973), pp. 3–11.

[13] R.E. Brown, "What the Biblical Word Meant and What It Means," in his *The Critical Meaning of the Bible* (New York: Paulist, 1981), pp. 23–44.36f.

[14] J. Barr, "Biblical Theology," *IDB Suppl.*, 104–11.

[15] Cf., however, J.D. Smart, *The Past, Present, and Future of Biblical Theology* (Philadelphia: Westminster, 1979).

[16] B.S. Childs, *Biblical Theology in Crisis* (Philadelphia: Westminster, 1970), pp. 13–87, points also to the controversy on the Bible between Fundamentalists and Modernists which was fought between 1910 and 1930 in American Protestantism.

[17] For the following, see J. Barr, "Biblical Theology," p. 105.

[18] See, e.g., T. Boman, *Hebrew Thought Compared with Greek* (Philadelphia: Westminster, 1961); D. Hill, *Greek Words and Hebrew Meanings: Studies in the Semantics of Soteriological Terms* (Cambridge: University Press, 1967), and the review of this book by J. Barr, "Common Sense and Biblical Language," *Biblica* 49 (1968):377–87.

[19] Cf. especially J. Barr, *The Semantics of Biblical Language* (Oxford: University Press, 1961), pp. 206–19, and the review of the *status quaestionis* by A.C. Thiselton, "Semantics and New Testament Interpretation," in I.H. Marshall, ed., *New Testament Interpretation: Essays on Principles and Methods* (Grand Rapids: W.B. Eerdmans, 1977), pp. 75–104.

[20] See, e.g., O. Eissfelt, "Israelitisch-jüdische Religionsgeschichte und alttestamentliche Theologie," *ZAW* 44 (1926): 1–12. This distinction is already found by J.P. Gabler (1753–1826); see the discussion by H. Boers, *What is New Testament Theology?* (Philadelphia: Fortress, 1979), pp. 23–38.

²¹ Cf. O. Cullmann, *Christ and Time: The Primitive Christian Conception of Time* (Philadelphia: Fortress, 1964); *Id., Salvation in History* (New York: Harper & Row, 1967).

²² O. Betz, "Biblical Theology, Historical," in *IDB* I (1962): 436. For a historical review, see also G. Hasel, *Old Testament Theology: Basic Issues in Current Debate* (Grand Rapids: Eerdmans, Rev. ed., 1975), pp. 15–34.

²³ For Hebrew Bible, see J. Muilenburg, "Old Testament Scholarship: Fifty Years in Retrospect," *Journal of Bible and Religion* 28 (1960): 173–81, and G.E. Wright, "Old Testament Scholarship in Prospect," *ibid.,* 182–93.

²⁴ H.J. Cadbury, "New Testament Scholarship: Fifty Years in Retrospect," *ibid.,* p. 196.

²⁵ R.M. Grant, "American New Testament Study, 1926–1956," *JBL* 87 (1968): 42.

²⁶ *Ibid.,* p. 50.

²⁷ E.C. Colwell, "New Testament Scholarship in Prospect," *ibid.,* p. 203.

²⁸ See also K. Stendahl, "Method in the Study of Biblical Theology," in J.P. Hyatt, ed., *The Bible in Modern Scholarship* (Nashville: Abingdon, 1965), pp. 196–209.

²⁹ For differing methods in biblical theology, see, e.g., G.F. Hasel, "Methodology as a Major Problem in the Current Crisis of Old Testament Theology," *BTB* 2 (1972): 177–98. However, difficulties in methodology seem to be rooted in different conceptualizations of what biblical theology should be. Cf. Hendrikus Boers, *What is New Testament Theology?,* for such a perspective.

³⁰ K. Stendahl, "Biblical Theology, Contemporary," *IDB* I (1962): 422.

³¹ *Ibid.,* p. 424.

³² *Ibid.,* p. 431.

³³ K. Stendahl, "Method in the Study of Biblical Theology," p. 199.

³⁴ H. Boers, *What is New Testament Theology?,* p. 85.

³⁵ A. Dulles, S.J., "Response to Krister Stendahl's 'Method in the Study of Biblical Theology,' " in J.P. Hyatt, *The Bible in Modern Scholarship,* pp. 210–11.

³⁶ R. de Vaux, "Method in the Study of Early Hebrew History," pp. 15f. Cf., however, G.E. Mendenhall's criticism of R. de Vaux's proposal and the traditional division of academic labor, *ibid.,* pp. 30f.

³⁷ The trenchant critique of historical criticism does not so much pertain to its methods but to its rationalist and agnostic presuppositions. Among others see, e.g., P. Stuhlmacher, *Historical Criticism and Theological Interpretation of Scripture* (Philadelphia: Fortress, 1977); D.C. Steinmetz, "The Superiority of Pre-Critical Exegesis," *Theology Today* 37 (1980): 27–37.

³⁸ Cf., e.g., O. Kaiser and W.G. Kümmel, *Exegetical Method: A Student's Handbood* (rev. ed.; New York: Seabury Press, 1981); R.N. Soulen, *Handbook of Biblical Criticism* (Atlanta: John Knox Press, 1976); D.J. Harrington, *Interpreting the New Testament: A Practical Guide* (Wilmington: M. Glazier, 1979); E. Krentz, *The Historical-Critical Method* (Philadelphia: Fortress, 1975); J.H. Hayes and C.R. Holladay, *Biblical Exegesis: A Beginner's Handbook* (Atlanta: Knox Press, 1982); K. Berger, *Exegese des Neuen Testaments* (UTB 658; Heidelberg: Quelle & Meyer, 1977); and the popular account of J.J. Collins, "Methods and Presuppositions of Biblical Scholarship," *Chicago Studies* (Spring 1978): 5–28.

[39] Cf., e.g., W.A. Beardslee, *Literary Criticism of the New Testament* (Philadelphia: Fortress, 1970); D. Patte, *What is Structural Exegesis?* (Philadelphia: Fortress, 1976).

[40] For a discussion and review of the "social world" study, see the contributions in *Interpretation* 37 (1982): 229-77.

[41] See, e.g., R. Polzin, *Biblical Structuralism* (Missoula: Scholars Press, 1977); I. Soter, "The Dilemma of Literary Science," *New Literary History* 2 (1970): 85-100.

[42] P. Hernadi, "Literary Theory: A Compass for Critics," *Critical Inquiry* 3 (1976/77): 369-86, 369.

[43] L.E. Keck, "Will the Historical-Critical Method Survive? Some Observations," in R.A. Spencer, ed., *Orientation by Disorientation,* p. 124.

[44] See, e.g., E. Schweizer, *Luke: A Challenge to Present Theology,* p. 12: "Historico-critical methods are certainly not necessary for the salvation of the individual believer. But if we prohibited them or limited their functions anxiously, we would forget that God became incarnate in the earthly history of a human being, called Jesus of Nazareth. If on the other hand, we thought that historico-critical research were just everything and the only basis of faith, we would forget that it was God who became flesh in this history."

[45] Cf. J. Rhode, *Rediscovering the Teachings of the Evangelists* (Philadelphia: Westminster Press, 1969), and especially N. Perrin, *What is Redaction Criticism?* (Philadelphia: Fortress, 1970).

[46] See, e.g., L.E. Keck, *The New Testament Experience of Faith* (St. Louis: The Bethany Press, 1976), for such an account.

[47] Cf. V. Furnish, *The Love Command in the New Testament* (Nashville: Abingdon, 1972); Pheme Perkins, *Love Commands in the New Testament* (New York: Paulist Press, 1982).

[48] Cf. E. Schüssler Fiorenza, ed., *Aspects of Religious Propaganda in Judaism and Early Christianity* (Notre Dame: University Press, 1976); D. Senior & C. Stuhlmueller, *The Biblical Foundations for Mission* (Maryknoll: Orbis Press, 1983).

[49] Cf. my " 'For the Sake of Our Salvation.' Biblical Interpretation as Theological Task," in D. Durken, ed., *Sin, Salvation and the Spirit* (Collegeville: The Liturgical Press, 1979), pp. 21-39, for such a proposal.

[50] Cf. R. E. Brown, "Hermeneutics," in *JBC* II (1968), 605-623; R.E. Palmer, *Hermeneutics* (Evanston: Northwestern University Press, 1969); R. Lapointe, "Hermeneutics Today," *BTB* 2 (1972): 107-54; and A.C. Thiselton, *The Two Horizons: New Testament Hermeneutics and Philosophical Descriptions with Special Reference to Heidegger, Bultmann, Gadamer, and Wittgenstein* (Grand Rapids; Eerdmans, 1980), for reviews of the problems and literature.

[51] Cf. P. Ricoeur, *Interpretation Theory: Discourse and Surplus of Meaning* (Texas: Christian University Press, 1976); *Id., Essays on Biblical Interpretation* (Philadelphia: Fortress, 1980), and J.W. Van den Hengel, *The Home of Meaning: The Hermeneutics of the Subject of Paul Ricoeur* (Washington, D.C.: University of America Press, 1983), pp. 192ff.

[52] Cf. G.N. Stanton, "Presuppositions in New Testament Criticism," in I.H. Marshall, ed., *New Testament Interpretation,* pp. 60-71.

[53] Cf. his "Is Exegesis without Presuppositions Possible," in S.M. Ogden (ET and ed.), *Existence and Faith* (London: Hodder and Stoughton, 1961), pp. 342-51.

[54] For the following, cf. A.C. Thiselton, "The New Hermeneutic," in *New Testament Interpretation*, pp. 308-33 (literature).

[55] Cf. T. Peters, "The Nature and Role of Presuppositions: An Inquiry into Contemporary Hermeneutics," *International Philosophical Quarterly* 14 (1974): 209-22.

[56] P. Stuhlmacher, *Historical Criticism and Theological Interpretation of Scripture*, p. 90.

[57] A.C. Thiselton, "The New Hermeneutic," p. 310.

[58] Sandra M. Schneiders, "Faith, Hermeneutics and the Literal Sense of Scripture," *ThSt* 39 (1978): 733.

[59] *Ibid.*, p. 735.

[60] *Ibid.*, p. 733.

[61] Cf., e.g., E. Cardenal, *The Gospel in Solentiname* (Maryknoll: Orbis, 1976), p vii: ". . . the commentaries of the *campesinos* are usually of greater profundity than that of many theologians."

[62] For a concrete example of how such a critical evaluative hermeneutic proceeds, see my "Discipleship and Patriarchy: Early Christian Ethos and Christian Ethics in a Feminist Theological Perspective," in L. Rasmussen, ed., *The Annual of the Society of Christian Ethics* (Waterloo: CSR, 1982), pp. 131-72.

[63] P.D. Hanson, "The Responsibility of Biblical Theology to Communities of Faith," *Theology Today* 37 (1980): 40.

[64] A. Schlatter, "Atheistische Methoden in der Theologie," in *Zur Theologie des Neuen Testaments und zur Dogmatik* (ThB 41; München: Chr. Kaiser Verl., 1969), pp. 138f.

[65] See my articles, "Feminist Theology as a Critical Theology of Liberation," *Theological Studies* 36 (1975): 602-26; "Towards a Liberating and Liberated Theology," *Concilium* 15 (1979): 22-32; and my forthcoming "Claiming the Center," in Buckley/Kalven, eds., *Womanspirit Bonding* (New York: Pilgrim Press, 1984).

[66] Cf., e.g., J.H. Cone, "Christian Faith and Political Praxis," in B. Mahan/L.D. Richesin, eds., *The Challenge of Liberation Theology* (Maryknoll: Orbis, 1981), p. 60: "If faith is the belief that God created all for freedom, then praxis is the social theory used to analyze the structures of injustice so that we will know what must be done for the historical realization of freedom. To sing about freedom and to pray for its coming is not enough. Freedom must be actualized in history by oppressed peoples who accept the intellectual challenge to analyze the world for the purpose of changing it." And: "The truth of the gospel then is a truth that must be done and not simply spoken. To speak the truth without doing the truth is to contradict the truth one claims to affirm." (p. 61)

[67] J.E. Weir, "The Bible and Marx: A Discussion of the Hermeneutics of Liberation Theology," *Scot. Journal of Theology* 35 (1982): 344. Cf. also J. A. Kirk, "The Bible in Latin American Liberation Theology," in N. Gottwald/A. Wire, eds., *The Bible and Liberation* (Berkeley; Radical Religion, 1976), pp. 157-65.

[68] See especially L. Cormee, "The Hermeneutical Privilege of the Oppressed: Liberation Theologies, Biblical Faith, and Marxist Sociology of Knowledge," *Proceedings of the Catholic Theological Society of America* 32 (1978): 155-81.

[69] See, e.g., Schubert Ogden, *Faith and Freedom: Toward a Theology of Liberation* (Nashville: Abingdon, 1979), and my critique of his objections in "Toward a Feminist Biblical Hermeneutics: Biblical Interpretation and Liberation Theology," in *The Challenge of Liberation Theology*, pp. 91-112.

[70] See my book, *In Memory of Her: A Feminist Theological Reconstruction of Christian Origins* (New York: Crossroad Publ., 1983), pp. 41-96.

[71] Cf. F. Herzog, "Liberation Hermeneutic as Ideology Critique," *Interpr* 27 (1974): 387-403; D. Lockhead, "Hermeneutics and Ideology," *The Ecumenist* 15 (1977): 81-84.

[72] See J. L. Segundo, *The Liberation of Theology* (Maryknoll: Orbis, 1976), pp. 8f. See also the evaluation of Segundo's work by A. Hennelly, *Theologies in Conflict: The Challenge of Juan Luis Segundo* (Maryknoll: Orbis, 1979); A. J. Tambasco, *The Bible for Ethics: Juan Luis Segundo and First World Ethics* (Washington, D.C.: University of America Press, 1981).

[73] Cf., e.g., E. Tamez, *Bible of the Oppressed* (Maryknoll: Orbis, 1982), who, however, has very little to say about women.

[74] This was underlined by both B. Birch's and T. Ogletree's response to my paper on "Discipleship and Patriarchy," *op. cit.*, pp. 173-89.

[75] For a different position emphasizing the prophetic traditions in the Bible as such a liberating tradition and principle, see, e.g., R.R. Ruether, "The Feminist Critique in Religious Studies," *Soundings* 64 (1981): 388-402; *Id.*, "Feminism and Patriarchal Religion: Principles of Ideological Critique of the Bible," *JSOT* 22 (1982): 54-66.

[76] J.L. Segundo, *The Liberation of Theology*, p. 179.

[77] J. Donovan, "Feminism and Aesthetics," *Critical Inquiry* 3 (1976/77): 608; *Id.*, *Feminist Literary Criticism: Explorations in Theory* (Lexington: University Press, 1975), who argues for a "prescriptive" criticism or a criticism that exists "in the prophetic mode" over and against a "purely aesthetic criticism and judgment" of literature.

[78] J. Barr, "The Bible as a Document of Believing Communities," in H.D. Betz, ed., *The Bible as a Document of the University* (Chicago: Scholars Press, 1981), p. 38.

[79] This seems to me the most one can say about the "overall theological coherence" of the canon. See the review by B.W. Anderson of B.S. Childs, *Introduction to the Old Testament as Scripture*, in *Theology Today* 37 (1980): 100-108. For a contrasting evaluation of B.S. Childs and J. Sanders, see E.E. Lemcio, "The Gospels and Canonical Criticism," *BTB* 11 (1981): 114-22, and J. Sanders' response, pp. 122-24. For an integration of "canonical" criticism into liberation theology, see L.J. White, "Biblical Theologians and Theologies of Liberation: Part I; Canon-Supporting Framework," *BTB* 11 (1981): 35-40; *Id.*, "Part II; Midrash Applies Text to Context," *ibid.*, 98-103.

[80] *RSR* 7 (1981): 283.

[81] See my "Toward a Feminist Biblical Hermeneutics: Biblical Interpretation and Liberation Theology," and the responses by A.C. Wire, B. Birch, B. Gaventa, D. Setel at the AAR panel sponsored by Feminist Hermeneutic Project/Liberation Theology Group at the AAR annual meeting in New York in 1982.

[82] See, e.g., S. Bann, "Towards a Critical Historiography: Recent Work in Philosophy of History," *Philosophy* 56 (1981): 365-85, and the exchange between P.H. Nowell-Smith, "The Constructionist Theory of History," and L.J. Goldstein, "History and the Primacy of Knowing," *History and Theory: The Constitution of the Historical Past* 16 (1977): 1-52.

[83] Cf. G. Leff, *History and Social Theory* (New York: Doubleday, 1971); R. Stephen Humphreys, "The Historian, His Documents, and the Elementary Modes of Historical Thought, *History and Theory* 19 (1980). 1-20.

[84] Cf. especially Hayden White, "The Value of Narrativity in the Representation of Reality," *Critical Inquiry* 7 (1980): 5-28; *Id.*, "Historicism, History, and the Figurative Imagination," *History and Theory: Essays on Historicism* 14 (1975): 43-67; *Id.*, "The Politics of Historical Interpretation: Discipline and De-Sublimation," in W.J.T. Mitchell, ed., *The Politics of Interpretation* (Chicago: University of Chicago Press, 1983), pp. 119-43.

[85] Cf. N. Schrom Dye, "Clio's American Daughters: Male History, Female Reality," in J.A. Scherman & E. Torton Beck, eds., *The Prism of Sex: Essays in the Sociology of Knowledge* (Madison: University of Wisconsin Press, 1979), pp. 9-31.

[86] See also the Inaugural Address of W. Sibley Towner, "Enlisting Exegesis in the Cause of the Church," who shared with me an unpublished copy at the 1983 Theology Institute at Villanova University. Cf. also E.C. Ulrich and W.G. Thompson, "The Tradition as a Resource in Theological Reflection: Scripture and the Minister," in J. & E. Eaton Whitehead, eds., *Method in Ministry: Theological Reflection and Christian Ministry* (New York: Seabury Press, 1980), pp. 31-52.

[87] Cf. also E.W. Said, "Opponents, Audiences, Constituencies, and Community," in *The Politics of Interpretation*, pp. 7-32.

[88] G.A Shaw, *The Cost of Authority: Manipulation and Freedom in the New Testament* (Philadelphia: Fortress, 1983), p. 275. Although there are many problems with its exegetical readings, the book's hermeneutic is pointing in the direction of biblical scholarship as scholarship for Christian liberation praxis.

[89] W.C. Booth, "Freedom of Interpretation: Bakhtin and the Challenge of Feminist Criticism," in *The Politics of Interpretation*, pp. 51-82.

[90] Cf. also G. Strecker, "'Biblische Theologie'? Kritische Bemerkungen zu den Entwürfen von Harmut Gese und Peter Stuhlmacher," in D. Lührmann and G. Strecker, eds., *Kirche. Festschrift fur Günther Bornkamm zum 75. Geburtstag* (Tübingen: JCB Mohr, 1980), pp. 425-445.443f, who argues for a more critical clarification of the presuppositions of the interpretative process than a "hermeneutics of consent" can allow for.

[91] Cf., e.g., R.R. Gillogly, "Spanking Hurts Everybody," *Theology Today* 37 (1980): 415-24; S. Brooks Thistlethwaite, "Battered Woman and the Bible: From Subjection to Liberation," *Christianity and Crisis* 41 (1981): 303-13. Cf. the review of interpretations by W.M. Swartley, *Slavery, Sabbath, War and Women: Case Issues in Biblical Interpretation* (Scottsdale: Herald Press, 1983), who argues for the Bible as "resource" and "guide," but does not sufficiently take into account the violence perpetuated by biblical texts.

[92] P. Hernadi, "Clio's Cousins: Historiography as Translation, Fiction and Criticism," *New Literary History* 7 (1975/76): 247-57.

[93] *Ibid.*, p. 250.

[94] This is also recognized by F. Hahn, "Probleme historischer Kritik," *ZNW* 63 (1972): pp. 14–17.

[95] For the literature and discussion, see my book, *In Memory of Her,* pp. 68–95.

[96] J.A. Sanders, "Hermeneutics," in *IDB Suppl.,* p. 407.

[97] J. Barr, "The Bible as a Document of Believing Communities," p. 40.

[98] *Ibid.*, p. 39.

[99] Cf. my forthcoming "For the Sake of·the Truth Dwelling Among Us: Emerging Issues in Feminist Biblical Interpretation," in J. Weidman, ed., *Visions of a New Humanity* (New York: Harper & Row, 1984).

[100] W.J. Mommsen, "Social Conditioning and Social Relevance of Historical Judgments," *History and Theory: Historical Consciousness and Political Action* 17 (1978): pp. 32f.

[101] Cf. also the excellent contribution of F. Schüssler Fiorenza, "Critical Social Theology and Christology: Toward an Understanding of Atonement and Redemption as Emancipatory Solidarity," *Proceedings of the Catholic Theological Society of America* 30 (1975): 63–100. For "solidarity"as the goal of biblical interpretation, see K. Berger, *Exegese des Neuen Testaments,* pp. 242–69.

Creation in an Evolutionary Worldview

Bruce Vawter, C.M.

As an old, unreconstructed Scholastic, irremediably indoctrinated into the system at an impressionable age, I find it useful at the beginning of any discussion to define its terms. We intend to talk about (1) creation in (2) an evolutionary (3) worldview. Of these terms—creation, evolution, worldview—perhaps the third can be most quickly dealt with, if for no other reason than that it is the least consequential.

Though it bears the semblance of one of those "Anglo-Saxonisms" rooted in our language, "worldview" is actually an English neologism, an importation from the German *Weltanschauung*. I am saying nothing against such importations, which are the stock-in-trade of every language and not only English, since they so often supply for the lack of native resources which is revealed only by exposure to an exotic vocabulary,[1] or which—as in this instance—may call attention from a cognate language to a linguistic development that should have occurred and unaccountably did not.

I am suggesting that, in German or in English, "worldview" does not primarily signify any particular outlook, mindset, or analysis of the physical composition of the cosmos. It signifies, rather and primarily, an outlook on the age, the life, and the condition of mankind.[2] I hope that I will not be accused of naïve etymologizing, or worse, of etymological pedantry, especially since I shall again shortly be invoking etymologies.

I am as aware as anyone else, I hope, that etymologies do not define the ultimate meaning of a word or an expression in any living language; use alone does this. That is what gave rise to the old Scholastic common-sense distinction between the definition of a term *quoad nomen*, "what the word says," and *quoad rem*, "what the term really means." I would, however, like to suggest that more weight .should be accorded etymologies—the first meaning of a word—than

37

sophisticated scholars of today are generally prepared to grant. Mankind's perennial fascination with etymologies, which is evidenced nowhere better than in the Bible, tells us something about their importance in human communications. It is not always simply when a writer or speaker makes conscious advertence to a word's origins that etymologies become important;[3] as the linguistic analysts and structuralists are fond of telling us, we are as much controlled by the language we use as we are in control of it. Thus, the "genuine" meaning of a word—the *etymon* of its inception—may still exercise a decisive influence on what we are really saying, whatever may be our intentions. Or, in other words, there is something to the formula (I think it was Müller's) that language is "the petrified philosophy of a people."

So, I do not apologize for the opinon that, in our thought-world, "worldview" signifies primarily an outlook on the age, the life, and the condition of mankind. Nor do I believe that the other languages that come into our purview in consideration of creation in an evolutionary worldview; namely, the classical and biblical languages, will lead to any contrary conclusion. *Mundus* in Latin and *kosmos* in Greek add up to fairly the same thing: the marvellous *display* which surrounds mankind and which he can only admire. We shall have occasion quite shortly to bring this concept of the created world into harmony with the biblical one. Biblical Hebrew had no term for "world" or "universe." Eventually, the language applied to this entity the term *'ōlām,* which really means "age" (cf. the Greek *aiōn)* and which, therefore, confused a spatial image with a temporal one—if, indeed, this is a confusion and not, rather, a response to instinctive human paradigms where time and space are rated as one. At all events, when we speak of "worldview," we are concerned with no scientific construct to be embraced or toppled, but merely with the casual eye that we of the human species care to cast upon the great panoply that surrounds us.

The Concept of Creation

It is frequently remarked, as though it were a rebuke uncovering a defect, that the Hebrew word *bārā',* used in the book of Genesis and translated "create(d)," actually signifies nothing more or less than a marvellous act of God—always having God as its subject—having no necessary connection with creation in the technical sense of the word.[4] That "technical sense" of the verb "create," however, seems to be a fairly modern and certainly philosophical one, quite unrelated to ancient languages and ancient concerns.[5] The "technical sense," to be more precise, is the philosophical—or, perversely, one might say, the anti-philosophical—concept of *creatio ex nihilo sui et subiecti:* creation which is the result of no emanation or of the reordering of preexistent matter. Obviously, Hebrew had no word to express such a complex and sophisticated idea. But, then again, what other language, ancient or modern, has such a word? I am perfectly disposed to accept Robert C. Neville's judgment in his most recent publication, *The Tao and The Daimon*, [6] that such an idea may be integral to what we of the twentieth century entertain under the concept of God. It was not, however, a concept entertained by our predecessors in the faith, or at least until fairly recent times it was not.

If the Norman Conquest had never occurred and we were still speaking Old English, we would express the idea of creation by use of the verb *scieppan*. It is cognate with the German *schaffen*, *Schöpfung*, the Scandinavian *skabe*, and so forth, and has its modern equivalent in our contemporary verb "to shape." Such a verb accurately describes the creation of man as it is figured in Gen 2:7, but just as obviously it is the description of no *creatio ex nihilo*. Nor have we benefitted by deserting our Germanic heritage in favor of Latinisms. *Creare*, hence our "create," has a semantic spread that ranges from the more disreputable produce of human ingenuity expressed in politics, through human procreation, all the way to craftsmanship, and basically the same must be said of the Greek Old Testament and New Testament *ktizō, ktisis*. In other words, there is no such thing, now or in ancient times, as a verb or a noun that expresses the concept of "creation" with that metaphysical precision that nowadays attaches to it.

It is true, a concept can exist, at least for some people who use a language, even when the language itself has no precise word for the concept. So it is in English, of course. Language, after all, was not invented by the philosophers, which is probably a very good thing; it was simply adopted by them. It is even possible to say that the concept of *creatio ex nihilo* can—probably—be found in the Bible, at least in those parts of the Bible that pertain to its secondary canon. In the Wisdom of Solomon 11:17 it is said of God that he is one who had *ktisasa ton kosmon ex amorphou hylēs:* "had created the cosmos from amorphous matter." This expression could be construed as a reference to the Genesis story of Gen 1:2 *tōhû wābōhû*, but more probably it derives from the Mesopotamian-Greek-Roman picture of creation as the emanation out of primordial chaos. In 2 Maccabees 7:28 the mother of the seven martyred sons exhorts her youngest to "look at the heaven and the earth and see all that is in them and acknowledge that God made them not from what is, and that so the human race came into existence." "Not from what is" (*ouk ex ontōn*) means, obviously, "from non-existent things," i.e., *ex nihilo*. But this is, equally obviously, a late, Greek thought introduced into the Old Testament. It is not, of course, a bad thought simply because it is late and Greek. But it is, nevertheless, aberrant from the rhythm of development of the idea of creation in biblical religion.

Not only is creation in the technical, philosophical sense a notion alien to biblical religion, it is also fair to say that creation in any sense, or specifically in the biblical sense of the creation stories of Genesis 1-3, is, as a theologoumenon in its own right, a relatively late affirmation made of the God of biblical revelation. In fact, it may be questioned whether even in that relatively late time creation did become a distinct theologoumenon in its own right. Both in the Hebrew Old Testament and in the Greek New Testament, which is, in the main, its ideological descendant, "creation" is but an aspect, even if in some sense an initial aspect, of the principal activity which is assigned to God; namely, that of "salvation." God is, first of all, a savior, and a creator only in respect to that.[7] Theologians have used the term "second creation" for the theology of such New Testament passages as Col 1:15-19, as though the New Testament author had taken the notion of creation and applied it typically to illustrate God's salvific work in Christ. To the contrary: the so-called "second creation" is what the Bible understands by "creation" itself, without any further qualification.

What is frequently translated "creator" in what appear to be ancient formulas applied to the chief gods of Canaan, Mesopotamia, or Israel, I am convinced really signifies that serene lordship over all which is the condition of—in Israel at least—*Heilsgeschichte*.[8] I am aware that practically every people and culture have produced etiological stories of creation, simply to respond to Aesopian curiosity about the origins of things, without concern for deeper theological questions. Barbara C. Sproul has recently done us the service of compiling a truly remarkable collection of creation-myths derived from Africa, the Near East, the Far East, the Americas, Australia, and farther outreaches, all of which share a good number of taxonomical similarities.[9] There is also no denying that the earlier, Yahwistic story of creation in Gen 2:4b-3:24 participates in some of this taxonomy, just as the same Yahwistic source pursues etiologies in 4:17-26 (origins of the arts and crafts), 6:1-4 (origin of the *Nephilim*), 11:1-10 (tower of Babel and the origin of languages), etc. However, no one has to read these chapters of Genesis very closely in order to recognize that, while etiologies may be the Yahwistic author's heritage and hobby, his real interest lay in far deeper issues. He constructed—he did not merely copy—a creation myth out of elements which we can see were put together in another combination and directed towards a quite different specific end in Ezekiel 27-28. Specific end, solely. In both cases the mythology has been tailored to the concept of a God working, not outside, but within history, for good or for ill. Creation as an act to be contemplated in itself and for itself, though it may exist in the Bible, is at best a later luxury tolerated by the Bible and almost invariably subordinated to what the Bible considers far more basic concerns.[10]

To go back to the word *bārā'*. It does, of course, mean "create" (in the sense of some marvellous act of God) more often than it means anything else. But, in its most significant use in the Priestly creation story of Gen 1:1–2:4a it has obviously been taken from the vocabulary of Second Isaiah where it habitually appears in parallel with *gā'al*, "redeem, vindicate." There is no question that this is the underlying idea of creation in the first and most dramatic portrayal of creation that occurs at the beginning of the book of Genesis. "When, at the beginning, God *created* the heavens and the earth (= the universe), the earth (what is now the habitable world) was *tōhû wābōhû* (an unformed void) and darkness was upon the face of the deep (= *tĕhôm*, the primordial waters that were thought to lie beneath the earth)." Note the word "created": in this construction it is still waiting for an object. Then comes a next clause: *wĕrûāḥ 'ĕlōhîm mĕraḥepet,* which can be rendered in various ways. I prefer to render it with the *New American Bible* and the *New English Bible;* namely, that "a mighty wind was sweeping over" the untamed waters of primordial chaos. This picture makes perfect sense in the context of a salvific concept of creation. With what do we begin? Total chaos, with no question about its origin. Then we move to creation, and then only. Isa 45:18 is not singing out of chorus when it proclaims that "the Lord who created the heavens, who formed the earth and made it, did not create it a chaos, he formed it to be inhabited." And so, we have the object of the verb *create,* which occurs only in 1:3, when God said, "Let there be light." It is the beginning of the Hexaëmeron, the ordering of creation. Creation, in the biblical sense, or at least in the sense of the Priestly author of Genesis who has preempted most of biblical thinking on the subject, means the order, propriety, tidiness that have been decreed for the world of man as it ought to be. He is the same author who, from the same sense of propriety or the lack thereof, has theologized the ancient Near Eastern flood story by introducing it into the Genesis account of origins in the guise of the creator God's reversal or withdrawal of the creation process, his permitted reversion of the cosmos to primordial chaos, requiring, according to the terms of Gen 9:1–17, a new creation, frequently using the identical language of Gen 1:1–2:4a, suitably modified now to the situation of the "historical" man, represented by the descendants of Noah who have replaced, in the (at least vaguely known) real world that begins to be depicted in Gen 10:2, the shadowy figures of prehistory who inhabited Eden and the regions to the east, including Nod, and wherever the *Nephilim* were given birth.

The Concept of Evolution

If *creatio ex nihilo* is not really a biblical concern in any genuine sense, why should there be any need to make a composition between creation in the biblical sense and a perspective on the cosmos that is dictated by evolutionism? There are, I suppose, at least two possible areas of conflict. Physicists who investigate the microcosm tend to discern no pattern other than random in the distribution of subatomic particles. If the distribution is random for the microcosm, why should it not be for the macrocosm? And if so, what is to be said of order as a touchstone of the notion of creation? And secondly, the biblical notion of creation is undeniably static, the total antithesis of what is meant by evolution. When Gen 1:11-12.21.24-25, etc., speaks of the "kinds" (*minîm*, "distinctions") into which the various creatures of the world have been ordinated, the evident meaning is that once and for all time certain genera and species, to use more recent terminology, have been fixed by the will of the creator. Both of these affirmations, I suggest, at least if baldly asserted, are anti-evolutionary and incompatible with modern science.

But, let us look at both propositions a little more closely. First of all, I would certainly agree with William Frost when he protests that a false dichotomy between science and religion has been created through a "philosophical exaggeration of the biblical stories."[11] I am not so sure, however, that I would like to share his exuberance over the fact that science is, or at least some science is, despite what I have just said, tending more and more towards discerning on its own a fundamental scheme of order in the universe. I know that some science or, more precisely, some scientists have indeed been talking in such terms, invoking such concepts as "design" and "teleology" as proper to the evolutionary process itself, even though they do not use these words which are of theological provenance. I am not comforted by this trend, in which I see far less a support to traditional theology than the mystical ruminations of the shamans of a scientism which is, in all but name, the theology of another religion, in all but name. To take one example, we have seen on our television screens explorations of the marvels of the universe about us which have had as their underlying premise the rather vague and fuzzy notion of what we used to call "nature" that has somehow controlled its own destiny, becoming what it has and what it shall be by, as it were, willing it so. I do not recognize in these excursions any buttress to the traditional biblical doctrine of creation; they propose, rather, an unacceptable substitute for it.

I am much more comfortable when science adheres to its own ground-rules and does not attempt to become a religion, just as I am much more confortable when religion sticks to its ground-rules and does not try to pass off its doctrines as science—a subject to which I shall turn in a few moments. By its own definition, science is restricted to observable physical phenomena. We are speaking, of course, of science in the contemporary sense of the word, not "science" in the medieval sense, by which was meant the study of any organized body of knowledge, including philosophy and theology. Science, in this contemporary sense, is precluded from such considerations as "design" and "teleology." It can detect "patterns," of course, which are the raw material for the conclusion of "design," since patterns, taxonomy, statistics, are part and parcel of the observable phenomena. But, when "design" is proposed as a conclusion from observed patterns, we have left the area of the physical, the natural, and entered into the realm of metaphysics. Of its own resources, science has no authority to draw any such conclusion, and certainly no right to extrapolate from the microcosm to the macrocosm. If it does so, it has not only usurped the prerogatives of philosophy and theology; it has also rejected its own scientific credentials.

The other potential conflict of creation-theology with evolution-science that I have mentioned, is obviously, far more fundamental. The biblical view of the created world is static: what is is as it was determined to be at the moment of creation. The evolutionary view, on the contrary, is exuberantly dynamic: what is is in transition to what may be and may or may not differ from what it was. I do not think it necessary to rehearse the evidence that supports the evolutionary view, not only in the biological area in which I have no competence but must depend upon an alien scholarly consensus, but also in the area of the human spirit where I do have a certain experience. Suffice it to say that I accept evolution as a law of human life, physical and spiritual. The original sense of "evolution," after all, means nothing more or less than to realize whatever is one's innate potential.

The Bible certainly has such a concept of evolution, of self-realization, at least in the individual. If it does not apply the concept to the human race in general, the reason is—unlike some modern empiricists—it does not extrapolate from the particular to the general, and also—perhaps as part of the same phenomenon—it did not philosophize. It remains that, without philosophy, the Bible does and continues to express to its readers and hearers an outlook on mankind that can be duplicated nowhere else in the contemporary Near Eastern world. One can look, for example, at Israel's unique development over the ages of the legal principles, ethical and moral standards, theodicy, even its mythology—all of which began as the common property of all those who peopled the ancient Near East—and compare the dynamism which historical criticism can verify in this development with the virtually timeless and unchanging affirmations found from millennium to millennium in the hieroglyphic papyri and cuneiform tablets of Egypt, Syria, Canaan, and Mesopotamia. Without professing it, without having the word, the Bible reveals an evolutionism from first to last. It could hardly be otherwise, once we take seriously the implications of the fact that Israel's grasp at ultimate reality was thought to be the result of historical revelation, constituting Israel and its tradition receptive and eager to the idea of change and to the expectation of the unexpected, a unique island in an archipelago of surrounding perennial, unchanging, totally predictable nature religions.

These considerations are far more important to our purposes than the fairly obvious ones of the biblical authors' ignorance of entities like neutrons or protons. Or, like atoms: a word, which I need not remind you, means "the indivisible." "Atom" was coined by philosophers and scientists to denote the ultimate, irreducible element in the composition of matter. We now live in a world which, for better or worse, and, unfortunately, more often for worse rather than better, depends upon the division of this indivisible, the reduction of this irreducible. Subatomic particles are now being calculated in the scores. There is no reason, as far as I can see, for the Bible to have to apologize for its rudimentary science any more than the old myths had to apologize to Thales and Heraclitus who demythologized them,[12] or Thales had to apologize to Newton, or Newton to Einstein. Without what went before, nothing that followed could ever have occurred. We can cheerfully dismiss as superseded and "revised" a biblical assumption of fixed species just as we must, cheerfully, or otherwise, dismiss as superseded and revised the pre-1940s dogma of the indivisibility of the atom. In any case, the Bible's rudimentary science was always an assumption, never an assertion. The Bible is a work of religious testimony, revealing in the process the limitations and shortcomings of its authors in matters of historical, scientific, or statistical fact.

At this point I would like very much to take this discussion into the positive realm and open up for you a vision in which the theological premise of creation and the scientific premise of evolution would be seen to coexist in perfect harmony to their mutual enrichment. Alas, I cannot do this, for I lack the necessary talents. One person who possessed those necessary talents could have been the late Père Pierre Teilhard de Chardin, and it is hardly necessary for me to recall to you the contribution of his *Le phénomène humain.* I have read this book several times, not always with the comprehension that I would have liked, but always with keen appreciation. It is well known that in 1962 the Holy Office of the Roman Catholic Curia issued a *monitum,* a caution—not a condemnation—against too hasty an acceptance of Teilhard's innovative thought. It is not always as well recognized that Sir Julian Huxley who, rather than any Catholic bishop or religious superior, provided the *imprimatur* of his book, also rejected the principal of Teilhard's theses, in fault of which he probably would never have written at all:

> Though many scientists may, as I do, find it impossible to follow him all the way in his gallant attempt to reconcile the supernatural elements in Christianity with the facts and implications of evolution, this in no way detracts from the positive value of his naturalistic general approach.[13]

Teilhard, priest, theologian, metaphysician, scientist, archeologist, and anthropologist, was unable to satisfy the watchdogs either of religion or of science that some kind of satisfactory synthesis had been achieved. What he could not do, I certainly do not propose that I can. Furthermore, I have been much impressed by a recent article by Donald Goergen,[14] whose central thesis is that the way to the understanding of the Teilhardian synthesis lies in mysticism, which I regret to say is one closed to me.

Creationism

If, however, I cannot do what I would like, I may at least attempt what I can. What I can attempt is to demonstrate the fatuity of the alternate response of creation faith to the challenge of evolution that has issued in such inappropriate reactions as go by terms like "creationism" or the oxymoronic "creation-science."

"Creationism" and "creation-science" are buzz-words for dealing with a situation that is both pragmatic—even cynically pragmatic —and also is founded in high principle. (1) It is pragmatic and even cynically pragmatic. These terms are legislative ploys to subvert the law of the land—the American Constitution as interpreted by the Supreme Court of the United States—by introducing under the fictitious guise of a secular discipline into the curriculum of the public schools of our country a religious doctrine which is at the same time a highly sectarian religious doctrine. And (2), these terms, nevertheless, deserve to be examined dispassionately as the felt conviction of many among us that there is as much evidence—or lack of it—from the empirical data to affirm as to deny an evolutionary beginning of the world and of man.

To begin with (1), legislative ploys, let us consider specifically the most notorious of the lot, Act 590 of the 73d General Assembly of the State of Arkansas of 1981, which defined "creation-science" in the following terms:

> the scientific evidences and related inferences that indicate: (1) Sudden creation of the universe, energy, and life from nothing; (2) The insufficiency of mutation and natural selection in bringing about all living kinds from a single organism; (3) Changes only within fixed limits of originally created kinds of plants and animals; (4) Separate ancestry for man and apes; (5) Explanation of the earth's geology by catastrophism, including the occurrence of a worldwide flood; and (6) A relatively recent inception of the earth and living kinds.[15]

Now surely, no one can read or hear a text like this and not acknowledge that "creation-science" so called is nothing other than an attempt to assert a vision of cosmic and human origins that has been extracted from a literalistic reading of the book of Genesis of the Judeo-Christian Bible. District Judge William R. Overton, who presided over the issue of the constitutionality of this Act and eventually permanently enjoined its implementation, recognized that the proponents of the Act had engaged in a "religious crusade" and that the Act itself had "as its unmentioned reference the first 11 chapters of the Book of Genesis."

I have just used the word "literalistic" in a pejorative sense, which I would like to distinguish from "literal." All my life I—and I think I can speak for most of my colleagues in the biblical enterprise—have devoted every talent to discerning what is the literal sense of the biblical word. The literal sense is not, of course, what words mean by dictionary definition or what idiom means when it is reproduced woodenly—what do you do with "nel bel centro" in Italian, "beau faire" in French, or "was für ein Mensch" in German, except to recognize that such ideosyncratic manipulations of words add up to idiom, which is at the heart of language, the means of communication, and has very little to do with glossary? The literal meaning of a text is what the text actually means when the writing is examined in terms of its historical context, the intent of its author, and the literary and linguistic conventions of which he was heir and of which he made use. A literalistic interpretation of the same text is, frequently, a lexical exercise in what its component words could mean, or could be made to mean, were they divorced from these selfsame controls of historical and literary criticism.

It is a literalistic reading of the Bible that underpins such excursions into bad theology as creationism. In turn, what motivates the literalistic reading, which, as I have just said, can be quite manipulative, is a doctrinal assumption of biblical infallibility and inerrancy. James Barr has correctly asserted the problematic in his basic work on the subject:

> What is the point at which the fundamentalist use of the Bible conflicts with the use of it by other people? The 'plain man', asked this question, will commonly say that a fundamentalist is a person who 'takes the Bible literally'. This, however, is far from being a correct or exact description. The point of conflict between fundamentalist and others is not over *literality* but over *inerrancy*. Even if fundamentalists sometimes say that they take the Bible literally, the facts of fundamentalist interpretation show that this is not so. What fundamentalists insist is not that the Bible must be taken literally but that it must be so interpreted as to avoid any admission that it contains any kind of *error*. In order to avoid imputing error to the Bible, fundamentalists twist and turn back and forward between literal and non-literal interpretation. The dominant fundamentalist assertions about the Bible, namely that it is divinely inspired and infallible, do not mean that it must be taken literally, and are not so interpreted in the conservative evangelical literature; what they mean, and are constantly interpreted as meaning, is that the Bible contains no error of any kind—not only theological error, but error in any sort of historical, geographical or scientific fact, is completely absent from the

> Bible. In order to expound the Bible as thus inerrant, the fundamen-
> talist interpreter varies back and forward between literal and non-literal
> understandings, indeed he has to do so in order to obtain a Bible that is
> error-free.[16]

There, indeed, is the problem. The creation story of Gen 1:1–2:4a speaks of a creation that it portrays as a six-day work. As was brought out at the Arkansas creationism trial through the testimony of Professor George Marsden, while the earlier fundamentalists or evangelicals experienced no difficulty in accommodating Darwinism to biblical creation-faith, there has been since World War I a progressive hardening of attitudes which has nothing to do with the attempt to get at the literal meaning of Genesis but speaks volumes about what was going on in the minds of the interpreters. From the desire to make an accommodation or harmonization of the biblical and scientific data,[17] commonplaces in the early days of the Darwinian revolution, we now run the gamut to pronouncements like those of Henry M. Morris: "Sometimes, evolution is described as God's method of creation, in an attempt to make it more palatable to die-hard creationists, but this device has never been satisfactory, either to evolutionists, or creationists."[18] And, "this philosophy [evolution] is really the foundation of Satan himself and of every evil system which he has devised since that time to oppose the sovereignty and grace of God in this universe."[19] To try to interpret the "days" of the Genesis story as the geological ages that had been revealed by science was a brave attempt, even though it may have been misguided, ventured by creationist and scientist alike in their first confrontation. Why did it later come to be regarded as an enterprise of Satan by the spiritual heirs of William Jennings Bryan? Professor Marsden, if I follow him, has associated the change with the disillusionment with German science, brought about in the Anglo-Saxon world by World War I. While I do not associate evolutionism peculiarly with German science then or now, I do not think the assignment of ultimate responsibility capable of final resolution. Suffice it to say that the fundamentalist reading of the Genesis creation story has shifted from a soft to a hard-line literalism out of no new exegetical resources but out of a sectarian and doctrinal posture. Whence comes the posture?

Whence, indeed, the assumption of biblical infallibility and inerrancy? It comes, of course, from the atavistic yearning of all of us to have some kind of immediate contact with ultimate truth. I accept without any qualification ever the formulation of the Second Vatican Council (in the fifth and final redaction of its formulation) that

> the books of Scripture must be acknowleged as teaching firmly, faithfully, and without error that truth which God wanted put into the sacred writings for the sake of our salvation.[20]

I can hardly conceive of anyone belonging to the main-line tradition of biblical religion having any difficulty with the formulation. This is simply the Catholic, Lutheran, and Calvinist conception of what is meant by "biblical religion": we accept the Bible as the testimony to the experience that has founded us, and we wish to live in its tradition and to hear its voice as the guidance of our future steps. And that is all. Whence, then, this bibliolatry, this iconization of a body of Semitic and Levantine literature as having the oracular character of a divinely inspired encyclopedia of all relevant knowledge?

It comes, as I have just suggested, from the natural but impossible-of-fulfillment desire for total assurance, for once-for-all answers, to the fundamental questions of a human enquiry. The quest can never, of course, be greeted with success because it is quixotic and chimerical. For Protestantism—and, to be sure, the phenomenon is peculiarly though not exclusively Protestant—it represents a *reductio ad absurdum,* to the extent that Protestantism could never have existed without the preexistence of a firmly defined canon of normative Sacred Scripture.[21] It is at the same time, however, a betrayal of Protestantism insofar as, having rejected ecclesiastical magisterium, it has ended by canonizing for itself a "paper pope."

It has also squandered its heritage of biblical religion by trivializing the biblical word. As Conrad Hyers has aptly observed, biblical literalism so called "sells its symbolic birthright for a mess of tangible pottage."

> Biblical materials and affirmations—in this case the symbolism of Creator and creation—are treated as though of the same order and the same literary genre as scientific and historical writing . . . [T]he symbolic richness and power—the *religious* meaning—of creation are largely lost in the cloud of geological and paleontological dust stirred up in the confusion . . . The literalist, instead of opening up the treasurehouse of symbolic imagination, digresses into more and more ingenious and fantastic attempts at defending literalism itself. Again and again the real issue turns out to be not belief in divine creativity but belief in a peculiar theory of Scripture, not faith but security.[22]

With this, let us now turn, finally, to (2), to the proposition that there is as much empirical evidence to affirm a creational as there is to affirm an evolutionary origin of the world and of mankind—accepting for argument the creationists' premise that the one position excludes the other.

Actually, the proposition is defended less by tendering any positive empirical evidence in favor of creation than it is by finding flaws in the fabric of supposition that supports the hypothesis of evolution,[23] an enterprise at which the evolutionists are probably more expert than the creationists. It remains a fact that evolution, admittedly an hypothesis, as an hypothesis works in ways that others do not. Creation, on the other hand, is not a working hypothesis to account for things the way they are. Creation is a matter of faith which does not necessarily exclude evolution but which, in any case, is something apart and nonfalsifiable by empirical evidence, a matter of religion and not of science. The term "creation-science" is a logical absurdity. It also proved to be a will-o'-the-wisp, a broken reed, for those who depended upon it to provide an alternative to "evolution-science." When the creationists had achieved their apparent victory in Arkansas by the enactment of Act 590 — before it was declared unconstitutional — they had already been chagrined to have to confess that there were no textbooks and no teachers prepared to present creation as a science and not as a religious affirmation.

All that empirical evidence can do for us is to reveal the god of the philosophers: the first cause of the cosmos. I know that in the post-Kantian world even this ability has been denied, but I continue to accept its basic premises.[24] However, in any case, it is a misreading of Christian history to conclude that the god of philosophy was ever to be identified with the God of biblical revelation.

Thomas Aquinas, in his famous "five ways" of the demonstration of God's existence, did not start from the scratch of curiosity but from the itch of revelation. What he set out to do was to demonstrate that the God who had been revealed to him through biblical faith and whom he accepted in this faith was also acceptable as a logical explanation of the workings of the universe. It was not the other way round. It may be debated whether Aquinas held that it would be theoretically possible to sustain by reason the proposition of an eternal cause of an eternal universe, a timeless contingent forever dependent on a timeless necessary;[25] what is quite certain is that he held, and the mainstream of Christian tradition held with him, that only by revelation, accepted in faith, could there be an affirmation of creation in time, and time, for that matter, as the consequence and not the condition of creation. That is the only concept of creation that is meaningful in biblical, Christian, or Jewish terms.

On the contrary, what our modern pragmatic creationists are proposing, in their theologically illiterate way, is a vastly different thing. In their single-minded determination to intrude "creator" and "creation" by any title whatsoever into the creation-evolution dialogue, they have hit upon, in a sort of groping fashion and not really understanding it, the concept of the god of the philosophers, which a more informed historical and philosophical erudition would have taught them, in the language of Blaise Pascal, can never be the God of biblical or Christian faith.

In the "Findings of Fact," filed by the creationist defendants in the Arkansas litigation concerning Act 590, we find these truly remarkable words appearing in paragraph 35:

[T]he terms or concepts of "creation" and "creator" are not inherently religious terms or concepts. In this sense, the term "creator" means only some entity with power, intelligence, and a sense of design. Creation-science does not require a creator who has personality, who has the attributes of love, compassion, justice, etc., which are ordinarily attributed to a deity. Indeed, the creation-science model does not require that the creator still be in existence.

Truly, this is to sell a priceless birthright for a worthless mess of pottage. But, it is far more. As Etienne Gilson outlined its consequences some years ago, it is a betrayal of the whole Christian enterprise:

The world of Aristotle owes its divine maker everything, except its existence. And that is why it has no history, not even in history. Hermetically sealed against any kind of novelty, the existenceless world of Aristotle has crossed century after century, wholly unaware of the fact that the world of philosophy and of science was constantly changing around it. Whether you look at it in the thirteenth, fourteenth, or sixteenth century, the world of Averroes remains substantially the same, and the Averroists could do little more than eternally repeat themselves, because the world of Aristotle was an eternally self-repeating world. It has opposed Christian theologians when they taught that God could have made another world than the one He has made. It has resisted Christian theologians when they maintained that, in this God-made world, there take place such events as are the work of freedom and escape necessity. Because theology was, before anything else, a history full of unpredictable events, it has branded theology as a myth, and science itself has felt the weight of its hostility. Itself scientifically sterile, there is not a single scientific discovery against which, so long as it lasted, it did not raise an indignant protest. And no wonder, for, since the world of Aristotle has no history, it never changes and it is no one's business to change it. No newness, no development, no history, what a dead lump of being the world of substance is![26]

I ask a candid world, are not these, without their knowing them, the ideological underpinnings of the modern-day fundamentalist creationists?

Creation, in the traditional theological sense, opposed the eternalism of the ancient Mediterranean world, first expressed in the ancient Near Eastern myths and then demythologized and philosophized in Greek science and philosophy. Initially, creation in this traditional sense found its natural ally in the idea of evolution.[27] I strongly suspect, once the temporary clouds of confusion and superstition have dissipated, as they inevitably must, that this natural alliance will be taken up again, to the enrichment of our understanding of our common human condition and of our relation to the God who made us.

NOTES

[1] The examples of this phenomenon are countless. There is no French for "gentleman": *gentilhomme* no more does the job than "opener" and "good word" translate *apéritif* and *bon mot* respectively; all these expressions are needed, in any language, for cultivated communication. When the late Frank Sheed received an honorary doctorate from the Holy See, conferred at the University of Tours (thought to be historically and geographically allied to the expatriate English College of Douai which had flourished during the Elizabethan repression of Catholicism), he was amused to discover that there was no precise French equivalent for the second term of a title for which he was particularly noted: *Theology and Sanity*. The subject could be endlessly pursued. Particularly during the period of the Nazi tyranny, the term *Zivilcourage*, denoting the courage to exhibit civil disobedience to unjust laws, came to be widely used. It will not be found in most German dictionaries, suggesting that it has no native roots in the language.

[2] Ultimately from the English *wer*, "man," + *eall*, "all." Cf. the modern German *Weltall*.

[3] So G. B. Caird, *The Language and Imagery of the Bible* (Philadelphia: Westminster, 1980), pp. 44–46.

[4] *bārā'*, which may have originally meant something like "incise" or "engrave," has been adopted as a technical term in the late OT, following Second Isaiah, to denote the special work of God (who always appears as the subject of the verb), especially in relation to his saving work for Israel. This verb, in view of the Deutero-Isaian associations, adds a determined soteriological connotation to the idea of creation in Genesis and elsewhere. Otherwise, *bārā'* easily parallels with *'āśâ*, "make," *yāṣar*, "bring forth," *kûn*, "establish," *yāsad* or *bānâ*, "build," *ḥādǎs*, "renew," etc. See the discussion in C. J. Botterweck-H. Ringgren, *Theologisches Wörterbuch zum Alten Testament*, I, 769–77.

[5] Cf. Fausto Salvoni, "Creazione dal nulla? Ricerca su Genesi 1,1–2," *Ricerche Bibliche e Religiose* 17 (1982): 210–44.

[6] *The Tao and the Daimon: Segments of a Religious Inquiry* (Albany: Suny Press, 1982).

[7] Mati Lai Pandit, "Creation: Text and Context," *Indian Theological Studies* 19 (1982): 318–38.

[8] This, I am sure, is the meaning of *qnh* ("possessor") which runs through Akkadian, Ugaritic, and Hebrew formulas and which is conventionally translated by others "creator." See my article, "Prov. 8:22; Wisdom and Creation," *Journal of Biblical Literature* 99 (1980): 205–16.

[9] *Primal Myths: Creating the World* (New York: Harper & Row, 1979).

[10] Cf. Hartmut Gese, "Die Einheit von Psalm 19," in Eberhard Jüngel *et al.*, eds., *Verifikationen: Festschrift für Gerhard Ebeling zum 70. Geburtstag* (Tübingen: Mohr, 1982), pp. 1–10. He holds that the psalm does not incorporate "an old creation hymn" but is rather an original composition from the end of the fourth century. In any case, there is no question of a *creatio ex nihilo*. Similarly, the "creation" doxologies in Amos 4:13, 5:8–9, 9:26, which certainly do in part celebrate creation (though again not creation "from nothing"), are best taken as redactional in the final postexilic production of the book and not as some hymn adapted by the eighth-century prophet Amos.

[11] "Genesis and the New Physics," *The Ecumenist* 20 (1982): 52-54.

[12] H. and H.A. Frankfort, *Before Philosophy* (Harmondsworth: Penguin, 1951), pp. 253-62.

[13] *The Phenomenon of Man* (New York: Harper & Brothers, 1959), p. 19.

[14] "Recent Studies of Pierre Teilhard de Chardin," *Spirituality Today* 34 (1982): 261-72.

[15] All of my quotations having to do with the Arkansas trial have been extracted from the transcripts provided by the court reporters, a copyright interest in which has been asserted by them. In the citations I have made I think I can vouch independently for their accuracy. At the same time, they must be consulted with some caution. For example, in my own testimony where the word "exegesis" surfaced, the court reporters heard (more than once) "Text of Jesus."

[16] *Fundamentalism* (Philadelphia: Westminster, 1978), p. 40.

[17] At the famous Scopes Trial, William Jennings Bryan stated: "It seems to me just as easy to believe that God created the world in six million years, six hundred million years, whatever you want, as to believe he created it in six days." (Court reporters' transcripts.)

[18] *The Troubled Waters of Evolution* (San Diego: CLP Publishers, 1974), p. 10.

[19] In *Studies in the Bible and Science* (Philadelphia: Presbyterian & Reform Publishing Co., 1966), p. 102.

[20] Walter M. Abbott, S.J., editor, *The Documents of Vatican II* (New York: Guild Press, 1966), p. 119.

[21] Cf. James Barr, *Holy Scripture: Canon, Authority, Criticism* (Philadelphia: Westminster, 1983), pp. 2-3. See also Alan D. Falconer, "Protestant Fundamentalism," *Doctrine and Life* 33 (1983): 4-13.

[22] "Biblical Literature: Constricting the Cosmic Dance," *The Christian Century* 99 (August 4-11, 1982): 823-27.

[23] For example, Howard Morrison, "The irrationality of biological evolution," *Homiletic and Pastoral Review* 82 (Aug.-Sept., 1982): 63-69.

[24] Cf. Brian Davies, O.P., "The Cosmological Argument," *New Blackfriars* 64 (1983); 100-13.

[25] Cf. Pasquale Mazzarella, "Creazione partecipazione e tempo secondo San Tomasso d'Aquino," *Studia Patavina* 29 (1982): 309-35.

[26] *Being and Some Philosophers* (Toronto: Pontifical Institute of Mediaeval Studies, 1949), pp. 72-73.

[27] Cf. Lenn E. Goodman and Madeleine J. Goodman, "Creation and Evolution: Another Round in an Ancient Struggle," *Zygon: Journal of Religion and Science* 18 (1983): 3-43.

Interpretations and Reinterpretations of the Fall

W. Sibley Towner

I. *Introduction*

> Of Man's first disobedience, and the fruit
> Of that forbidden tree, whose mortal taste
> Brought death into the World, and all our woe,
> With loss of Eden, till one greater Man
> Restore us, and regain the blissful seat
> Sing, Heavenly Muse. . . .
>
> That. . . . I may assert Eternal Providence
> And justify the ways of God to men. [1]

It is all there in Milton's poem, is it not? The Fall of man, embracing woman, I mean, just as it was interpreted to you and me at our mother's knee. Never mind that Milton was a Protestant of the Reformed stripe, a seventeenth-century Calvinist who shared the dour outlook on the human condition of his sixteenth-century Genevan mentor. His description of the Fall, though more poetical and therefore memorable than most, was strictly mainline. Not only would Calvin have recognized it, but so would Luther. So would Augustine, the teacher of them all, for it was he—standing in the tradition of Paul, as he understood the apostle—who established the basic lines of thinking about the Fall and about biblical anthropology that remained normative in the church down to the rise of modern biblical scholarship, and that frequently inform the catechesis of children and shape the ideology of ordinary believers even today. For St. Augustine, human nature before the Fall was fundamentally different from what followed it. The crisis in the Garden resulted in an altered anthropology, which alteration was transmitted by Adam and Eve to all their progeny forever, just as mutations in human genes, resulting from the sin of nuclear warfare, might be transmitted forever from sperm to egg. This fundamental change in human nature is spoken of by Augustine in the *City of God:*

[Before they sinned, our first parents'] love to God was unclouded, and their mutual affection was that of faithful and sincere marriage; and from this love flowed a wonderful delight, because they always enjoyed what was loved. Their avoidance of sin was tranquil; and, so long as it was maintained, no other ill at all could invade them and bring sorrow. . . . As happy, then, as were these our first parents, who were agitated by no mental perturbations, and annoyed by no bodily discomforts, so happy should the whole human race have been, had they not introduced that evil which they have transmitted to their posterity. . . .[2]

Augustine speaks for the ages when he identifies the sin that led to the Fall as rebellion, a "despising of the authority of God." As punishment, the fallen couple, the new humanity, began to experience the flesh as a burden, tied up in the bonds of hard labor and death:

Not to live in the absolute independence he affected, but instead of the liberty he desired, to live dissatisfied with himself in a hard and miserable bondage to him to whom by sinning he had yielded himself, doomed in spite of himself to die in body as he had willingly become dead in spirit, condemned even to eternal death (had not the grace of God delivered him) because he had forsaken eternal life.[3]

The fuse that lit the fire of rebellion was lust, good old lust. Augustine could prove it because the first couple became ashamed of their nakedness and moved to cover it only *after* their sin. Somehow, then, human sexuality became inplicated in the Fall, and human nature universally and forever after sought to cover the private parts. Augustine even carried his readers to the public facilities:

Consequently all nations, being propagated from that one stock, have so strong an instinct to cover shameful parts, that some barbarians do not uncover them even in the bath. . . .[4]

Finally, all of this came about because of Satan, the fallen angel who was envious of the unfallen condition of the man and woman. For Augustine, the serpent was not itself Satan, but was Satan's mouthpiece, chosen because, "being slippery, and moving in tortuous windings, it was suitable for his purpose." And Satan also employed his knowledge of human nature to attack the woman first because she was

The weaker part of that human alliance, that he might gradually gain the whole, and not supposing that the man would readily give ear to him, or be deceived, but that [through lust] he might yield to the error of the woman.[5]

Here, then, are the principal components of the Augustinian analysis of the Fall. Before the sin of Adam and Eve, recorded in Genesis 3, human nature was different. It was innocent, trusting, spontaneously loving, tranquil, and above all, immortal. The Fall consisted in rebellion against God's sovereignty, in a grab for independence, manifested in eating the forbidden fruit. Satan promoted this out of jealousy, using the slippery serpent as his mouthpiece, and attacking the weaker sex initially, but relying on Adam's lust to carry the tragedy to its conclusion. Post-fall humanity suffers sexual shame and pain in childbearing as a consequence, together with the curses of drudgery and death, and no human being can escape this universal blight, for the new sin-prone, death-fated anthropology is inherited with the father's sperm and the mother's milk.

If we fall twelve centuries forward in time from Augustine to Milton, we find that nothing much has befallen the Fall. True, a Reformation had happened, and in England the Puritan revolution was underway. But, the fundamental interpretation of the origin of sin and death remained essentially the same in all branches of western Christianity. The opening lines of "Paradise Lost," with which this essay began, described the Fall as disobedience, manifested in the eating of the forbidden fruit. Before the Fall, human nature was perfection itself:

> Two of far nobler shape, erect and tall
> Godlike erect, with native honour clad
> In naked majesty, seemed lords of all,
> And worthy seemed; for in their looks
> The image of their glorious Maker shone,
> Truth, wisdom, sanctitude severe and pure. . . .
> For contemplation he and valour formed,
> For softness she and sweet attractive grace;
> He for God only, she for God in him. [6]

But such nobility was doomed:

> Who first seduced [our grand parents] to that foul revolt?
> The infernal Serpent; he it was whose guile,
> Stirred up with envy and revenge, deceived
> The mother of mankind, what time his pride
> Had cast him out from Heaven, with all his host
> Of rebel angels. . . . [7]

Satan and the serpent have now become identified, and the first couple are enmeshed in a dualistic struggle of cosmic dimensions. In that sense, Milton's Calvinism represents an advance over Augustine. But, the result is the same. First comes the fall from sexual innocence.

> . . . he scrupled not to eat
> Against his better knowledge, not deceived,
> But fondly overcome with female charm.
> Earth trembled from her entrails, as again
> In pangs, and Nature gave a second groan.
> Sky loured and, muttering thunder, some sad drops
> Wept at the completing of the mortal Sin
> Original. . . .
> As with new wine intoxicated both,

> They swim in mirth, and fancy that they feel
> Divinity within them breeding wings
> Wherewith to scorn the Earth. But that false fruit
> Far other operation first displayed,
> Carnal desire inflaming. He on Eve
> Began to cast lascivious eyes; she him
> As wantonly repaid; in lust they burned. . . .[8]

Then opens the Pandora's box of all the ills that beset humankind: shame, anger, hate, mistrust, suspicion, discord, and "sensual appetite, who, from beneath Usurping over sovran Reason claimed Superior sway. . . ."[9]

The trajectory from Augustine through Milton down to our own time is direct and uninterrupted. The concept of the Fall, espoused in these classic shapers and exponents of the western theological tradition, is enshrined in catechisms and confessions, dogmatic theologies and pontifical directives, and so has come to be part of our own personal heritages.

II.   The Fall in Christian Orthodoxy

Only a few illustrations will suffice to demonstrate the extent to which this normative understanding has influenced our dogmatic formulations. The "Decree Concerning Original Sin," promulgated in the fifth session of the Council of Trent, June 17, 1546, reads in part as follows:

> . . . the first man Adam, when he transgressed the commandment of God in paradise, immediately lost the holiness and justice in which he had been constituted, and through the offense of that prevarication, incurred the wrath and indignation of God, and thus death . . . and together with death, captivity under his power who thenceforth *had the empire of death, that is to say, the devil.* [10]

The Tridentine definition goes on to anathematize anyone who contends that Adam, by his sin of disobedience, "has transfused only death and the pains of the body into the whole human race, but not sin also, which is the death of the soul."[11] To deny that original sin was involved in the Fall was perceived to deny the explicit words of the Apostle Paul, "By one man sin entered into the world, and by sin death; so sin passed upon all men, in whom all have sinned."[12]

One seeks in vain any substantive difference between this formula for the Fall and that set forth less than two decades later in the *Scots Confession of 1560* (produced in four days, and read line by line in the Scottish Parliament). It affirms that before the Fall

> In the whole nature of man, no imperfection could be found. From this dignity and perfection man and woman both fell . . . both conspiring

against the sovereign majesty of God. . . . By this transgression, generally known as original sin, the image of God was utterly defaced in man,
and he and his children became by nature hostile to God, slaves of
Satan, and servants to sin. And thus everlasting death has had, and shall
have, power and dominion over all who have not been, are not, or shall
not be reborn from above. [13]

The *Westminster Confession of 1647,* still the confessional standard
of many English-speaking branches of the Reformed faith, reiterates
the same tradition a century later, with the simple additions of an at-
tribution of the Fall to the permissive will of God (through which he
could glorify himself in the gracious salvation of some sinners and also
in the just damnation of others), and a heightened emphasis on the
total depravity of humankind which resulted from the Fall of Adam
and Eve:

1. Our first parents, being seduced by the subtlety and temptation of
   Satan, sinned in eating the forbidden fruit. This their sin God was
   pleased, according to his wise and holy counsel, to permit, having
   purposed to order it to his own glory.
2. By this sin they fell from their original righteousness and communion
   with God, and so became dead in sin, and wholly defiled in all their
   facilities and parts of soul and body.
3. They being the root of all mankind, the guilt of their sin was im-
   puted, and the same death in sin and corrupted nature conveyed to
   all their posterity, descending from them by ordinary generation.
4. From this original corruption, whereby we are utterly indisposed,
   disabled, and made opposite to all good, and wholly inclined to all
   evil, do proceed all actual transgressions. [14]

The traditional dogmatic understanding of the Fall, enshrined in
these confessional texts, has the virtue of tidiness and rational
coherence. It accounts for the origins of evil and of death, and it ex-
onerates God from responsibility in the matter. So central did the doctrine of the Fall come to be regarded that bulwarks were erected
around Genesis 3 by the guardians of the faith to prevent any erosion
of that sober theologumenon. For example, in 1909, the Pontifical
Biblical Commission pronounced:

The Catholic exegete must hold as historical, among other things, that
woman was formed from the first man (Gen. 2:21-23); the unity of the
human races, sprung from one couple (Gen. 3:20); the divine command
to test the obedience of our first parents (Gen. 2:17); the Serpent that
tempted Eve (Gen. 3:1-4); the fall from a previous state of perfection
characterized by justice, integrity, and immortality. [15]

Neat as the position may have been, however, it has also wrought in-
calculable mischief in the hearts of believers throughout the ages.
Modern believers and unbelievers alike tend to hold as patent nonsense
the notion that all human sin and all death are generically descended

from a single act by a single pair of human beings who lived at a single moment in time, or that the cause of their original transgression was Satan in the guise of a snake. Seriously under review now are the concepts of original sin and total depravity which are derived from the doctrine of the Fall. Augustine, Calvin, Luther, Trent, Westminster, and the other councils, fathers, and confessions of the church to the contrary notwithstanding, we have had to put behind us the Fall in its traditional formulation as we now try to grapple with the ever more profoundly experienced realities of human sin and evil.

What has brought about so great an ideological revolution? Certainly secularization, with its strong sense that human beings have within themselves what it takes to free themselves from the terrors that beset them, has played a major part in breaking the hold of the Augustinian formulation of the Fall on Christian orthodoxy. Freudian psychology, too, has given us a new map of the human mind which sees rebellion against parental authority, the struggle against the threat of death, and the drive to extend the dominion of the human ego all as inevitable and necessary aspects of the human experience.

However, particularly for those who view scripture and doctrine from the perspective of believers, the rise of historical-critical biblical studies accounts for much of the relief from the heavy hand of dogma about the Fall. Thanks to critical reading of Genesis 1-11, the conviction is now very widespread among us that the story of Adam and Eve is not an historical account at all, and that the Primeval History is fundamentally a theological treatise, written in narrative, history-like style. Both the discovery in ancient Mesopotamia of other accounts of creation comparable to the biblical account and the breakthroughs by form-criticism in showing that the narratives of Genesis exhibit the literary qualities of "faded myth," now recast as a saga of human origins, have eliminated any need to treat Genesis 3 as an actual historical account of the origin of evil and sin. No longer do we need to suppose—in opposition to every kind of anthropology, commonsensical or scientific—that human nature underwent any kind of profound change as the consequence of one simple human act, committed at a moment in time.

III.   The Texts in Question

Historical-critical reading demands that Bible stories be read literally, with more precise attention to detail than any ancient rabbi or Tennessee evangelist ever lavished upon them. Accordingly, modern commentators take us back to look again more closely at the key texts, Gen. 3:1-19 and Rom. 5:12-21 (cf. I Cor. 15:20-28). In Gen. 3:1, the serpent is presented as "more subtle than any other wild creature." This subtlety is not regarded negatively, but is simply stated as a fact. If the serpent is intended to be a symbol for anything beyond itself, the writer gives us no clue to that effect. It is simply the cleverest of all creatures, so clever, in fact, that it can tempt the woman by promising her the knowledge of good and evil which comes to those who eat the fruit of the tree which God placed off-limits but left temptingly visible smack-dab in the middle of the Garden. This knowledge, too, is not perceived in any negative way. The effect of the disobedience of the woman and the man is a simple awareness of their nakedness. To deal with this awareness, they create the first inadequate garments for themselves. But, the fig leaves do not eliminate their new-found shame. Indeed, their shame gives them away. On an evening walk in the garden, Yahweh finds them in hiding; he questions them, receives their confessions of disobedience, and pronounces their punishments. The woman must now experience pain in childbearing. She must submit to her husband's rule. The man must now win bread from the ground, the very dust from which he came and to which he and the woman inevitably return. This he must do with sweat and toil. At the end, lest they sample the fruit of the other tree and live forever, the man and the woman receive the heaviest blow of all. They are expelled from paradise. Period.

That is the story, literally read. That is all it says, though that surely is plenty. Neither sexuality nor Satan caused the Fall; it happened. No word is to be found to identify death as a consequence of the Fall; no hint suggests that all of nature and all human beings were forever corrupted through this one couple's sin. Nowhere is it said that human nature was irrevocably altered in a fundamental way that afternoon in the garden. Nor is the serpent Satan at all. It is not even the female temptress, the night-hag Lilith, whose head it so often wears in the medieval paintings. It is just a snake. That is all that the biblical account says—it never has said any more than that. Does it not seem odd that it would have taken the rise of biblical criticism to recall to the great dogmatic tradition the simple testimony of the text?

The picture is somewhat different in Paul's transformation of this story in Rom. 5:12-21. The Apostle was an heir of an extended tradition of reflection on the theme in post-Old Testament Judaism, a hint of which is seen in the late work II Esdras 7:118:

> O Adam, what have you done?
> For though it was you who sinned,
> The fall was not yours alone,
> But ours also, who are your descendants.

True to this tradition, Paul attributes all sin to one man, and all death as a consequence to that one sin (Rom. 5:12). However, a critically literal reading of Paul on the Fall shows that the entire point of his discussion is to create an exact antithesis between the guilt and death which flow from one man's trespass and the free gifts of grace and life which flow from another man's obedience. Paul sums up his argument in the famous verse 18: "Then as one man's trespass led to condemnation for all men, so one man's act of righteousness leads to acquittal and life for all men." One can only assume that Paul is very serious about this parallel and that his purpose in establishing the solidarity of humankind with the fallen Adam is to establish the premise that the redemptive work of Christ extends to all humankind. In short, Paul's use of the Fall in Rom. 5:12-21 is as the necessary foil to his soteriology; it is not intended in the first instance to make historical claims about the origin of evil or to denigrate human nature as it now is in contrast to what it once was. Note also that Satan has no more role to play here than in Genesis 3.

Such direct and literal readings of these texts, demanded by criticism, bring a welcome relief from the burden of traditional interpretation which presses down upon these texts. One wonders, in fact, what drove the Western interpretive tradition to go so far afield with them. That puzzle is only aggravated when one realizes that the Eastern theological tradition about the disobedient act in the Garden, derived from Irenaeus, never did view it as a disaster of universal tragic import. The Irenaean theodicy saw the Fall as a movement from childish innocence toward adult maturity. The Fall was not a spoiling of the divine image in the human being, for that image abides in us. It was, indeed, the work of a frail creature, but it was a "fall upwards." Though it caused a delay and complication in God's redemptive work, it had the salutary effect of promoting spiritual development. [16]

Perhaps the time has now arrived for our Western tradition to redefine the doctrine of the Fall in a leaner, healthier way, at least as sensible as that of Irenaeus. If that is the case, this salubrious development can take place in part because biblical criticism has demanded that theology read the texts carefully again and take them seriously for what they say, even while recognizing them to be theological and not historical writings. Critical reading of Genesis 3 has, in fact, cleared the way for a rich variety of new interpretations of that text which will, in turn, require enriching revision of the traditional doctrine of the Fall.

IV. Redefinitions of the Fall

A. *In dogmatic theology.* The process of redefinition of the concept of the Fall has long been underway, not only in the literature of biblical criticism, which is the initial locus of the discussion, but also in dogmatic literature itself. One can be sure that revisions in the traditional theological standards are well advanced when they reach expression in new confessional formulations, since such formulations must attain broad-based assent in the church in order to be regarded as truly reflecting the faith of a people. Three brief citations will suffice

to show that Christian believers have been thinking about the Fall and
wish to speak differently about it now. The first citation is taken from
the Second Vatican Council's "Pastoral Constitution on the Church in
the Modern World," *Gaudium' et Spes.* In the paragraph on "Sin" in
the chapter entitled "The Dignity of the Human Person," the Constitution discusses the Fall as follows:

> Although he was made by God in a state of holiness, from the very dawn
> of history man abused his liberty, at the urging of personified Evil. Man
> set himself against God, and sought to find fulfillment apart from God.
> Although he knew God, he did not glorify Him as God, but his senseless
> mind was darkened, and he served the creature rather than the
> Creator. [17]

The paragraph continues by averring that experience confirms what
revelation teaches—human life is a struggle of light and darkness,
good and evil, "for sin has diminished man, blocking his path to fulfillment." Christ's work is to liberate the human person and to cast out
the "prince of this world" (John 12:31). At Vatican II, then, the formal
terms of the doctrine of the Fall were maintained—pristine holiness
succeeded by darkened, senseless mind; loss of harmony with creation;
role of personified evil. But, the document is subtle. It does not
specifically link all human ills with one couple's sin; it merely says that
in our experience we are beset with manifold evils and feel ourselves
bound in chains. So, the story of Adam must be our story. Evil is personified, but that is a claim more cautious than saying that evil
originated with an anti-god. In short, the story of the Fall contained in
Genesis 3 is now being regarded as paradigmatic of the human experience, and not as an actual historical account of the origin of sin
and of human woe.

The *Confession of 1967,* the current standard of the United
Presbyterian Church, makes no mention whatever of Adam or the
Fall, pre- or post-lapsarian human nature. Under the heading, "The
Sin of Man," it simply acknowledges the universal reality of human sin
and its consequences: rebellion, despair, and isolation. An attenuated
statement of the rich Calvinistic sense of total depravity is offered in
these sentences: "All men, good and bad alike, are in the wrong before
God, and helpless without his forgiveness. Thus all men fall under
God's judgment." [18]

The proposed confession of the Presbyterian Church in the United
States also avoids a hard line on the doctrine of the Fall, but discerns
an analogy between the original parents and all the rest of us. In the
paragraph entitled "The Human Race Has Rejected Its Maker," the
confession says:

> Though they were made to be like God,
> Man and woman broke community with God,

Refusing to trust and obey him.
Their community with each other was broken
   By shame and murder, lust and pride.

We confess that in all generations
   Men and women have rejected God again and again.
At times we seek in pride to become gods,
   Denying the good limits that define us as creatures.
At other times we draw back in apathy,
   Refusing to fulfill our human responsibilities.
The antagonisms between races, nations, and neighbors,
   Between women and men, children and parents
   Between human beings and the natural order,
   Are manifestations of our sin against God. [19]

This version in a very gentle way suggests an analogy between Adam
and Eve and all the rest of us; in no way, however, does it suggest that
original sin is inexorable and endemic, but only that sin is a reality for
all of us. The broken relationship of God and humankind occurs, not
in a moment, but over many ages and many ways ("shame" may refer
to Adam, "murder" to Cain, "lust" to the Generation of the Flood, and
"pride" to the Builders of the Tower!). Nowhere does Satan figure in
this, nor does sexuality. The Fall consists in refusal to trust and obey,
resulting in broken community. There is a Fall in every generation
when people attempt to become like God and to reject the limits that
define us as creatures.

   B. *In the critical literature of biblical study.* If one asks how a
revolution in outlook as great as that suggested by these substantially
altered confessional statements could have taken place, the answer
must, at least in part, attribute the change to the work of critical
reading of the biblical text itself. In the following pages, summaries
and responses to a number of modern interpretations of Genesis 3 by
biblical critics are put forward as evidence of the diversity and the in-
novativeness now present in the critical literature about the Fall narrative. The selections are chosen because they represent particularly influential or distinctive readings. No Jewish commentators are included
simply because, since the days of the Pharisees, Judaism has not really
had a doctrine of a Fall and original sin and Jewish commentators tend
not to read Genesis 3 through those filters. A famous critical commentary from the turn of this century will be examined simply in order to
set the stage for the general lines of critical discussion in the ensuing
decades. Then, the main stream of critical understanding of Genesis 3
and the Fall will be examined. This examination will begin, not with a
biblical critic at all, but with famous studies by Karl Barth and
Dietrich Bonhoeffer which had powerful effects even upon biblical
critics in ensuing years. Catholic criticism will be integrated into this
discussion, particularly as the effects of Vatican II on biblical scholar-

ship become clearly felt. At the conclusion of the voyage down the main stream, two of the most recent commentaries will be set forth as evidence that standard reading of the Genesis 3 narrative is now completely in abeyance and that a very fresh and open attitude toward the text is abroad in the land. In every case, I attempt to discern the new insight or approach which the commentator brings to bear on the story, rather than to recount his entire discussion. In any case, most follow the consensus regarding the proper way to read Genesis 3, which, for the purposes of this essay, will be encapsulated in the discussion of the commentary by John Skinner.

It is regrettable that space precludes incorporating into this survey examples of the rich array of literary responses to the story of the Fall. These range from "Humpty-Dumpty" and "Rock-a-bye Baby" to William Blake's poem, "The Garden of Love," poetry by Walt Whitman, William Butler Yeats, and Archibald MacLeish through William Golding's *Lord of the Flies*, [20] John Steinbeck's *East of Eden*, and Arthur Miller's *After the Fall*. [21] Literary renditions lie outside the scope of this essay on modern critical reading of the Bible, but they lie very much within the broad range of human questioning for which the Bible provides profound response.

1. *Critical interpretation at the turn of the century.* John Skinner's *A Critical and Exegetical Commentary on Genesis*, in the International Critical Commentary Series, remains a highly influential work, even though it was first published in 1910. [22] I select his discussion as a way of entering into the mainstream of critical opinion, which was already in full flow by his time. Skinner acknowledges his debt to Wellhausen, Gunkel, and Strack before him, as well as to his contemporary, S. R. Driver. The potential effect of critical realism upon the dogmatic understanding of the Fall is already fully visible in Skinner's work, as will now become evident.

Although his study of the history of religions suggests to Skinner that behind the present story lurk the ancient Near Eastern legends of the serpent as a god or a demon, in the story as it now stands, the creature is merely the cleverest of all animals. "The Yahwistic author does not speculate on the ultimate origin of evil; it was enough for his purpose to have so analyzed the process of temptation that the beginning of sin could be assigned to a source which is neither in the nature of man nor in God." [23] The serpent is not really even a liar. Skinner enlists Gunkel for support when he remarks that

> the facts are all, in the view of the narrator, correctly stated by the serpent; he has truly represented the mysterious virtue of the tree; knowledge really confers equality with God (3:22); and it is also true that death does not immediately follow the act of eating. But at the same time the serpent insinuates a certain construction of these facts: God is envious, inasmuch as he grudges the highest good to man. [24]

Skinner acknowledges the new sense of shame which, in the aftermath of the sin, the intelligent couple draw from the fact of their nakedness. However, he specifically rejects any connection between sexual shame and sin, not to mention any thought that the forbidden fruit was an aphrodisiac! The new knowledge is "the kind of knowledge which comes with maturity to all."[25] Skinner then concludes his commentary with the contention that the curse contained in vv. 14-19 is the "key to the significance of the story of the Fall." By that he means that the point of the whole story is etiological and that "certain fixed adverse conditions of the universal human lot are traced back to a primeval curse uttered by Yahweh in consequence of man's first transgression."[26]

Skinner's critical insistence on asking for the plain meaning of the text and the intention of the author is typified by his rejection of any sense of a *Protoevangelium* in the conflict between the seed of the serpent and the seed of the woman. While acknowledging that 3:15 was indeed regarded as a christological reference in medieval theology and even by Luther, he points out that no victory is ever promised to either party in this conflict, that a message of hope would be out of place in the midst of a curse, and that the serpent represents no principle of evil greater than himself. His conclusion: The verse is intended to be an etiology of the unremitting hatred of humans for snakes and is a clear effort to deprive the serpent of any holy or wise image which it may have had in the religions with which Israel came into contact.

In his concluding discussion of Genesis 3, Skinner distinguished three religious and moral truth-claims of the passage from the crude mythological motifs of forbidden fruit on magical trees and talking serpents living in a fabulous Garden. The first religious truth-claim springs from the etiological desire to give an explanation of the hard, pervasive facts of human experience. The farmer must sweat and labor, and his wife must bear children in pain. Even so, he says, "It is doubtful if death be included in the effects of the curse."[27] He goes on to show that death was the natural fate of being made from the dust (v. 19) and that the exclusion of the man and woman from access to the tree of life (v. 23) implies that they were naturally subject to death. "Nor does it appear that the narrative seeks to account for the origin of sin. It describes what was, no doubt, the first sin; but it describes it as something intelligible, not needing explanation . . ."[28] The second religious idea is contained in the theme of the knowledge of good and evil. Skinner rejects the idea that this has to do with knowledge of right and wrong, for surely God would not have intended to withhold from human beings the power of moral discernment. He thinks that the frequently advanced suggestion that the knowledge unlocks the secrets of nature has more to recommend it, but finally he sides with Gunkel in accepting the notion that the knowledge which the human beings learn from the tree is that which is proper to the adult as opposed to

the child. "Man's primitive state was one of childlike innocence and
purity; and the knowledge which he obtained by disobedience is the
knowledge of life and of the world which distinguishes the grown man
from the child."[29] In short, he adopts a basically Irenaean view of the
Fall as a "fall upward," a step necessary to human maturation.

As to the sin of the first couple, Skinner takes the position that has
become practically normative. "Man was tempted by the desire to be
as God, and Yahweh does not will that man should be as God. Sin is
thus in the last instance presumption — an overstepping of the limits of
creaturehood, and an encroachment on the prerogatives of deity."[30]
The only place in which Skinner seems to maintain some tie to the
traditional understanding of the Fall is on the question of whether this
sin was somehow hereditary: "The consequences of the transgression,
both privative and positive, are undoubtedly transmitted from the first
pair to their posterity; but whether the sinful tendency itself is regarded as having become hereditary in the race, there is not evidence
to show."[31] The understanding of God contained in the story Skinner
describes is as follows. God is not threatened by the human violation of
limitations. The world is his world, and he can act with stern justice in
handling human rebellion. But, nonetheless, he is a God of compassion. "That is the real *Protevangelium* which lies in the passage: the
fact that God tempers judgment with mercy, the faith that man,
though he has forfeited innocence and happiness, is not cut off from
fellowship with his creator."[32]

Here, then, is a summary of this early critical interpretation of
Genesis 3. Adam is not regarded as a historical figure. The serpent is
not Satan, and the sin is finally violation of the limits imposed on
humanity. Only in the matter of original sin and its transmission to all
humankind does Skinner seem to allow something of the traditional
understanding of the intention of Genesis 3. To him, the Yahwist is in-
conclusive as to whether human nature underwent a profound change
with the Fall. If he thinks it did, he makes nothing of it. Not every
commentator in subsequent generations even down to the present day
accepts all of Skinner's findings, of course. But, his interpretation
represents the state of the art as it reached Karl Barth, Dietrich
Bonhoeffer, and the other theologians who have been most influential
on our generation.

2. *Critical interpretation during and after World War II.* All
critical interpretation of the Fall sustained profound influence from
the work of Karl Barth. No dogmatic theologian of our time has taken
the Bible and biblical criticism more seriously, and the "higher critics"
have frequently repaid him the honor by taking his biblical commentary as seriously as if it were their own. Although biblical criticism rises
and falls on its dispassionate objectivity, it cannot entirely free itself
from the theological milieu in which it works. Thus, communications

run back and forth between dogmaticians and critics to their mutual enrichment. Although it is not possible here to discuss Barth's treatment of the account of Adam and Eve in the Garden in any detail, suffice it simply to say that the Fall is understood to be a "move to self-help in paradise." When Adam "tried to help himself . . . he [became] catastrophically helpless. Such is the human subject when he tries to live out his subjectivity otherwise than in the framework of the free grace of God, and therefore in the obedience of thankfulness."[33] Obviously, he is not talking of any historical personage, but rather of the prototype, whose behavior is paradigmatic of all humanity. The history of Adam, which is our history, is a constant re-enactment of the little scene in the Garden of Eden. There never was a golden age. There is no point in looking back to one. The first man was immediately the first sinner. But, "he has not bequeathed [sin] to us as his heirs so that we have to be as he was. He has not poisoned us or passed on a disease. . . . No one has to be Adam. We are so freely and on our own responsibility. Although the guilt of Adam is like ours, it is just as little our excuse as our guilt is his."[34]

But, Adam is also the very antithesis of the new Adam through whom reconciliation and salvation for all men are effected. So, the real meaning of Adam was properly captured by Paul in Rom. 5:12–21:

> It is in relation to the last Adam that this first Adam, the unknown of the Genesis story, has for Paul existence and consistence, and that in what is said of him he hears what is true and necessarily true of himself and of all men. It is beyond the threshold which Jesus Christ has crossed, and every man in Him, that he hears in Him the sentence on himself and all men as a Word of God and not of man—a sentence against which there can be no appeal passed on the man of sin, who was every man, but who no longer exists now that God has had mercy on all with the same universality with which he once concluded all in disobedience.[35]

For the great Reformed theologian Barth, then, Adam has no significance at all as a historical figure, nor is his fall anything other than the first example of that which has been repeated endlessly in human experience. It is neither endemic nor genetically transmitted, nor was human nature spoiled by the Fall of Adam. The whole story has no significance at all except as a backdrop to the account of the universal election of all human beings in Jesus Christ.

A second dogmatic theologian has given us an interpretation of the account of the Fall in Genesis 3 which has had a lasting impact on critical and theological commentators alike. I refer to Dietrich Bonhoeffer in his work, *Creation and Fall*.[36] Although he was fully aware of the historical critical method and the results of that method when applied to Genesis 3, Bonhoeffer elected to use medieval typology to the fullest and even risks the charge of allegorizing in his treatment of the text.

Bonhoeffer opens with the first couple placed in a garden in which
stands the tree of the knowledge of good and evil. Since Adam is innocent, he cannot know what good and evil are; however, he understands
that this tree is the tree of prohibition. Like Skinner, Barth, and
modern interpreters generally, Bonhoeffer understands the tree as a
limit in the midst of the Garden. To have a limit is to be a creature,
even if the creature is free. The tree in the middle of the Garden is the
symbol or metaphor for that creaturely limit of the human being. The
limit at the edge of the Garden is the limit of human technology and
achievement, and that is a movable limit. But, "the limit in the middle
is the limit of [human] reality, of . . . true [human] existence." [37]
Adam understands that limit as grace, and so it is, for to know good
and evil is to know pleasure and pain, pleasure in the midst of pain,
and even the pleasure and pain of death. To break out of the limit of
perfect trusting obedience in the middle of the Garden is to be thrust
out into a world where life becomes a commandment, where life is
always haunted by knowledge that escape in death is forbidden, even
when death might be the pleasure of the absence of pain.

Now, the Temptation and Fall occur in a world entirely created by
God and without any need for any *diaboli ex machina*. The serpent is
not Satan, Eve is not the seductress, the tree of knowledge is not a
divine "dirty trick." What these things really are remains ambiguous.
"It is not the purpose of the Bible to give information about the origin
of evil, but to witness to its character as guilt and as the infinite burden
of man." [38]

The serpent subtly raises a question about the word of God: "Did
God say, 'You shall not eat of any tree in the garden'?" The hint is
dropped that something is wrong in God's word, that there is a defect
in the limiting word of God. "The serpent knows of a greater, nobler
God, who does not need such a prohibition." [39] The question is a
religious one, asked by a "pious" serpent, and as such, it is more
dangerous than other kinds of evil questions. It is evil in that "the false
answer is contained within it, that within it is attacked the basic attitude of the creature toward the Creator. Man is expected to be judge
of God's word instead of simply hearing and doing it." [40]

There now follows the first religious conversation, which is to say a
conversation about God that seeks to get beyond God. The serpent
portrays God's truth as a lie: "You will not die . . . you will know good
and evil." So, it becomes the serpent's truth against God's truth, "You
shall surely die" (2:17) versus "you shall not die, but be like God" (Gen.
3:4-5). When the man becomes like God, he is no longer *imago dei,*
that is, "bound to the word of the Creator and living from him"; now
he is *sicut deus,* "like God," that is, "bound to the depths of his own
knowledge about God, in good and evil." [41]

With the act of sin, the limit in the midst of the Garden is trans-
gressed, and the human being is without a limit. The human being is

no longer simply a creature, but is now a creator in his own right. Being like God means "going behind the given word of God and procuring his own knowledge of God." It is "disobedience in the form of obedience,"[42] that is to say, it is religion.

Bonhoeffer's interpretation reaches its most profound depth in his ensuing discussion of Gen. 3:7. Unlike many critical commentators, he perceives the discovery of nakedness to be the discovery of sexuality. But, he allegorized sexuality as he has allegorized other aspects of the story. Originally, the man and woman lived in the garden with no sense of duality, no sense of good and evil. Now, a new sense of duality is expressed, first of all, in relation to Eve. Formerly, she had been for Adam a limit, which Adam had accepted. He loved her because she was human, fit for him but other than he. Now that he is no longer a unity in himself (knowing good and evil), he perceives Eve's otherness — once a limit of grace — as a hateful thing. Now, she is over against him, at variance with him. So, he "makes use of his share in the woman's body," and he puts forward a claim of possession over her, "thereby denying and destroying the other person's creatureliness."[43] The sexuality of the man who has broken over the limit is the denial of any limit. It is an "avid impotent will for unity in the divided world"[44] — avid in its desire for the old lost unity, and impotent because in possessing and propagating, it finally destroys itself. The desire to cover the nakedness is of the essence of a divided world of good and evil, for nakedness is the essence of unity and unbrokenness.

The curse which follows the transgression is at the same time a promise. First, the human being will always have to battle with the serpent, "the power of religious godlessness."[45] Adam and Eve will win that battle from time to time — that is the promise; but, the serpent will always bruise their heels. Second, the woman must always bear her children in the dividedness of good and evil — passionate pleasure increased by pain, and pain increased by pleasure. Third, the community between man and nature is also affected. Now, the cursed ground becomes rebellious; the earth creature must work it. Yet, the ground will still sustain us. Because the curse is God's curse, it is a blessed curse. We can still live, and by making garments, God affirms us in our new fallen way. He issues orders for our preservation.

We live, but we are always on the way to death. God was right — on the day we ate of the tree of the knowledge of good and evil, we died the death of being like God. Now we have to live out of our own selves, and we cannot. But, real physical death is also a promise of grace, because it means the end of the enmity, of the painful community of man and woman, and the struggle with the cursed ground.

Bonhoeffer's treatment of the Fall agrees with essential findings of the biblical criticism of the preceding decades — the story of the Fall is prototypical rather than historical; it is not a story of cosmic dualism, pitting God against the great serpent Satan; it is not an account of the origin of evil and never was intended to be, and it does not proclaim the coming-into-existence at a moment of time of an ontologically changed humanity. Yet, Bonhoeffer enriches the story, remythologizes it, by means of the literary device of allegory to make it an account of the battle between mature sophistry, expressed as religion, and childlike innocence. His reading, though beautiful, is radically consistent with his hermeneutic of a religionless Christianity.

Dogmatically tendentious and non-historical-critical as Bonhoeffer's reading of the Fall may be, it has flowed back into the work of biblical scholarship itself. One biblical writer who has taken Bonhoeffer seriously is Gerhard von Rad, whose commentary on Genesis is perhaps the most influential of all the modern ones.[46]

Like Skinner before him, von Rad begins by ruling out the presence in the story of any living myth. While myth undoubtedly lies behind it, in its present form the story is not interested in the mythic dimensions of any of its images. The serpent, for example, is neither Satan nor any other demonic power. This means that the onus of guilt rests directly on the human being. Nonetheless, there is a subtle distortion in the serpent's question: "Did God say you shall not eat of any tree of the garden?" (v. 1). Von Rad, the historical critic, accuses the serpent of lying and supports his charge out of the highly allegorical and imaginative reading of the theologian, Bonhoeffer: "Man's ancient folly is in thinking he can understand God better from his freely assumed standpoint and from his notion of God than he can if he would subject himself to his Word."[47]

The temptation is to become like divine beings, knowing good and evil; here, von Rad draws upon a semantic analysis to show that "knowing" means "experiencing," "becoming acquainted with." He even quotes Wellhausen: "To know in the ancient world is always to be able to as well." Good and evil encompass all possibilities; therefore, to know good and evil is to know everything. But, to know everything is to break out of all limits of the possibilities of human existence — another insight shared with Bonhoeffer and with the mainstream of modern interpretation.

The transgression itself takes place without any special notice, almost as though it were inevitable. Shame follows, and fear at the rustle of God's steps in the Garden. Nakedness, which in time became a matter of extreme sensitivity in Israel, embarrasses the man. Adam's impulse to "put the blame on Mame" signifies immediately that the primal community of people with one another has now been destroyed. Now, there is a new solidarity of sin, and yet, it is not a true solidarity either, but more like a common experience of isolation. Like the other critical commentators, von Rad stresses that the curse which follows is primarily etiological in its function. The curse against the serpent explains the reason reptiles move in a peculiar way, without setting foot on the ground, and the reason there are abiding fear and hostility between snake and human. Beyond that, however, argues von Rad, the writer uses the serpent to symbolize that evil present in the world which singles out the human being, "lies in wait for him, and everywhere fights a battle with him for life and death."[48]

The agonizing contradiction in which the woman is placed by the curse has three aspects: pregnancy and *painful birth,* which derive from her *desire* for man, which desire does not, alas, yield fulfillment but rather humiliating *domination.* As for man, a break occurs in the affectionate relationship between himself and the soil. What ought to have been and was a natural, mutually enriching sustenance is now a dogged struggle. Von Rad points out that work itself is not the punishment, for Adam had work to do even in paradise (Gen. 2:15). It is that the work is now so unsatisfying and yields so little in relation to the effort expended.

On the question of the relation of death to Adam's sin, von Rad follows the critical flow away from the pre-critical interpreters. Though scripture does teach that "the wages of sin is death" (Rom. 6:23), it is impossible to say that in this case death is a punishment. "One cannot say that man lost a 'germ of immortality' any more than one can say that a material modification occurred in him, as a consequence of which he must now fall prey to death; the narrator already said in ch. 2:7 that man was created of dust."[49] In other words, no new anthropology accompanies the loss of innocence, no mortality in place of an earlier immortality. It must be acknowledged that the threat of death is a note sounded much more audibly after the primeval crunch on the forbidden fruit; nevertheless, the man and the woman did not, in fact, die after their sin but were cursed to go on living.

Will the human beings now grasp for the tree of life as the only available antidote for the living death to which they have now been condemned? Again von Rad draws upon Bonhoeffer: "Man has stepped out of the state of dependence, he has refused obedience and willed to make himself independent. The guiding principle of his life is no longer obedience but his autonomous knowing and willing, and thus he has really ceased to understand himself as creature."[50] Lest this ex-creature who is now like a god seize the tree of life and so escape the ban of death, whether now or in the future, God sends him out of the Garden. Such an expulsion must also be regarded as a grace, for to live forever in the condition of fallenness would surely be unbearable.

For a proper grasp of von Rad's understanding of the Fall, it is important to read Genesis 3 in the context of the entire primeval history. For von Rad, Genesis 1-11 is a story, not of one fall only, but of four. Adam's fall is only the first and, in some ways, the least significant. The relationship of the four falls to each other is progressive; each one marks a further deterioration in the divine-human relationship, and with each comes a curse. But, with all but the last, God provides a means of grace which makes survival of the human species possible. The first fall is this one, the sin of Adam and Eve in the Garden. As we have seen, the punishment is banishment from the garden and the loss of effortless humanity. But, continuance is possible. God makes breeches of skin for his human beings so that they can survive. East of Eden, beyond the barred entry of Paradise, humankind will still be able to wrest a living from the earth and to bear offspring.

The second fall is that of Cain. The son of the slayer of effortless humanity now becomes a slayer of humanity itself. His penalty is more severe: condemnation to fruitless wandering over the face of the earth. However, the mark of Cain is a means of grace, for because of it, he will not be slain by those into whose villages and suburbs he wanders. It is a mark of his election, one might say, for Cain was more elect than the righteous Abel who, by his death, was rejected (Barth).

The third fall is that of the generation of the flood, whose sin was concupiscence, titanic lust. In punishment they are extirpated, but God provided a way back for humanity, nonetheless. On board the single little boat that bobs on the surface of the waters are creatures enough of every kind and people enough to repopulate the earth.

The fourth and most terrible fall of all is that of the generation of the Tower of Babel, who thought to make themselves a name in order to shore up their autonomy against the whole cosmos. Their penalty was the most severe of all—dispersion, the mixing of tongues, alienation, the utter breakdown of human community. From this final fall there is no escape! No provision of grace accompanies it. But for the genius of the Yahwist we might have been left with this doleful prospect, but, in attaching the primeval history to the history of Israel, he finally discloses the road back from Babel. In linking Babel with Abraham, a slender thread ties the universal history of fallen humanity to the salvation-history of Israel. In that one man and his posterity, whose name will be made great by God, the nations of the earth will find a blessing. Through that one man the curse of Babel will at last be undone.

In the Yahwistic account of the Fall there are loose ends, traces of myth and evidences of conflation. Yet, by taking each part in the context of the whole and making a virtue out of the fact that things do not fit together entirely perfectly, the narrative is enhanced. The J writer understood his limitations and respected the fact that he, too, was fallen. "He limits himself to pointing out the great disorders of our present life—shame, fear, and the dissonances in the life of the woman and the man—and ascribing them to human sin."[51] Though he gives no account of the origin of evil, his story is a theodicy after all. It does acquit God of responsibility. Yet, whether the Fall was a necessity, whether culture could have come into being and history gotten underway without human sin, is left open to question. The Yahwist knew not to say too much. But, what he said was a story of remarkable poignancy. Von Rad sums it up as follows:

> Man was completely surrounded by God's providential goodness but incomprehensibly he denied God obedience. Paradise is irreparably lost; what is left for man is a life of troubles in the shadow of a crushing riddle, a life entangled in an unbounded and completely hopeless struggle with the power of evil and in the end unavoidably subject to the majesty of death.[52]

3. *Critical interpretation in the 70s.* The most magisterial commentary on the Book of Genesis to appear in our time is that by von Rad's student and successor at Heidelberg, Claus Westermann.[53] Fortunately for the English-speaking reader. Westermann summed up the theological import of his work on Genesis 1–3 in a small work entitled simply, *Creation.*[54] It is revealing for his entire approach that he prefers to entitle his discussion of the Fall (Genesis 3) simply "the offense." He wastes no time in showing why:

> First of all, it must be stated that in the Old Testament the text did not have [an] all-embracing meaning. It is nowhere cited or presumed in the Old Testament; its significance is limited to primeval events. The Old Testament knows nothing of a narrative which says that man sank into a state of corruption, that from that moment on he was "fallen man."[55]

Westermann's debt to the mainstream of critical discussion is evident in this approach, and it becomes clearer as he proceeds. However, he has his own cutting edge. For example, he acknowledges that the serpent can be examined from the point of view of the phenomenology of religion (as Skinner does), or it can be related allegorically to the principle of evil (as von Rad tends to do). But, both of these miss the point, according to Westermann. The intention of the narrator is "to present defection as a human phenomenon."[56] Under certain circumstances, the human being can be seduced; it happens in religion, politics, and private life. In this case, the defection is from the proper relationship with God; Adam and Eve overstep their limits in their drive for knowlege like God's knowledge. And, the results have positive aspects — the human beings get insight which they did not have before. In some ways, Westermann's, like Skinner's, is a fall upward — his strictly literal reading of the text leaves him no alternative!

The punishment is formulated as a series of curses. This personal address begins with the serpent, and it speaks of the suffering and enmity which tragically interrupt the harmony of the created order. It is etiological. It speaks of what is, in fact, the case, rather than prescribing a future destiny. The whole creation groans in travail — that's a fact! The same is true of the curses upon the woman and the man. The condemnation to bear children in pain is not a law which precludes any attempt to improve maternity care. It is simply an account of life as it was and — to the degree that conception, pregnancy, and birth belong to the woman—will always be. The decree of submission to the husband "should not be regarded as an eternally valid norm. It describes life as it then was."[57] And yet, to pretend that the verse has nothing to say to every generation, including our own, is nonsense. If anything, an era of equal rights of women and men has freighted the relationships of the sexes, particularly in marriage, with ambiguities greater than ever. Westermann is one of the few recent commentators to acknowledge this so clearly.

Something similar can be said of the man's fate. Work is not bad, nor is the lightening of toil through technology a bad thing either. "But this does not alter the fact that in all work which is undertaken seriously and enthusiastically, worthwhile results presume difficulty, thorns and thistles, sweat."[58] Death, far from being a punishment, is a limitation on the necessity and burden of work. It is the only way that human beings can finally transcend work and find rest.

The goal of the story, and perhaps its original punitive element, is expulsion from the Garden. This, too, is etiological—it acknowledges that human beings experience God as one who is far off. Yet, the very moment of negation and abandonment is joined with two preceding verses that affirm the human creature. The woman is to be called the mother of all living. The primeval, God-given blessing of fecundity is still in force, and the future is still open. And then, in his act of clothing the naked couple in skin garments of his own making, "God accepts man just as he is with his weakness . . . God removes from him that constant feeling that he is a sinner; he does not wish that man be always conscious of his sins."[59]

In the light of this close reading of the key text Genesis 3, what can be said about the Fall? Westermann is clear. The notion that Adam was "an historical individual whose 'Fall' was passed on through him to his descendants . . . has no foundation at all in the narrative. . . . Paul's interpretation of Genesis 2–3 follows the interpretation of late Judaism [Cf. II Esdras 7:118]; it did not have its origin in Paul's encounter with Christ."[60] The Augustinian tradition of the Fall is based on the failure to understand Genesis 2–3 as a "primeval happening, and so something quite separate from our own history."[61] The narrative is really a discussion of the dilemmas and ambivalences in which human beings actually exist. It is not doctrine, but a rendition of human existence fraught with guilt and death, yet continuing under the care and blessing of God. From now on, if the question of the beginnings of the human race arises, theology will need to make common cause with anthropology and social psychology in order to gain a purchase on the matter. But, to that dialogue Genesis will contribute the conviction, profoundly rooted in our tradition, that "man's development . . . is inseparable from his understanding of himself as he stands face to face with the divine power."[62]

The fascinating thing about Bruce Vawter's book, *On Genesis: A*

New Reading, [63] is the contrast which it presents to his study of Genesis two decades earlier, *A Path Through Genesis.* [64] The earlier work appears to walk a cautious line in its treatment of the doctrine of the Fall. It maintains the basic position on original sin, the infection of subsequent humanity from the original couple, the profound change in anthropology which took place in the moment of the Fall, and the identification of the serpent with Satan. The woman in 3:15 was Eve, and her seed is the human race "which would conquer Satan." But, because the final fulfillment of the prophecy of the "seed" is identified with Christ, "the woman" who bore the seed is finally to be identified with the Blessed Virgin. Thus, Vawter maintained the presence in the text of the *Protoevangelion.*

The impact of Vatican II, together with Professor Vawter's own years of additional reflection and experience, result in a rather dramatic shift in his later work, *On Genesis: A New Reading.* He seems now to be much closer to the opinion represented very succinctly by H. Haag in this sentence: "The present opinion of Catholic and evangelical dogmatic theology, according to which the primeval state was a chronological phase at the beginning of human history . . . does not accord with the Bible. The Bible knows no 'sinless man' and consequently no state of innocence." [65] Furthermore, regarding the advent of death in the world, Vawter can say, "It is never said in Genesis, despite what an uncritical construction of 2:16 might lead [the reader] to believe, that prior to his 'fall' man had been created immortal by God." [66]

Vawter seems more like Bonhoeffer than some other modern interpreters in his willingness to recognize the sexual overtones in the "knowledge of good and evil." Unlike Bonhoeffer, however, his reason for this is his contention that the story is to be seen against the background of Canaanite fertility religion. (Vawter points out that Baal is often associated with the symbol of the serpent.) In support of this claim, he notes that the penalty for Eve also has sexual overtones; her desire will be for her husband, and out of that desire will come pregnancy (3:16). He acknowledges the ancient notion that the tree might bestow potency. He points out that after eating, the man and the woman experience shame at nudity (3:10-11); and, finally, he sets the whole story against its larger ancient Near Eastern context, observing that in the Gilgamesh Epic, the primitive man Enkidu leaves his affiliation with the beasts and moves toward wisdom like the gods after he has achieved union with a cult prostitute.

The knowledge of good and evil was God's prerogative; in seizing it, the human beings violate the principle set forth in Job 28:28: "The fear of the Lord, that is wisdom; and to depart from evil is understanding," For Vawter, then, the Fall is bound up with the issue of wisdom. In seeking sufficiency in human knowledge and especially in sexual knowledge, the first couple inaugurate a tendency to substitute for wisdom which is truly appropriate to humankind their own kind of wisdom. Paul speaks, too, of that wisdom that looks for God but cannot find him because it rejects his own disclosure of himself: "Has not God made foolish the wisdom of the world? For since, in the wisdom of God, the world did not know God through wisdom, it pleased God through the folly of what we preach to save those who believe" (Rom. 1:20–21).

Like so many other modern commentators, Vawter feels that Genesis 3 should not be regarded as an account of the origin of evil, but simply an admission of what we have always known; namely, that the human capacity to do wrong is a fact of life: "While this story depicts a 'fall' of man in the sense that he commits the sin, misses the mark, transgresses a commandment imposed upon him . . . still, it is not a fall in the sense that man after has become anything else that man was before. The potential for transgression is always present . . ."[67] The decision of the man also to eat is not to suggest that woman bears some special guilt, contrary to Sirach 25:24:

> From a woman sin had its beginning,
> And because of her we all die.

On the contrary, "the 'fall' as J depicts it is collective, a social act."[68]

In his more recent book, Vawter joins Westermann and others in pointing out the high degree of etiological significance attached to the curses. Something which is etiological is not going to be normative; therefore, these curses are not law. The reference to the crushing of the serpent's head and the striking at the human heel in 3:15 is not a mandatory war cry in the fight against Satan, but is simply an explanation of the continuous and violent enmity between these two creatures. Vawter assigns to Irenaeus of Lyons (A.D. 130–200) the honor of being the first to detect in this passage the *protoevangelium*. But, Vawter is no longer in his camp. In spite of what he said in his earlier work, Vawter now says:

> The passage is part of a curse and a condemnation, not a prognosis of future blessings. It predicts a protracted hostility, even a protracted battle, but not a victory of one side or the other. . . . The offspring of the woman, despite the "he" of the personification, is a collective body, not an individual, not David any more than it is Christ. . . . Thus far and no further runs the literal sense of verse 15, the only sense with which we have to do in this book.[69]

Thus is critical reading triumphant with its insistence on taking the plain meaning of the Bible seriously as the starting point of all interpretation!

At the conclusion of his treatment of Genesis 3, Vawter returns to the broader question of the relationship of that narrative to the dogmatic notion of a Fall of humanity. He affirms the doctrine of

original sin, showing its importance as a repudiation of the Pelagian
heresy which argued that human beings could achieve their own salvation. He sees no reason to quarrel with the normal teaching of both the
Old and the New Testaments that people are born into a sinful world
and are themselves sinners in need of redemption. But, he no longer
believes, if he ever did, that Genesis enables us to speak historically
about how this state of affairs came about. Human beings were
capable of transgression from the beginning—there was no alteration
of anthropology, no move from immortality to mortality:

> There was, therefore, no "fall" in the sense that men and women
> became something other than what they had been created. The story
> does try to account for man's alienation from God, why his life is
> bounded with frustrations, and why he is under the sentence of death.
> According to the story, however, immortality was not a gift to be
> forfeited, but rather one that he failed to obtain.[70]

Vawter then proceeds specifically to oppose the teaching of Pope Pius
XII (in the 1950 encyclical, *Humani Generis*) that all human beings
are descended from a single couple (the theory of monogenism). Says
Vawter, "[the Yahwist] may very well have thought that the human
race originated in such a fashion, but if so he simply took it for granted
and did not make it a part of his message. The story of the 'Fall' is a
paradigm of human conduct in the face of temptation, not a lesson in
biology."[71] Vawter looks forward to the flowering of theological discussion exactly of the sort that has, in fact, been taking place. He calls
upon the theologians

> to redefine the doctrine in such a way as not to historicize unduly the
> myth of Genesis or to create out of Romans 5:12 a new myth of Adamic
> origins for all mankind . . . this kind of redefinition is going on apace. Its
> fruition cannot but help to restore Genesis to its position as illustrating
> the frailty of the man we know and the mercy of the God with whom he
> places himself in contest.[72]

The great mainstream of interpretation which we have been ex-
amining is best summed up by James Barr.[73] Barr is willing to give
Adam a break. He was not such a terrible sinner, after all. The Book
of Genesis does not understand that all human sin goes back to Adam
and that the tragedy of human experience is all the result of one
catastrophic human sin. What the story of Genesis 3 is talking about is
frustration. Death is the frustration of "a life in which things are not
going to work out for man."[74] The knowledge for which the man and
the woman gave up their chance at immortality is also fraught with
ambiguity and frustration:

> Man became like God through his knowledge of good and evil, and this
> is the center of the human problem: knowledge of the past, which is

memory; knowledge of the self and of others; the power and need to make moral judgments, to harness the power of moral judgment to the ambitions, prejudices, and self-affirmations of the self, to take to oneself the power of judging which properly belongs only to God. Man's knowledge . . . thus builds him up, but it also casts him down; it constructs his world, but it also means that it does not work. . . . For all man's talents, his life lies under frustration, and the final sign of that frustration is the swinging sword in the hand of the angel, guarding and barring the way to the free life.[75]

Theologians will, of course, offer a number of ways out of that dividedness and frustration, and the history of Christian thought about fallen humanity will include talk, on the one hand, about self-realization and the achievement of authenticity within the existential moment; and, on the other, about the eschatological restoration of human unity and ultimate access to immortality.

4. *A very recent reading, and two radical ones.* The final portion of this survey of interpretations and reinterpretations of the Fall in modern critical biblical literature will examine three recent treatments which carry the mainstream of critical reading even further away from the traditional understanding of the doctrine of the Fall. The first of these is found in the 1982 commentary by Walter Brueggemann, *Genesis: A Bible Commentary for Preaching and Teaching.*[76]

Like his predecessors and mentors, Bonhoeffer, von Rad, and Westermann, Brueggemann is clear on what Genesis 3 is not. An Augustinian notion of the Fall is not to be found there, nor anywhere else in the Old Testament, for that matter. Only in the prophets can one begin to discover any truly pessimistic estimate of human nature. The rest of the Old Testament could really take its stand with the Deuteronomist who could write:

> For this commandment which I command you this day is not too hard for you, neither is it far off. . . . But the word is very near you; it is in your mouth and in your heart, so that you can do it.[77]

Furthermore, says Brueggemann, Genesis 2–3 is not another failed attempt to account for the existence of evil, nor an account of the origin of death. At best, this text is "a reflection . . . on troubled anxiety-ridden life."[78] Nor is the story an account of the loss of sexual innocence, even if we grant that snakes are often phallic symbols in primitive literature and in the imagination and dreams of today. Sin and sex are not linked here any more than sin and death are. The protagonists of the story and its writer alike are, finally, not concerned with "the danger of sex, the origin of evil, the appearance of death, or the power of the Fall." Rather, their concern, like ours, is "the summons of this calling God for us to be his creatures, to live in his world on his terms."[79] And, the tragic ending which we expect fails to materialize. God will not inflict death. The curse is heavy.

> But it is less than promised, less than legitimate. The miracle is not that
> they are punished, but that they live . . . God's grace is given in the very
> sentence itself. Perhaps "by one man comes death" (Rom. 5:12). But the
> news is that life comes by this one God (cf. John 6:68-69) . . . . [this] is a
> story about the struggle God has in responding to the facts of human
> life. When the facts warrant death, God insists on life for his creatures.[80]

What was once thought to be an account of a cosmic moral disaster,
then, proves to be a story of God's persistence in love. Yes, it is an
etiology for the human agenda of distrust, broken community, and
subordination of women. But, none of that was part of God's original
agendum. From the side of God, the story is the first episode in God's
long, long struggle to respond faithfully to a faithless people. The
lesson which human beings might most appropriately draw from it is
that already perceived in the text by Bonhoeffer; namely, "the
recognition and honoring of boundaries leads to well-being. . . . It
probes the extent to which one may order one's life autonomously,
without reference to any limit or prohibition."[81] A grab for wisdom at
the expense of trusting obedience destroys essential human values.
Fear, which has to do with punishment, not perfect love, emerges (I
John 4:18-20). Human community now stands in need of reconciliation with God and with each other (cf. II Cor. 5:18-19). Anxiety arises
out of the rejection of God's providential care and the autonomous effort to secure human well-being. Yet, all of this does not add up to a
biblical doctrine of a single fall with profound ontological implications; rather, it is a commentary upon the distortion which human beings actually experience in every age when they reject their God-given
vocation, scorn their permission modestly to enjoy the good gifts of the
Garden, and break across into the area of prohibition outside the
sphere of human competence.

In both method and perspective, Phyllis Trible's 1978 book, *God
and the Rhetoric of Sexuality*,[82] takes a more radical approach. Simply
by never mentioning the term "Fall" nor alluding to the history of the
doctrine deriving from Augustine, Trible neatly dissociates herself
from any attempt to make Genesis 2-3 into a factual account of the
origin of sin, the corruption of the divine image, and the like. For her,
the account is simply "A Love Story Gone Awry."

Reading from an explicitly feminist perspective and using
rhetorical-critical methods which enable her to discern cor-
respondences across the architecture of the story, Trible describes it in
three scenes. In the first of these, "Eros Created" (Gen. 2:4b-24),
human community comes into being through the sexual differentiation of the "earth-creature" (*'adam*) into man (*'ish*) and woman
(*'ishsha*). In the second scene, "Eros Contaminated" (Gen. 2:25-3:7),
this joyous, primal human communion is disrupted by disobedience—the vigorous and decisive disobedience of the woman and the
bland, passive disobedience of the man. Finally, in scene three, "Eros

Condemned" (Gen. 3:8–24), the consequences of "turning God-the-subject into God-the-object; [of] exchanging God-the-authority for God-the-deceiver; and [of] asserting human autonomy over divine providence"[83] are developed. What was nurturing differentiation within common humanity now becomes the battle between the sexes. Speaking of the judgment against the woman that her husband should henceforth rule over her (Gen. 3:16), Trible writes:

> Where once there was mutuality, now there is a hierarchy of division. The man dominates the woman to pervert sexuality. Hence, the woman is corrupted in becoming a slave, and the man is corrupted in becoming a master. His supremacy is neither a divine right nor a male prerogative. *Her subordination is neither a divine decree nor the female destiny.* Both their positions result from shared disobedience. *God describes this consequence but does not prescribe it as punishment* (emphases mine).[84]

Statements such as these reveal, I take it, how Trible would respond to questions of historicity and normativity in the Genesis narrative of the Fall. The story is just that—a story. But, it is also an exquisitely wrought, profoundly successful evocation of the melancholy realities of the day-to-day experience of women, men, and serpents; furthermore, it is an acknowledgment that human relationships could be and, therefore, ought to be wholly other than they are.

The most radical of all of the modern historical-critical interpretations of Genesis 3 which I have chosen to survey is that of Richard S. Hanson. Written in a popular vein, Hanson's book, *The Serpent Was Wiser,* is forthright. The tree of the knowledge of good and evil "means, simply, the tree of growing up. . . . Its fruit will wean one away from his parents."[85]

By such words, the stage is set for an Irenaean theodicy of maturation, and Hanson does revive that theodicy, tinged with hues drawn both from developmental psychology and from tragic literature. Genesis 3 is no Fall narrative, but is a story of maturation, of risk-taking and adventure, of willingness of the youthful Adam and Eve to leave the safety of the Garden and to fulfill the vocation given them to subdue the earth and have dominion over it. Adam and Eve are compared to the Israelites who finally dare to leave Egypt in search of liberty, to the prophets who followed their calling in spite of the personal dangers, and to Jesus, who left his home town and set out on a road that led to death. "The notion of a fall becomes necessary only when one begins with the concept of the perfect man," argues Hanson.[86] But, that notion is finally foreign to the Old Testament. It belongs to what Hanson calls the "Orphic world of thought," which links the notion of a fall to the conception of pure spiritual perfection trapped in imperfect and inadequate materiality. "But the Genesis story which we are considering does not begin with such a perfect creature. It begins with a real specimen, a child of the earth . . . who must await the realization of his potential."[87] Like J. Moltmann, Hanson contends, "Only the future can reveal the perfect man."[88] Paul's Adamic Christology identifies the perfect Adam who never was with the Christ who will be the perfection of all of us.

Hanson even advances a kind of aesthetic argument in appreciation of the sin of Adam. The grasp for the fruit of the tree of knowledge was a necessity if human beings were ever going to realize their potential. "Call it the rebellion of man, the rise of man, or better still, the story of man's discovery of himself."[89] Though the crunch on the forbidden fruit was in direct violation of God's express command, it was an inexorable part of coming of age. It was tragic, not because it introduced death (who says there would have been no death in the Garden when the man and the woman curled up in quiet final innocence under the tree of life, going gentle into the good night?), but because it introduced the fear of death. But, without that fallen knowledge, there could be no ambition, no raising of monuments, no need to create children or novels, no "rage against the dying of the light" (Dylan Thomas), none of the other virtues that flow from the knowledge of death. In short, Hanson finds in Genesis 3, not a Fall, but a profound dilemma. The position reflects the mounting consciousness of the last few decades that rebellion against the yoke of authority is both an inevitable and a necessary element in human maturation. Another Old Testament scholar, B. Davie Napier, reflecting on the story of Genesis 3 down lines similar to these, puts it this way:

> *You* are the problem, God.
> You *force* us into disobedience —
> If disobedience it really is,
> and that's a matter simply of perspective.
> The theologians want to call it pride
> or even by the stronger term, rebellion.
> The pious make the charge apostasy
> and hypocrites will cry idolatry.
> But this is nonsense, God. It is our nature
> (you ought to know, who mixed the hot ingredients)
> to spurn the docile role of subjugation;
> to be not merely creature but creator;
> to stand alone; to cherish in ourselves
> all requisite resources for renewal;
> > to mount with wings as eagles
> > to run and not be weary
> > to walk and not to faint.[90]
>
> > You give us all creation, to be sure —
> > then shake a disembodied godly finger
> > in our face about a special tree.
> > Well, God Almighty, if you are almighty
> > let us be free of you — or let us die![91]

As for the serpent, Hanson looks upon it almost as favorably as did the Ophites, those ancient Christian gnostics, who thought it was a hero because it gave *gnosis* to humankind. He toys with the idea that, psychologically at least, the serpent speaks for God, bringing "ennoblement to man by assuring him of his godlike possibilities." It is the serpent who urged the man and the woman to act out the *imago dei* in them and to spread their wings and fly. But, the serpent too must experience judgment, because "the creative urge [= the serpent] is neither above God nor his rival."[92]

Hanson's approach works for those who view the Genesis 3 account as literary and prototypical, theological and evocative, rather than as a factual account of the beginnings of human sin. Anyone who does not share that viewpoint might, of course, accuse Hanson of making God the author of evil through his mouthpiece, the serpent. Such an opponent might even quote the bitter words of Omar Khayyam:

O, Thou who Man of baser Earth didst make,
And who with Eden didst devise the Snake,
    For all the Sin wherewith the Face of Man
Is blackened, Man's Forgiveness give — and take![93]

Obviously, Hanson would reject the suggestion that the text hints that God ultimately is responsible for the Fall. But, he finds in Genesis 3 a profound dilemma: "How can one live in freedom and responsibility apart from sinning?"[94]

V. *Concluding Observations*

This essay set out to chronicle the "interpretations and reinterpretations of the Fall" in modern biblical scholarship. Though the nuances and special insights have grown richly varied since historical criticism restored interest in the literal meaning of the text of Genesis 3, the essential reinterpretation is quite univocal in all the literature of the main stream. There is no Fall in scripture, if by Fall one means the doctrine of the shattering of the divine image in humankind, the loss of immortality at an early moment in human history, and the inexorable transmission of the original sin through human genes ever after. There is no account of the origin of evil and no primeval encounter with Satan. What Genesis 3 offers us is a paradigm, a story about every human being rebelling against the commandments of God and thus discovering alienation and despair. It is a powerful, primitive rendition of a reality which all of us know full well — the truth that life is a pilgrimage from innocence to maturity through a land fraught with the dangers of loving and hating, growing powerful and cowering in humiliation, living and finally dying. It is a story about God, too, whose name is not only Yahweh but also Immanuel and who will not leave his beloved creatures to their fates even when they defy him to his face or thrust a spear in his side.

I find it difficult to think of humanity without a Fall. The concept of a Fall-less history requires some further maturation in me, away from the religion of my Sunday School and my dogmatics textbooks. But, I find it growingly exhilarating, as well. Perhaps I can at last see us, not as creatures helplessly mired in sin, helpless to extricate ourselves in any way, but rather as people and peoples who can hope to make significant strides toward emancipation from the evils of hatred and greed.

Genesis 3 is a story about growing up, and grow up we must now, in a big hurry, for we live in a world in which the instruments of evil and death cannot be left in the hands of adolescents. But, if this world is not hopelessly fallen, then grow up and cope we can.

If this world is not hopelessly fallen, perhaps we can hope one day to bring an end to the destructive enmity which characterizes the relations of men and women — the battle between the sexes.

If this world is not hopelessly fallen, perhaps we can imagine and, with God's help, put in place genuine innovations in achieving a just distribution of wealth among the peoples of the world.

If this world is not fallen after all, we can even dare deny this deadly premise: that the use of nuclear weapons to deter evil is necessary in a fallen world!

NOTES

[1] John Milton (1608–1674), *Paradise Lost* (1667), Book I, lines 1–5, 24–26.

[2] Augustine (354–430), *The City of God*, Bk. XIV, 10.

[3] *Ibid.*, sect. 15.

[4] *Ibid.*, sect. 17.

[5] *Ibid.*, sect. 11.

[6] Milton, *op. cit.*, Book IV, lines 288–93, 296–98.

[7] *Ibid.*, Book I, lines 33–38.

[8] *Ibid.*, Book IX, lines 997–1004, 1008–1015.

[9] *Ibid.*, Book IX, lines 1129–31.

[10] "Decree Concerning Original Sin," paragraph 1, promulgated in the fifth session of the Council of Trent, June 17, 1546. Cited from John H. Leith, ed., *Creeds of the Churches* (Garden City, NY: Doubleday, 1963), pp. 405–406.

[11] *Ibid.*, p. 406.

[12] Rom. 5:12, as rendered in the Tridentine decree.

[13] "The Scots Confession," chaps. II and III, in *The Proposed Book of Confessions of the Presbyterian Church in the United States* (Atlanta: General Assembly of the PCUS, 1976), p. 49.

[14] "Westminster Confession," Chapter VI, para. 1–4.

[15] Cited by Carlos Mesters, *Eden: Golden Age or Goad to Action,* trans. Patrick J. Leonard, C.S.Sp. (Maryknoll, NY: Orbis, 1974), pp. 7–8.

[16] A detailed comparison of the eastern and western views of the Fall is given in N. P. Williams, *The Ideas of the Fall and of Original Sin* (London: Longmans, Green, and Co., 1927), esp. pp. 165–314. See also John Hick, "The

Problem of Evil," in *The Encyclopedia of Philosophy,* vol. III (New York: Macmillan, 1967), pp. 136–40.

[17] Walter M. Abbott, S. J., ed., *The Documents of Vatican II* (New York: Guild Press, 1966), p. 211.

[18] "Confession of 1967," Para. 9:13.

[19] "A Declaration of Faith," Chapter 3, lines 110-25, *The Proposed Book of Confessions, op. cit.,* p. 52.

[20] Selections from these and many other works are brought together in the source book by Terry Otten, *After Innocence: Visions of the Fall in Modern Literature* (Pittsburgh: The University of Pittsburgh Press, 1982).

[21] Several of these longer modern "Fall" accounts are analyzed by F. Parvin Sharpless, *The Myth of the Fall: Literature of Innocence and Experience* (Rochelle Park, NJ: Hayden Book Company, Inc., 1974).

[22] John Skinner, *A Critical and Exegetical Commentary on Genesis,* International Critical Commentary (Edinburgh: T & T Clark, First ed., 1910; Second ed., 1930).

[23] *Ibid.,* second ed., p. 73.

[24] *Ibid.,* p. 75.

[25] *Ibid.,* p. 76.

[26] *Ibid.,* p. 78.

[27] *Ibid.,* p. 95.

[28] *Ibid.*

[29] *Ibid.,* p. 96.

[30] *Ibid.,* p. 97.

[31] *Ibid.*

[32] *Ibid.*

[33] Karl Barth, *Church Dogmatics,* Vol. IV, Part 1, trans. G. W. Bromiley (Edinburgh: T & T Clark, 1956), paragraph 60, "The Pride and Fall of Man," p. 466.

[34] *Ibid.,* pp. 509–510.

[35] *Ibid.,* p. 513.

[36] Dietrich Bonhoeffer, *Creation and Fall,* trans. John C. Fletcher (London: SCM Press, 1959).

[37] *Ibid.,* p. 51.

[38] *Ibid.,* p. 65.

[39] *Ibid.,* p. 67.

[40] *Ibid.,* p. 68.

[41] *Ibid.,* pp. 71–72.

[42] *Ibid.,* p. 74.

[43] *Ibid.,* p. 79.

[44] *Ibid.,* p. 80.

[45] *Ibid.,* p. 86.

[46] Gerhard von Rad, *Genesis,* Old Testament Library, trans. John H. Marks (Philadelphia: Westminster Press, 1961).

[47] *Ibid.,* p. 86.

[48] *Ibid.,* p. 90.

[49] *Ibid.,* p. 92.

[50] *Ibid.,* p. 94.

[51] *Ibid.,* p. 97.

[52] *Ibid.,* p. 98.

[53] C. Westermann, *Genesis,* Biblischer Kommentar, 3 vols (Neukirchen-Vluyn: Neukirchener Verlag, 1966–83).

[54] C. Westermann, *Creation,* trans. John J. Scullion, S. J. (London: SPCK, 1974), esp. chapter 4, pp. 89–112.

[55] *Ibid.,* p. 89.

[56] *Ibid.,* p. 92.

[57] *Ibid.,* p. 101.

[58] *Ibid.,* p. 102.

[59] *Ibid.,* p. 104.

[60] *Ibid.,* p. 108.

[61] *Ibid.,* p. 109.

[62] *Ibid.,* p. 112.

[63] Bruce Vawter, *On Genesis: A New Reading* (Garden City, NY: Doubleday, 1977).

[64] Bruce Vawter, *A Path Through Genesis* (New York: Sheed & Ward, 1956).

[65] H. Haag, *Der 'Urstand' nach dem Zeugnis der Bibel* (1968), cited by C. Westermann, *Creation,* p. 110.

[66] Vawter, *On Genesis,* p. 68.

[67] *Ibid.,* p. 79.

[68] *Ibid.*

[69] *Ibid.,* p. 84.

[70] *Ibid.,* p. 89.

[71] *Ibid.,* p. 90.

[72] *Ibid.,* pp. 90–91.

[73] James Barr, an unpublished sermon on the texts Genesis 3, Revelation 22:1–4, preached at Christ Church Cathedral, Oxford, Sexagesima Sunday, February 18, 1979.

[74] *Ibid.,* p. 2.

[75] *Ibid.,* p. 3.

[76] Walter Brueggemann, *Genesis. A Bible Commentary for Teaching and Preaching* (Atlanta: John Knox Press, 1982).

[77] Deut. 30:11, 14.

[78] Brueggemann, *Genesis,* p. 42.

[79] *Ibid.,* p. 44.

[80] *Ibid.,* pp. 49–50.

[81] *Ibid.,* p. 51.

[82] Phyllis Trible, *God and the Rhetoric of Sexuality* (Philadelphia: Fortress Press, 1978).

[83] *Ibid.,* p. 115.

[84] *Ibid.,* p. 128.

[85] Richard S. Hanson, *The Serpent Was Wiser* (Minneapolis: Augsburg Press, 1972).

[86] *Ibid.,* p. 39.

[87] *Ibid.,* p. 41.

[88] *Ibid.*

[89] *Ibid.*

[90] Isa. 40:31.

[91] B. Davie Napier, *Come Sweet Death. A Quintet from Genesis,* Rev. ed. (New York: Pilgrim Press, 1981), p. 27.

[92] Hanson, p. 52.
[93] *Rubaïyat of Omar Khayyam* (FitzGerald's translation), 58.
[94] Hanson, p. 49.

Interpreting the Economy of Salvation: Reconciling Prebiblical, Biblical, and Postbiblical Horizons of Experience

Robert North, S.J.

1. Prebiblical??

How can there be such a thing as a prebiblical situation? If there is a God at all, then his plan for men's happiness must perforce have been operative from the moment anything existed, no matter how much later his interventions into creation were to be *revealed*.

Catholic theology has usually and rather naïvely reckoned with a situation in which the very first man who ever existed is fully described in the Bible, in his relation to men's fall and God's own subsequent plan to save them. There was a brief flurry called the Pre-Adamites, pure hypothesis that a race of genuine *homo sapiens* existed before the biblical Adam, and all completely died out before him, so that they were not involved in his original sin.

Nowadays, more urgently pushing to the fore is the question of human life on other planets, and what relation it would have to the sin and salvation of Adam.

But such possibilities are mere fly specks on the vastly greater solid knowledge which we now have of the prebiblical horizon of human experience. This information has come through three channels, mostly within the last century: archeology, biology, and sociology. My participation in this symposium, on the basis of the above title assigned to me, would seem to be warranted and productive only on condition that I can show how these three sciences evoke areas of human experience paralleling the Judeo-Christian experience, and even challenging the way it has been lived by some adherents (often admittedly on a rather ill informed popular level, or in a "subconscious" where images and sentiments dominate).

Our first step will be to show that from archeology we now see Israel to have been a latecomer among the nations. Before the first societal situations recorded in the Bible, huge empires had flowered and declined even in the Mid-East, to say nothing of the immemorial culture and power structures of China.

This broadening of horizon does not automatically disqualify Adam. His name in the Hebrew text, if a name at all, is simultaneously a common noun, and a collective at that. If we translate "the (first) human being(s), whoever that may have been," then one could still maintain that there is no pre-Genesis horizon of human life at all. But, it would not be easy to carry through this hypothesis in relation to the kingdoms which involve Adam's nearest descendants.

There is a second channel of recent information about human situations long before the Bible, and that is Darwin. Darwinism has been thoroughly discredited in two of its aspects. One is the view, shared at least partly by Darwin, that living things can adapt their species-structure to changing environment by their own struggles, and transmit to their descendants these improved structures.

The other derided feature of what is called Darwinism is social. Not only species-structure, but every aspect of social life was held to be in a constant state of progress, so that the succeeding generation is always superior to the preceding, even sociologically.

A third twentieth century channel of information about when man had to get along without the Bible is the recent science of Comparative Religions. It is not a branch of theology, but of sociology: concerned not with what men *should* do, but with what they *in fact* do and have done since earliest recorded time.

In its origin, this science gave signs of hostility to Christianity and to theology, and pointed up barbaric parallels to what had been considered original innovations of the Judeo-Christian revelation: mothers of God, divine triads and divine men, redemptive sacrifice. But, the comparative religionists are generally faithful to their slogan of "Get the facts, without value judgments." And Christianity has by now learned that it can only benefit by taking a hard look at the facts, *all* the facts, accurately and dispassionately.

There was an interval (including my own seminary days) when bright Catholics nourished the slogan (also against Darwin and Babel), "Debunkers have nothing but *facts;* we have *The Truth.*" Most Christians today would be leery of any advocated "truth" which is frankly in violation of "the facts." Still, there was a measure of reasonableness in the slogan. For scientists, as for theologians, the genuine facts are, indeed, all-important. But, they are scattered, amorphous, unhomogenized. To convert them into a real body of knowledge requires the use of imaginative insight and intelligence—called by the scientist hypotheses, theories, or even laws (for him only quantitatively distinct from hypotheses); while theologians of the better sort, like you and me, recognize "the facts" as a major or at least minor *premiss:* about as close to the word syllogism as you will ever hear nowadays.[1]

Let us now take up how the study of the Bible and of Christianity and even life itself must be redimensioned by giving their fair human rights to all those prebiblical people and situations.

2. Archeology: Origins and Impact

Let me tell you briefly of the origins of archeology. Far back in the time of Jeremiah and Buddha, a Babylonian king named Nabonidus, or, according to some texts, his daughter, was the first to show interest in digging to find the foundations of century-old temples, and gathering the finds into a little museum display.[2]

Some experts sniff that what Nabonidus did was not archeology at all, but the same old obscurantist theology: kings superstitiously believed that new temples had to rise in the same place and manner as the old, not be transferred to a spacious, accessible beauty spot.

Of course, meanwhile many thoughtful men, even witch doctors and Confucian sages, had made careful note of what was known from the past, including its material remains. Markings that started as mere calendars or archives gradually began, including footnotes like "the damages due to an earthquake in that year." But, the word History and its prototypes began to appear only recently on the human horizon, nowhere yet in the Bible, but roughly contemporary with it in Herodotus and Thucydides. Their histories, like most others, are concerned with political and global movements, mostly wars, and with the personal eloquence and prowess of the *heroes* who succeeded in promoting or (like Pyrrhus) "winning" them.

The entry of the word archeology into our culture may fairly be credited to the Jewish contemporary of Jesus, Flavius Josephus. He did not really invent the word; he emphasizes that he frankly lifted both the word and the concept of a twenty volume record of the Jewish people from the twenty volume *Archaiología Romaïkē,* just written by Dionysius of Halicarnassus.

— Ology, as you know, is the Greek ending of almost all the names of sciences. "Archaic," also Greek, means simply old or "too old to be of practical relevance." Thus, Josephus like Dionysius purported simply to compose a "science of the old." This meant for them just "History," as you can tell by glancing through their books.

But, Josephus was gifted with a sharp eye for material realities: the stones in the high priest's breastplate, the masonry of Jerusalem's besieged walls. He had no Newtonian instinct to go out and experience these things in the raw, much less to contrive experiments for finding out about them. He noticed only what was already in written sources, which he copied out voraciously, without the slightest striving for consistency or proof.

Josephus included not only the data about material remains which caught his eye (which might be called archeology), but such other tidbits as enabled him to tell a rousing good story in excellent popular language. These skills, even more than the fact that he was writing a defense of the Jews, or the much more decisive fact that he described the cradle of Christianity in a way no Christian for a thousand years ever thought to do, brought his term *Archeology* into our culture, and also *Antiquities,* as it is often translated.

Josephus was imitated in his concern for tabulating material remains by two disciples of Origen. Moving from Alexandria to Caesarea around 230 A.D., Origen showed in his textual criticism the makings of a really great empiricist, though in his exegesis he inherited the allegorizing of Alexandria.

Origen's disciple and successor around 300, Eusebius, bishop in Caesarea, wrote two books of genuinely empirical character, a "Chronology" and an "Onomastic" or geography. And, after another century, Epiphanius of the same Caesarea school (later bishop in Cyprus), though concerned mostly with catching heretics in his "Basket" (*Panarion*), took time to write the highly archeological treatise, "On weights and measures."

But despite Caesarea, or *on account of* its allegorizing influence really, you could say that nineteen centuries of Christianity never got beyond the definition of archeology implicit in Josephus, "Such information about the material objects of daily life as can be ferreted out *between the lines* of books really written to describe more influential things like politics or war."

Thus, in 1800 A.D. the Western world in general could still regard

Adam in 4001 B.C. as the first human being and the occasion of God's earliest intervention on behalf of humanity. What happened around 1800 A.D.?

Napoleon's invasion of Egypt included also a veritable army of scholars, to record its monuments and its geology. Out of this enlightened despotism came two rather fortuitous offshoots of immense importance. One was the Rosetta stone, containing a Greek inscription with translations in two kinds of Egyptian. The other was its decipherment by Jean Champollion the younger. Some Church authorities of that time never forgave him for this unmistakable step toward a prebiblical horizon.[3]

Now, for the first time, became available whole libraries of documentation. Egypt, in case you never noticed, was the setting of a considerate proportion of our Bible. But, Egypt now disclosed also the imposing developments from a thousand years before. And, this included the religious revolution of a kind of "monotheist" who also hated war and believed in honesty in art: Akhenaten, 1370 B.C., a true hero for our generation.[4]

Egyptian hieroglyphs were well worth the effort. They are so beautiful and so relatively easy and so accessible, still standing all around Egypt, as well as on the fifteen obelisks of Rome and five others in power centers around the world.

But, with Canaan's Mesopotamian neighbors it was another story. The search there, too, was begun early, glamorously by the British politician, Layard, at Nineveh, more soberly by the Germans, Robert Koldewey at Babylon and Walter Andrae at Assur.[5] Tens of thousands of tablets in cuneiform script were unearthed, but they were cramped and scrawly in comparison with gorgeous Egyptian.

Nevertheless, the key to their decipherment was found: in Iran at Bisitun, by British officer Henry Rawlinson, copying from a sheer crag with death defying acrobatics. Rawlinson himself entered an international competition to see who could first and best decipher the cuneiform, and his results turned out dazzlingly identical with French and other entries.

And when the early Nineveh tablets turned out to contain stories of Creation and the Flood, not a word was whispered against the cramped eye strain writing any more. The sensational rewriting of "the Babel Bible" went to extremes equaled only by the Pan-Ugaritism and Pan-Eblaism of more recent date. Fortunately, an equilibrium was attained. But, there is no denying that we are now copiously informed about three powerful empires—the Hittites in Turkey, too, as well as Babylon and Egypt, more prominent in the Bible—and also about their predecessors a thousand years before the properly historical events of our Bible.

But, with all this, we still remained imprisoned, more or less, within the thousand some years allotted to Moses and the beginnings of documentary history. Anything before written documents was called "Prehistory" (*Vorgeschichte* in proper German still refers to periods preceding the written histories of *Greece* and Rome). Crude flint tools without inscription, numerous figurines (whether goddesses or toys), and some few samples of cave art (but not in Palestine as Neuville prematurely claimed) now inform us about man as early as two or even *six* hundred thousand years ago.[6]

Not much, it is true. Very few authors have had the courage to offer a course in "Neolithic Religion."[7] We have nothing so early about man's beliefs in creation or the deluge or monotheism. But, evidence is ample that the Bible is *not* "In the Beginning"—rather almost at the very end of man's cultural and religious history. To adapt Teilhard's image: if the whole time from which man's religious activity is known be represented as the twenty-four hours of a clock, then from Moses to us is the eight minutes before midnight! This prebiblical horizon revealed by archeology must enter into and even dominate our concept of when and how God determined to take personally in hand the reform of humanity.

We must pause to ask: Granted that there really did exist for thousands of centuries a world of humans, how can we call this a horizon of *experience,* a prebiblical horizon of experience? And, what can it have to do with our own spirituality and actual living? Is it not merely a bit of curious information, like the number of stones on Mars, which may enrich our horizons of *knowledge* without really becoming part of our *experience?*

Not so. These are not only real humans; these are our own parents. More than today's inhabitants of remote coral islands or even of parts of Manhattan, these men and women were bearers of our own genes. What little we are able to learn about the life and loves and terrors and religious consolations of the cave men who drew hunters on the rocks of Altamira or Anatolia, tells us something momentous about *ourself,* as we shall next examine.

3. The Prebiblical Half of Evolution

Beyond what was said earlier about Creation, Darwin opened for us a second window onto the prebiblical horizon. He was far from being the first to pose questions of science that threatened religion. The Galileo case is a scandal in the history of the Church, and this scandal has recently been faced squarely without whitewashing.[8] Meanwhile, there were Copernicus and Jesuits like Boskovitch who contributed submissively, yet inexorably, to the breakdown of a static astronomy.

But, stars are not people. Darwin put the pinch where it hurts. Darwin himself was a religious man and tried to interpret his finds as a proof of God's power and greatness, which indeed they were. But, in

the purely scientific area a major tenet of Darwinism has been rejected, or rather, the blame was thrown off on a Frenchman.

Lamarck claimed that the species mutations noted by Darwin, from
lower to higher animals including man, were due to "transmission of
acquired characteristics." To put it crudely, the giraffe was born with
a short neck, but he stretched it hard to reach food on the higher
branches, and when his offspring were born, they inherited his long
neck. This Lamarck thesis is even more reprobated today, because it
has been taken up avidly by the Russians and made to serve ideological
aims.[9]

It was a Catholic, the Abbot Mendel, who is currently held to have
proved that acquired characteristics are *not* transmitted. Then, how
does one species differentiate into another? i.e., how is "Evolution"
possible? Even Darwin more or less agreed to what is incongruously
called in biology the "sport" theory. This means that all changes in
heredity and genes are due simply to a "caprice," an *accident*. The
cases in which nature produces a freak or monster are known to our
experience; they are *relatively* few, but still they do add up. And, *some*
of these few cases, according to the prevailing theory, have
characteristics more suitable than the parent's for coping with the
changing environment.

Two splendid books describe the century long effort of Bible
believers to discredit Darwin and the whole theory of evolution. The
more scholarly but quite readable book by Gillispie describes the situation within the Protestant fold, mostly British and American.[10]
Wendt's book, translated from the German, tells in a more exciting
popular style the resistance of Catholics, especially the French.[11]

The war is not yet over. Within my lifetime the United States was
rocked by Bryan's effort to prevent teaching evolution in the schools.
Indeed, new lawsuits to the same effect, duly televised but less sensational, are happening every year.

Galileo's stumbling block had been that single passage of Joshua
10:13, where the sun stood still. Save for that, his whole new helicocen-
tric astronomy might well have been accepted without a ripple. Today, without even adverting to the known fact that the sun *does* move,
nobody considers Joshua 10:13 an exegetical impasse. In a similar way,
the main thrust of Darwin against Bible readers was that God did not
fashion a doll out of mud and blow in it to make living man, or then
take a rib out of Adam and make it into Eve (Gn 2:7,22). Before
"hermeneutics" came into vogue, it would have been hard to compare
those events to other apparently historical passages, like the Good
Samaritan or the Prodigal Son. Even today, people will say, "You may
want to think your grandfather was an ape, but I sure don't," and you
will not bring them around by saying, "My ancestor, if you please, was
a *Primate,* and I get much more satisfaction out of that than by thinking he was a pile of mud."

The Catholic Church took its usual sensibly slow and cautious good time in coming to terms with Evolution. Karl Rahner somewhere, I think, says that the real scandal was not that the Church took so long to admit scientific commonplaces, but rather that for a century, behind a façade of nominal acceptance of Church rejection, there was built up a complete system of "reconciling evolution with Catholic dogma," all ready to spring forth full panoplied when the go sign would be inevitably given.[12]

Any encyclical, though embodying from the first to the last stages of its composition the convictions of the reigning Pontiff, none the less is well known to be drafted for him by successive stages of experts and revisers. It is said that the earlier framers of the 1950 encyclical, *Humani Generis,* really intended it to decree that a Catholic could still not teach evolution; but, at some stage of its redaction a wise counsellor got them to put in the words, "cannot teach evolution *as a fact,* but only as a hypothesis" — which Science ultimately considers it anyway, since Evolution is not a metaphysical or mathematical "must," impervious to continuing experience.[13]

Humani generis ended up less delicate about the claim that "the first man" [i.e., Adam in Hebrew] may have appeared in different times and places. "It is in no way apparent how polygenism is compatible with original sin." But, loyal Belgian experts rushed into print, acclaiming this as an *invitation* to Catholic scientists to marshal their evidences in a way that will make the matter more "apparent."[14]

Knowledge about evolution and primal man is a prebiblical horizon. We do *not* maintain that the first chapter of Genesis in symbolic or borrowed language is really giving us an account of evolution. It does describe in a general sort of way the sequence from a formless whirl, to a planet of seas and earth, then primitive life forms taking shape and teeming in the sea and marshes, then others creeping and crawling up toward the mountains, and finally, those who could stand up and walk and fight, then eventually man. The fact that at each stage God is shown personally causing the emergence of a new species need not be taken to imply primary rather than secondary causality, just as when it says God caused the end of one day and the beginning of the next.

But, even if *we today* can handily take Genesis 1 as a condensed exposition of the evolutionary process, we must not forget that the person who wrote those lines twenty-five hundred years ago, or the rhapsodists of a few centuries earlier, could not possibly have been describing an evolution they knew nothing whatever about, nor did anyone else until millennia later. *God* knew, it is true, even if those mere men did not know. But, the situation is like that which most exegetes today maintain regarding Second Isaiah. God could not have had any *motive* for describing in detail events which his hearers could not possibly understand, as if he were to have given in David's time a telescoped account of the wars of Caesar and Hitler.

"Prediction of the future" is, of course, like any *miracle*, God's prerogative, but a prerogative in which even omnipotence is limited by motivation. Anyway, "prophecy" is now understood to mean something rather different from prediction. Most of what the prophets talk about is *history*, but *known* in such a way as to be a guide for the immediate future. Thus, prophecy is very nearly a synonym of salvation history. I respect the worldwide fervor for a return to *"real"* history," generated by Pannenberg, but I have expressed elsewhere how much he, too, ultimately has recourse to the kind of "meta-history" he combats. [15]

My own classification of the first chapters of Genesis is in dependence upon my colleague, Alonso-Schökel. They are a *philosophical* recapture of what *must* have happened at the very beginning to account for the way man is as we find him existing today. [16] Alonso, in place of philosophy, uses the more biblical term Wisdom, as had been felicitously pioneered already by Dubarle. [17] But, the biblical wisdom literature is basically a collection of *maxims*, distillations of the experiences of the past into rules of thumb for how we should be existing today: a very "ahistorical" equivalent of what we just described as salvation history.

Rather, it was the functions of a real philosopher or cosmologist, as we understand them today, which the author of Genesis 1ff was performing. The cosmologist, starting with the real reliable factual data which he has at hand (and which are of a very different order from those limited but nevertheless factual and reliable data which J and P had at hand), asks himself how there could ever have come into being a world exactly such as we find it today.

We have the big bang theory. We have the Kant-Laplace theory. We have also some reputable scientists who see creation as the only possible way to account for the *beginnings*. But, we have even scientists today who postulate *continuing* creation as the only way to compensate for the entropy which we will discuss below.

In much the same way, I submit, J of Genesis 2 and P of Genesis 1 were trying (each in his own very different way) to recapture what the first origins of woman's and man's world *must* have been in order to account for the physical state of affairs those two authors recognized around them in their own day. And, many fair critics admit that they succeeded not at all badly. But, this does *not* mean that they were describing the details of evolution, or taking sides on whether Darwin or Lamarck or Mendel or Dobzhansky was closer to the right track.

In a word, those worthy scholars, J and P, were audaciously reaching out for the prebiblical horizon of experience as an exercise of philosophy, not of history or science.

You may be inclined to react that, insofar as they succeeded and really got back to the roots of things, then there is no prebiblical horizon of experience after all; Page One of the Bible starts absolutely as far back as you can get. To some extent we must admit this, and agree not to quibble merely about terms; still, you would also admit that this view of Genesis lf and its relation to history and experience are quite different from any held by the normal believer.

In short, one may continue to maintain that whole eons of human experience, *prior* to the Bible, are at most "imaginatively conjured up" by writers who themselves lived thirty-one hundred years after the Adam they purported to describe.

4. Sociology and Psychology on a Prebiblical Horizon

The third recent window opened onto prebiblical horizons is Comparative Religion. We saw that this is a branch of sociology rather than theology: how people *really* act instead of how they *should* act.

But, it is equally a branch of *psychology*, and brings Freud into the picture.

Freud, you know, said the way we act today, especially if we are kinky, is due to some traumatic experience in the womb or shortly after. There have been some who claimed that Genesis 2–3 is really saying something similar. Humanity, as a whole, does often act irrationally (the *sinful* is, after all, irrational) because of a traumatic experience in the very moments of its earliest existence. [18]

The Existentialists, too, though most of them are (often with a show of reluctance) atheists, describe the frustrations of our human strivings in a way reflecting not only Genesis 3 but also Romans 7:24,19: "Unhappy man that I am! . . . the good that I will, I do not perform; what I do is the evil which I do not will."

In this sense not only Freud but also Sartre are waiting there for us on the first pages of the Bible, and how can we hope for a prebiblical horizon more revolutionary than those two?

But, there is a difference. Comparative Religion in its way assumed that religious behavior itself was the trauma. "Thou hast conquered, O pale Galilean, and the world has grown gray with thy death," wrote Swinburne. And, I confess to having seen the movie, *Rosemary's Baby*, without realizing until I was later told that the baby was Jesus, a normal happy baby of a normal happy mother, but swooped upon in his cradle by a vulture horde of blackrobes. These worthies made him the symbol of salvation-by-frustration, that is to say, "by doing everything repellent to nature and avoiding everything which nature desires" (à Kempis).

These are sobering thoughts for loyal Christians, especially of the celibate variety, and we are skating on thin ice when we try to grasp the admissible amid the prebiblical horizons opened out by comparative religious sociology and psychiatry. Yet, I believe their valid contribution can and must be sifted out from the murk of venom which has acclaimed in Church practice many of the commonest and most barbaric usages of people in widely diverse times and places.

Let us begin by pinpointing the origins of Comparative Religion as a discipline within the science of psychosociology. Sociology itself, as you well know, was invented out of the whole cloth only one hundred thirty years ago by a Frenchman named Auguste Comte. He had the somewhat right idea that Aristotelian scholasticism had so dominated men's thinking that it was directed toward a phantom of science. Comte proposed to substitute a science of the practical art of living; the lessons of success and failure are to be drawn from how men are actually observed to live. But alas, he too was still far too much the victim of scholasticism, and his so-called "Sociology" is a work of pure philosophy from start to finish, contributing only the name to a momentous science still waiting to be born.

The real fathers of modern sociology were Durkheim and Weber. And even Weber has to be left on the sidelines because his greatness was just as imposing in the field of exegesis as of sociology. His greatest works deal with "charisma," a New Testament term which he applies felicitously to Hebrew Prophetism, and also to the Hebrew Judges, as antithesis to bureaucracy. [19] He further had dazzling insights into the close interplay between wealth and religion from earliest times; one of the few notable points he missed is that the very invention of writing, and with it the whole of pre-McLuhan culture, was as a device for keeping the accounts of payment to workers for the building of temples at Warka near Ur in Mesopotamia around 3100 B.C.

Weber further follows the intimate interplay of money and religion down through China and India and, in "The Protestant Ethic and the Rise of Capitalism," raised hackles almost as enduring as his misunderstood fleeting characterization of the biblical Jews as a pariah people. [20]

The authentic sociology differs from its protoparent Comte chiefly in the use of statistical methods. Its model is perhaps Durkheim's work on Suicide. This book showed, just from counting cases, that the most general cause of suicide is *anomie* or muddledness, a lack of any clear, even if painful, goals to live for. A man with huge debts, even without a family, rarely escapes them by suicide; the people who do often live alone and with few ties to anyone else. A prime conclusion was that both Jews and Catholics, strongly integrated into organizations of constant mutual obligations, rarely commit suicide.

Thus, one of the first and still best sociology researches shows more favor than hostility to religion. Durkheim also wrote a very informative but more theoretical work on the ultimate components of religion. The study of the totem among aboriginals in Australia concludes that what the totem really represents is the clan itself as a whole; thus, the real object of worship is the whole body of the faithful. [21] Of course, this has overtones far different from Paul's saying that the Body of Christ which we worship is really we ourselves; it is because of the Eucharist (1 Cor 10:17) that "we who are many are one body." In this way we are set apart from the claims of communists and others that "our fellow-humanity" is the only worthy object of religious worship. Also provoking for Christians, but with perhaps some grains of insight not altogether valueless, is the important work of American pragmatist William James on the "Varieties of Religious Experience."

Works such as these were only partial avenues toward a general sociology of religion, or the roughly counterpart "Comparative Religion" (which really means much the same as "History of Religion" or even "Philosophy of Religion," with almost no diminution of sociological orientation). The very fact that religion was recognized to be so universal and so *operative* and so "computable" from the very earliest forms of human society should have been taken as a compliment to Christianity and a starting point for dialogue. But, it never was. May we say modestly that only the exegetical fraternity constituted a kind of exception? Critical exegesis from the start, even Catholic, felt the need of building up a library of "Comparative Religion" more or less like the locked off library sections on Wellhausen and Harnack: they were needed only in order to be refuted, but they were not ignored.

Yet, many Christian academic and pastoral authorities regarded with misgiving any burgeoning efforts to show how some of the most primitive and repugnant elements in pygmy style religions were very like the practices of Catholicism—or even like the more antiseptic expressions of Protestant belief. We can scarcely blame such hierarchs, as long as the goal of early Comparative Religion exponents seemed to be "Crush the Church (*écrasez l'infâme*)," rather than foster a mutually beneficial interaction between the societal and the churchly.

At any rate, the great classics of Tylor and Hubert-Mauss rather threw the Bible into the shade for people who had had a taste for it. Jephtha's daughter (Jg 11:39) was an Iphigenia (Lucretius 1:101!), a fate which Jonathan escaped only by vow violation (1 Sam 14:39). Not only Jephtha and Jonathan; also Jael, Judith, Job, Jonas! There is a barbarity in those stories, but their very inefficaciousness has something childlike that merits more sympathy than the blitzkrieg-juggernaut of warrior Yahweh's hegemony.

James Frazer, though more famous for his *Golden Bough* constantly appearing in new editions, left a three volume work, going through the Bible itself page-by-page and noting its relevance to his anthropological discoveries. [22] There we have prebiblical horizon with a vengeance: not that the populations he studied were anterior in time to Israel or Sumer, but they were plainly anterior to any contact with the Bible, despite very effective penetration of Anglo-American bible societies among cognate tribes.

Here are some examples of pagan or primitive practices which *sound* much like Christianity, drawn not from Frazer, but from my own forty years in Egyptian antiquities and in the surrounding (pre-)Muslim world. The Cairo museum shows several examples of a Divine Triad, each of whom was believed to be not only true God but also sharer in a single nature distinct from that of lesser gods. The outside wall of the innermost Luxor temple shows in detailed reliefs the birth of a divine king from the womb of a virgin mother, who had been fecundated by the god in the only apparent form of the human king. [23]

At a later date, Nilus in Migne relates how the bedouin of the Sinai desert precipitate themselves upon the camel they sacrificed, in order to drink some of its blood and thus be a united and strong tribe by all sharing in the same sacrificial blood. Similarity to 1 Cor 10:16 about the blood of Christ uniting and strengthening us was consolingly acceptable to Christian liturgists. But, Catholic scholars have recently exposed inauthenticities in the Nilus account. That fact has been overlooked by René Girard, whose four recent successes are intensely relevant to our theme, but will perforce occupy me in an entire research elsewhere. [24] Here I must note only that Girard, though his interpretation of Christ's death is rarely tolerable to Christians, nevertheless regards himself as in some sense defending the insights of a religion against the whole tribe of psychiatrists and religious-sociology gurus whom he excoriates.

Let us turn to another area, that of miracle. In the Christian polemic against well publicized Jewish and pagan wonder workers, like Apollonius of Tyana, it is remarkable that the factual reality of their miracles is never denied; only their motives are shown to be unworthy and un-divine in comparison with Jesus.

The practice of enforced celibacy among the Roman vestal virgins is too well known to need mention here, but it may be opportune to note that for centuries the term "chastity" was used both for that case and for the Christian counterpart. We are now more sensitive to the fact that chastity is a virtue for *all* married and unmarried people, while the intention of not having even legitimate sexual relations is called celibacy. It was totally unfree in the case of the Vestals. For Christian priests, at least as individuals and in the earlier stages of its acceptance, it is completely free.

A final example: in the early days of excitement about the Dead Sea Scrolls, one scholar claimed that in the Habakkuk Pesher the Master of Justice was expected to rise again ("appear in glory") after the Wicked Priest had had him put to death (by crucifixion, another scholar argued). This interpretation (in place of the viable alternative, it was the *Wicked Priest* who "appeared in" liturgical "display") was immediately denounced as blasphemous throughout the whole Catholic and Protestant world. But, the main point at issue seems to have been missed: whether or not some Qumran scribe wrote that their teacher arose from the dead, the fact they could have had such an *expectation* does not downgrade the uniqueness of Christianity. Not only the *resurrection* of Jesus and of us all, but the Trinity and Eucharist and virginal motherhood were all, as shown above, long standing yearnings of the human heart. The "originality" of Christianity must not be imagined to consist in its *difformity* from human religious longings, but in its nobler and absolute *fulfilment* of them.

Christian missionary scholarship did not remain indifferent to the challenge of debunkers. The name of Wilhelm Schmidt is held in veneration as a man who used objective anthropological methods to prove that the most original form of religion in any milieu whatsoever is monotheism, only gradually decomposing into the worship of many gods familiar from classic mythologies and from Tylor. Unfortunately, it has been recently recognized that some of the remote, inaccessible tribes, patiently studied by Schmidt, had not been, in fact, sufficiently immune from missionary "contamination," to which their monotheistic convictions would have to be at least partially attributed.[25]

But, search for the truth of the matter goes on perseveringly, and one of our most recent resources is a cooperative Catholic team effort, facing up with boldness and insight to the problem of monotheism on a prebiblical horizon.[26]

Without unduly anticipating what we have to say below under both "Hermeneutic" and "Ecumenism," let us note in both the function of what has come to be a key word for making anthropological categories commensurable with organized religion. That key word is "Symbolism." Undoubtedly, many of the things done in either biblical or primitive religions are intended to be *symbols* of truths or facts not easily expressible.

To say bluntly that the consecrated host is only a "symbol" of the Body of Christ rather than the real thing is a door slammed in the face of any Catholic dialogue, of course. But, the excitement aroused by a work of Schillebeeckx shows that when the terms are more sensitively chosen, some basis for discussion remains. It is true that Pope Paul VI expressed explicit disapproval of "transignification" as an updated equivalent of "transubstantiation." But, Schillebeeckx was fortunately able to make available to the Pontiff, in a dutiful and roundabout way, an early draft of the Council of Trent, in which several bishops flatly rejected the term "transubstantiation," because it was newfangled jargon that had never been heard in Catholic theology a couple of centuries before. To this at Trent the majority was able to reply that, as usages change and language changes, it becomes *necessary* to "invent" a new term in order to preserve the *genuine* underlying significance. Trent was progressively successful in thus imposing the neologism, "transubstantiation"—so successful that it is now defended as tenaciously as if it had been used by Jesus and the Apostles.[27]

In the New Testament we nowhere find either "person" or "trinity," and even "nature," as applied to God solely in 2 Pt 1:4, is held in common with *humans* rather than with the Spirit or Incarnate Son. Yet, the New Testament declarations do indeed make inescapable that Jesus and the Spirit are in some ways identical with God, in some ways different. But, it took three hundred years of pre-Chalcedon struggle, in which certain specific terms were for a while dominant and for a while discredited, before we reached our present terminology, satisfactory on the whole if kept in close relation to its historical origins. What was at stake in all those discussions of Chalcedon and Trent was not *whether*, but *to what extent* and *in precisely which cases*, the biblical language was literal, and in which cases symbolic. In other words, there was powerfully at play even then a force which today has become the in word, "Hermeneutic."

Our whole approach to the *originality* of the Bible, intimately tied up with its *possibilities* of interpretation, has been clarified (and that means *enriched* rather than threatened) by Comparative Religion. We would not want to defend immemorial positions by sticking our heads in the sand and saying that facts have no relevance simply because they embarrass us.

What we urgently need today is a single, consistent, comprehensive theory of symbolism which can be applied with surgical impartiality to biblical and extrabiblical practices.[28]

All this does not mean merely a technique for proving that Christianity is right and those primitive pagans were wrong. Someday we will be proud and happy to admit that God has revealed to pygmies in a mysterious (natural?, maybe) way certain truths about his being and their relation to him, which they then endeavored to express by rituals, imperfect like ours, but often even more instructive for being so childlike.

The editors of a recent French bible found it illuminating to use exclusively drawings by children.[29] We are reminded of a Candid Camera television program which showed a dozen children, answering the question of how the world first started. It was so transparently clear that the children were *symbolizing*. Each one expressed within his own framework of imagery or comprehension what some teacher or comrade or atheist had told him. Sister's classroom narration of a loving father, communicating his love, is even more moving in children's lingo. But, it was almost more plaintive and convincing to hear a child tell of a big machine, with buttons to be pushed, so that everything gradually came forth. This materialist picture, in order to make sense at all to the child, *presumed* everything we consider essential to a personal creator God.

Thus, we are coming to have a more ecumenical respect for the valid human and cultic insights of religions hitherto called childish and primitive, whether a hundred thousand years ago or just around the corner in some Voodoo hideout or Zen commune. Even Jonestown I am not forgetting, with its painful echoings of Abraham, trudging up the hill for human sacrifice.[30] (In that year, I had made up for my college theology class a "midrash" of how Abraham had "doubtless" acted prudently after all; a member of the class came to me afterwards with Woody Allen's biblical takeoffs in "Without Feathers," which really did exactly the same job much better!) Anyway, at Jonestown it is easier to separate out an overlay of gangster-television culture from some underpinning of genuine religious conviction. Even of those Christian martyrs who leaped into the fire without waiting to be forced, we were taught to say, "worthy of respect but not imitation."

We Catholics now recognize how other religions, perhaps only in small ways, perhaps even in greater, have been doing the job better than we have. To publish such a statement before the Second Vatican Council would have been unthinkable; today, following its very wording, we can cheerfully say that values from other religions must be recognized and incorporated into our own. The same Council also liberated us to say that the Bible is not a tool to be manipulated by the Church as she wishes, but a higher revelation of God "over against" the Church, judging the Church and aiding that comparative reevaluation of our beliefs and practices. We do not think for a moment that there is any different "truth" conveyed by God's Bible and God's Church. But, how in *both* cases that "truth" is embodied *in human terms* becomes easier to interpret with the help of prior human insights, the "prebiblical horizon of experience."

5. The "Biblical Horizons": a Re- and Pre-capitulation

This section may be rather brief because we need to point out only three things: first, the points on which Biblical data have already been focused in querying their relevance to more modern rediscovery of what preceded; second, the same for situations which we will next present as postbiblical; and third, mention of other areas which are currently most agitated in biblical studies.

What points, hopefully in pursuance of the duty and intention declared on our first page, have we already touched upon, in the hope of showing how mankind outside or without the Bible exhibits noteworthy experiences which can not only criticize but also constructively illuminate the true religion? You will recognize, from Genesis: creation, women's lib-or-rib, Abraham's date, Jonestown's relation to the sacrifice of Isaac. From Joshua-Judges: Galileo and the sun standing still; Max Weber's charisma versus bureaucracy; Jephtha with Jonathan-Jael-Judith-Job-Jonas. Kings era: annals, calendars, close link of temples both with money and with the invention of literacy; Nabonidus' museum; Eusebius' chronology and onomastic. Prophets:

"prophetic" history, "extrapolating" rather than predictive; Pannenberg against "meta-history" or salvation-history; "Second" (nonpredictive) Isaiah. Wisdom: Genesis 1 really a wisdom reflection.

From the New Testament: miracles and Apollonius; parables linked with Jonah and the Flood; "primitive" monotheism and Akhenaten; "trinity" and virgin birth in Egypt; "enforced" celibacy; the Eucharist as the community worshiping its own body. More generally, allegorizing "hermeneutic" and the *symbol*; "Facts versus truth," the very nature of certitude in science as against medieval theology; God's authorship of the *whole* Bible, even its dubious human statements, in a way that is never asserted of a Papal or even infallible decree.

What, indeed then, have we *not* already touched upon but intend to? Among specific passages we will notice only: the Joshua anathema and attitudes toward war and God as warlord; Third World theology, "the rice of life"; Christ all in all, as Teilhard's Omega point; Fuller Sense, French *relecture* and medieval accommodations, somewhat highlighted with the recent naming of de Lubac as cardinal.

If these represent the biblical data only incidental to areas prior or posterior to the biblical horizon, what is left to point to as the properly and strictly *biblical* issues of our day? For Old Testament history, four massive acquisitions of early twentieth century scholarship have been shaken, though not really dislodged: a) The Pentateuch sources JEPD, which were never more than a hypothesis at best (like Evolution!) and always had even more weaknesses than a well behaved hypothesis should, are under renewed attack, but, as usual, nothing really different is offered to replace them.[31] b) Unduly apologetic defense of the "historicity" of Genesis and Exodus, associated chiefly with the archeological great name of Albright, has been attacked (but varyingly), especially by Dever and Thompson in the Hayes-Maxwell history.[32] c) The equally great name of Martin Noth, which, for many of us, was a bulwark against Albright style patchwork defense of "traditional historicism," is under attack on the two fronts of "amphictyony" (all but dislodged as an explanation of Israel's Tribes, though I frankly remain faithful) and "deuteronomist" as compiler of the books Joshua through Kings (still holding valiantly, though linked with JEPD reappraisals).[33] d) The "Covenant" as basis of the whole Old Testament theology since Eichrodt and of Albright historicism in Mendenhall has been thoroughly relieved of some Hittite and other "parallels" by McCarthy.[34]

In the New Testament area, a whole new era of Christology was inaugurated by the publication of three essays in Dutch.[35] Out of them have emerged the volcanic Schillebeeckx volumes. These are commonly, and not without some basis, lumped together with Küng or even with Rahner by conservatives. Form criticism of the Gospels and more recently structuralism have been so thoroughly examined in the Schillebeeckx volumes that to save space we may be pardoned for resting with him the whole current case for updating New Testament research.[36]

At the close of this section on the properly "biblical" horizon, we may single out a movement as *bridge* between the biblical and post-biblical, a movement varyingly called "non-religious use of the Bible," "death of God," secularism, and linguistic analysis.

Chesterton said, "Christianity has not failed — it has just never been tried." From such a super-loyal son of the Church this could have meant only that the splendid presentation of Christ's doctrine and example in organized Catholicism was never tried on a global scale or even in the dominant societies as a whole. But, I do not think we are quite as loyal or naïve as Chesterton in supposing that the powerful and far flung structures of the Church have "tried" to the full the message of Christ. Anyway, the Second Vatican Council says loud and clear that even though we have tried, we have not tried enough; like Avis, we must try harder. We must try to be like Jesus rather than powerful or wealthy or dogmatic. We have reached a phase which, if not postbiblical, is at least posterior to hitherto existing relations between Church and Bible.

A kindred line of thought by Bonhoeffer has had immense resonance, doubtless in undue measure because he was a clergyman executed by the Nazis. Did you know, though, that he started out as a missionary in Barcelona, of all places? And, did you know that he spent a year's study in a New York seminary by which he was frankly not impressed? Less important perhaps for you to know is that he wrote a couple of books with titles sounding like exegesis, notably of Genesis 1-3, about which Dr. Towner has informed us enthrallingly. Bonhoeffer's even more influential works, smuggled out of prison, were edited by his friend, Eberhard Bethge, in a way which is frankly avowed not to distinguish neatly the exact parts which came from Bonhoeffer himself.[37] Taking all this fully into account, we realize he is a great thinker and a mammoth influence on the younger clergymen, both Protestant and Catholic, in our century.

Bonhoeffer's message is typically "not postbiblical, but post-what-*we*-have-been-making-of-the-Bible." Bible *sí*, religion *no!* He advocated a "non-religious interpretation of Bible themes," which, by a paradox worthy of Chesterton, turns out to mean "the *real* religion of the Bible which has escaped the attention of the organized (and, for him, Protestant) church." One reason he must have been trying to promote religion, after all, is that he claims religion ought to dominate the *center* of people's lives, when they are healthy, vigorous, powerful, loving, and earning. People's religion must not be relegated to the fringes, where they are altar boys or catechism pupils or scout troops or accident victims or the vast silent majority of tired, sick, old people who find in religion their only resources. Not that Bonhoeffer begrudged it in the least to *them*, even though he did not spell out how much *more* help it would be to them if it were essentially the domain of the strong, young power wielders.

More akin to our title, and yet fully in the Bonhoeffer line, is one of the few impressive theological movements "Made in U.S.A."—the Death of God. It came on early enough so that I still had strength to read thoroughly both the primary documents of Vahanian, Altizer, and Hamilton, and the flood of scandalized secondary literature.[38] Therefore, I can say with some assurance that virtually every one among the Christians denouncing these "godless or even blasphemous" formulations has read no further than the title, or at least had made up his mind already. The title was, indeed, chosen for shock value, but the goal of the two earnest Protestant ministers was deep and sincere. They were anticipated by Vahanian, whose claim plainly was not that God himself is dead, but that the *images* (drawn from our supreme values) which we have used to represent him are no longer operative, and must be changed in order not to leave us with a cold, dead phantom instead of a real, living God.[39]

Proceeding from this point, Altizer stressed rather that we have no other way of grasping God *except* by image, and when this fails us, God too is dead: to us, to our alive and younger generation; yet, Altizer was wholly taken up in the striving to make this God live again *for us*.[40] Harvey Cox took up and worked out these and some more original "post-God" reflections in *The Secular City*.[41] Largely with his help has arisen a genuine theological movement or "style" called "secularity" as a positive value, "the theology of this world," as distinct from the ambiguous Secularization (German *Säkularisierung*) or theft of church property.[42]

Paul Van Buren, in two works which I, against the common consensus of the virtuous, consider masterful, gathered up the numerous links connecting this "Death of God approach" to what had long been known in British linguistic analysis as the problem of "what we really mean by statements nominally made about God."[43] I find nothing to reproach in his formula borrowed from Braithwaite: From the beginning of time, every statement apparently made about God is really a declaration of the speaker's own commitment to a *course of action* based on a narrative which he himself recognizes to be only partly historico-factual.[44]

This programmatic formulation is generally attacked as "reductionism," on the ground that it reduces God to the status of a purely inner worldly value. But, that charge is unfair and false; it is a different thing to say that *statements* apparently about God are really statements about inner worldly values. When food was men's highest value, their God was visualized in terms of a rainmaker. When war became men's highest value, Yahweh was a warrior, and so were Jupiter and Thor. When a peaceful, patriarchal, very male society dominated, then God appeared as an old man with a long white beard. With Amos and Isaiah he becomes the guarantor of a social order of justice and brotherhood. It would take us too far afield to investigate the extent to which Jesus proposed a new image of God, rather than working within the Amos pattern developed by so-called Pharisee Judaism, or whether Paul, in turn, operates with any differing God image. Meanwhile, it was the very perfection of Jesus' own humanity which made *him* the henceforth insuperable expression of God among men; God incarnate *within mankind,* through and in one man, as we shall presently see in Teilhard.

Note that all these dying and reviving images of God are not postbiblical; in fact, almost all the examples were chosen squarely within the biblical horizon. In the Bible itself the two prongs of Braithwaite's statement are stunningly verified. First, when we talk about God, it is really not God we are talking about, as Anselm and Marcel said.[45] Aquinas explained this to mean that we can know God *only* by affirming of him some highest intrahuman value, which we then proceed immediately to *deny* of him, and conclude only that he is *"not* that but 'something' *better."*

And the second prong: our commitment to a certain highest in the order of human values is based on a narrative which we know to be only partly historical. The six days of creation, Eve from Adam's rib, Jonah in the whale, are profound theological teachings, which hardly anyone maintains to depend on the historical factuality of the events narrated. As for the New Testament, even the words of institution of the Eucharist we have in four different forms which cannot *all* be the one spoken by Jesus; and, a momentous Biblical Commission decree made secure for us the view that the Gospels are proximately the record of a *faith* based on specific facts, rather than a record of the historico-factual realities *upon* which that faith was based.[46]

Thus, the "God is dead" movement and Van Buren's "edges of language" are by no means a post-God horizon, but a horizon posterior to the dominance of human values previously considered worthy of representing God; a horizon posterior to our excessive security as to what people were really saying when they made statements about God. And, with this realization we are precipitated into "the New Hermeneutic," at the threshold of what we will treat under the title assigned to us as "Postbiblical."

6. Actualization: "life is for now, not centuries ago"

From a certain point of view, the expression "postbiblical horizon"—itself also doubtless chosen for shock value—is intended to raise the question of whether what the Bible *really says* is irrelevant for our time. An equivalent way of putting it would be: "the problem is to *sift out* of the biblical then-and-there interests some basic or even incidental content which is fully applicable here-and-now." Christians, furthermore, cannot ignore that the Old Testament as a whole is the record of a religion which, though it lives vigorously today, is rejected by us and held to be annulled, superseded, or at best transformed.

Is the Bible actual today? Take our attitude toward war, one of our most burning issues. What help can we hope to get from the Bible? Even in the New Testament it is rather approved and held up for imitation in parables and asides, or at least taken for granted like death and taxes. "Those who take the sword will perish by the sword" of Matthew 26:52 is indeed of unrivaled helpfulness, but it is matched by Luke's "let him who has no sword, get one" (22:36). Life is a warfare! (2 Cor 10:4). This message came through loud and clear in the Crusade era, and still dominated the "age of chivalry" in which an Ignatius Loyola could found what he frankly called "the shock-troops."

All this without even adverting to the Old Testament. When we turn to Joshua and Kings, all our energy is drained defending or explaining away the "anathema," massacre of innocent populations *after* defeat, prescribed or even prayed for (Ps 137H,9).[47] This looms so large that we scarcely feel called upon to defend the fact that from Abraham through Maccabees God himself is a Warrior, a leader of his people in battles often frankly aggressive.

At the side of thorny points like war or the God of Wrath, we have Jacob telling lies in Gn 27:20, defended by Augustine as "no lie but a mystery." We have polygamy and divorce. Almost the only thing we have about ecology—and it is more cuttingly relevant than the environmentalists like to admit—is Paul's (1 Cor 9:9) "does God have any concern about oxen?"

Summing it all up, the key *specific* issues of our own world seem so different from those of the whole Bible that we might well seem resigned to calling ours a postbiblical age. Our life must be lived *now*—even if it is to be lived for God—and not in a pattern of what he considered useful for people long ago and far away.

The Jewish users or even producers of the Hebrew Bible already experienced this malaise and coped with it by a device which is called "Midrash." The exact nature of this device is in the forefront of modern exegesis, and the experts do not exactly support the view which I will now present.[48]

We may take as examples Psalm 68 or 78H or Wisdom 16. Here we have the Exodus story retold with imaginative embroidering. The manna which "inside everyone's mouth turned to the taste which most pleased him" (Wisdom 16:21) or "Yahweh lunged up like a drunk out of sleep" (Psalm 78H:65) might well be called pure inventions, unfounded in the transmitted text, and of dubious taste. But, in my view they are simply a normal way of making the true facts "come alive" for listeners far remote. In just the same way today, when telling the Christmas story to children, we would not hesitate to supply details like, "Joseph blew on the fire," or "Mary shivered from the cold," which we know very well are not among the attested facts.

The later Bible books "took liberties" with the earlier text on which they were basing themselves, *not* in order to deceive or to proclaim these imaginative details for their own sake, but only because this was the best way of remaining *faithful* to the real "proclaimed facts" in a cultural setting which had already considerably changed. The rabbinic commentators continued this "Midrash" tradition in a way which, even to modern Jewish scholars, seems audacious: an "audacity" which ultimately is due more to the sweeping changes of the surrounding culture than to any disrespect of the commentators for the real underlying facts.

A more modern escape from the impasse of an "outdated Bible" has been offered by what is called "the fuller sense." This term has had quite a vogue, though it was really *invented* no more than sixty years ago, and by a Spaniard. But, it has been taken up enthusiastically, especially in France, and publicized in America, mostly by Raymond Brown.[49] In the momentous world of German exegesis or among Protestants in general it has hardly been recognized to exist.[50]

"Fuller Sense" (*sensus plenior*) means that, though God and the human writer are each truly the "author" of Scripture, still what God meant by the words can be different and deeper than was seen in them by the human author who chose them. It mostly comes down to this: Old Testament passages can be telling us something about Christianity even where they do not seem to. It might not be going too far afield to give as examples the Assumption or Immaculate Conception, known by God (but by no one else) to be contained in Genesis 3:15.

The "Fuller Sense" is not presented as identical with the "Typical Sense." The whole Old Testament, and certain specific persons or episodes within it, have long been held to be a "type" of Christ; that is to say, a genuine historical occurrence long before him, which, however, in due time the Christ-event "fulfilled" by experiences quite similar. Thus, the typical sense is a branch of the literal or historical sense.

Do not be misled by the term "fulfilled," which ultimately means the same as "fuller." Do not be misled either by the New Testament passage which most expressly calls Old Testament episodes a "type" of Christ, 1 Cor 10:4—in which, however, the examples chosen by Paul tend rather toward the zone of "pure accommodations" or metaphorical application. For this reason, even in some recent literature, the term "typology" is employed for *all* the applications or actualizations of the Old Testament by ardent Christian preachers. But, in Catholic manuals it has been firmly insisted that we only confuse the issue if we mix up the properly "typical" sense either with the "fuller" sense or with any type of "accommodation."

The "Fuller Sense," therefore, is held to be a meaning of the Old Testament itself, which was really intended by God and really contained *within* the words, though in a way altogether unknown both to the human author and to his readers. This fuller sense was presumably disclosed by the light of Christian revelation or developing Church dogma. It is prized as a way of making the Scripture "actual" in our time and thus conquering the menace of a "postbiblical horizon."

For two reasons, I join those who do not recommend the "Fuller Sense."[51] First, it is subject to no control. Though you and I and other exegetes of the better sort will use good sense and historic awareness in applying it, still the door is flung open to those who find Hitler or nuclear blasts "clearly intended by God" in apocalyptic biblical images.

Secondly, the "fuller sense" does not really go far *enough*. God's knowledge of the things which the human author is inspired to write is, indeed, greater than the author's own. It does indeed include details, like whether the "maiden" of Isaiah 7:14 is really the only "virgin in childbearing" known among humankind; or whether the liberating activities of Cyrus are mentioned in a scroll composed two hundred years earlier. God's knowledge of every item, not only in the Bible, but in *every* work of literature, is greater than the human author's, *infinitely* greater. This truly "fuller" knowledge of God is called "supercomprehensive," and means equivalently

> *To me the meanest flower that blows can give*
> *Thoughts that do often lie too deep for tears.*

In any single word or event, God sees the whole of reality, and we, in moments of insight, can catch tiny glimpses of that reality.

Thus, truly the whole of the past and present and future is a proper object of our rereading of a single banal statement, like "there was much grass in the place" (John 6:10). We can get just *anything* out of our reading, not only of the Bible, but of poetry or even sober history. This is the *value* of literature in general; it broadens the horizons of the mind. But, it is an entirely different matter to say that God is the *author* of a written statement or of a *meaning* within it, unknown to the human author and intended to become known only in the light of later events or teachings.

The objection to "fuller sense" which I have just voiced is essentially the conclusion of a recent and erudite French survey of "the Messianism of *relecture*" of the late, highly influential Belgian exegete, Joseph Coppens.[52] The term *relecture* is widely favored, not only in France and Belgium, but also in English and other languages retaining the French form. What is this *relecture* which has become an international term?[53]

It means "a rereading," but a rereading *in the light of* later revelation. Thus, it seems to have much in common with the "Fuller Sense" and precisely with the *elusiveness* of that term which we criticized above. I do not say that the informed users of the term *relecture,* and

especially those of French mother tongue, would agree that they
understand by that term the same thing as "fuller sense."[54] In any case,
relecture is a deceptively innocent term. Of course, we will always be
rereading the Scripture, and of course, it will always "mean more to us
each time." But, this is only partly because we gradually come to
understand better what the text really means or meant to the time and
milieu in which it was given. Another part of our relecture consists in
finding new applicability to our own spiritual life today, and that does
not quite mean discovering that the text really had within itself that
meaning all along.

What is the difference between relecture and eisegesis? Eisegesis is
also a fabricated word, a Greek coinage more popular in American
and German circles, to mean "getting out of the text something which
is not in it," the opposite of ex-egesis. Naturally, no one would own up
to doing eisegesis. But, the advocates of relecture ultimately have to
find their justification in a kind of "insight." Insight happens to be the
title of Lonergan's chief work, which, indeed, contains one of the best
justifications of properly exegetical method known to me.[55] But, insight is often loosely used: just as "intuition" (in the days before
women's lib) used to be defined as "the inner voice which tells a woman
she is right even when she is wrong." So also relecture risks having in
common with eisegesis that "it finds within the text something which is
not there."

Recent elevation of the French medievalist Henri de Lubac to the
Cardinalate focuses and indeed rather aureoles an aspect of his
thought which is highly relevant here. His four most learned volumes,
entitled Exégèse médiévale, (and some companion researches) show its
roots in Origen. This lifelong dedication of de Lubac succeeds in showing that for more than a thousand years within the Church the "literal
sense" was only a Cinderella among the four senses valued by
medievals. The other three are all what we would call "accommodations" or "spiritual applications" (not sifting out the properly "typical
sense," as we warned above).

In these and other volumes, de Lubac shows pained awareness that
his preceding researches had been favorably acclaimed by everyone except exegetes, of whom he honorably cites an imposing number.[56] But,
he suggests that these criticisms were without exception based on a
misunderstanding of his goals; he agrees fully with these exegetes that
it would be inopportune and wrong to try to foist on the Church of today a medieval "spiritualizing" exegesis in place of the historico-critical
methods now rightly dominating. His own goal was rather simply to
preserve from oblivion a vast episode of the past, embodying its own
lessons which ought not to be forgotten. We might call this (though he
does not use the term) an "exegetical archeology," which, like any
archeology, is instructive and necessary, but does not impose on later
generations the culture norms discoverable in past ages.

But, to one who continues doggedly to read through de Lubac's massive later volume, it is hard to believe that he is not somehow *recommending* this "spiritual insight" of medieval exegetes. And indeed, it *ought* to be recommended; "spiritual applications" will always be needed in our use of Scripture, but this is not automatically identical with *exegesis*. There is a problem here: how can we "actualize" Scripture, making it *relevant* to our vastly changed cultural conditions? Or, if you prefer, how can we find *within* the text itself a *measurable and controllable* basis for such applications? For me, the answer will be "hermeneutic," as I will admit below.

But, before leaving de Lubac, we must insist on the immense influence which his views on exegesis have had, even before the recognition accorded him by the Holy See in 1983. Read, for example, what Henri Crouzel has to say in the American *New Catholic Encyclopedia* near the end of his article, "Origen." It is hard to believe that current advocates of "actualization" look to de Lubac for no more than the sober view about modern exegesis attributed to him above.

Precisely these zealously "actualizing" exegetes tend to use the term "hermeneutic" or "new hermeneutic" as if it were quite synonymous with actualization. I will now mention another widespread correct but very partial, and to that extent misleading, use of the term. It is prominent chiefly in a Protestant collection entitled in English *Essays on Hermeneutics.*[57] When examined, these essays turn out to deal solely with the age-old question of how Christians can make the Old Testament utilizable, or how they can "find Christ in the Old Testament." This can indeed be done and can be best done by means of "hermeneutic." But, if hermeneutic means only or precisely this, it is in danger of being reduced to a kind of Bible-belt fundamentalism. The day is past when we can value the Old Testament solely as a haystack in which forty-some shining needles of messianic prediction can be found, verifiable only in Jesus of Nazareth, "so that no Jewish reader can remain unconverted in good faith."[58] Rather, our task is to show how, with the help of hermeneutic, the Bible can be actualized for *every* aspect of modern life. For the Christian, indeed, "to live is Christ" (Phlp 1:21), and it is no mere rhetorical exaggeration to say that Christ is the whole of our reality. In that sense, the only needed hermeneutic is its branch which deals with actualization, and the only needed part of that is its branch which deals with Christ. But, as soon as we have properly located our Christocentrism within this twofold subdivision, we have a more realistic and, on the whole, more Christian view of "hermeneutic."

In summary, then, hermeneutic should not be defined as a way of finding "Christ in the Old Testament," or "God's meanings unknown to the human author," nor as a *relecture* along the lines of Jewish midrash or medieval "spiritual applications." Rather, hermeneutic is more globally the method of *sifting out,* from what the text actually said to a remote culture, its *factors* which are of permanent validity, or in any case *relevant* to our problems of today. This is a technique required, not only for understanding the Bible, or laws, or art, but constantly for understanding the simplest statements ever made in human communication.[59] Human statements are often governed by patterns beyond our control, and this fact of life applies even to God's own statements if he chooses to make them in human language.

"Hermeneutic means *sifting out*" is my expression which most worried my confrère, Jack Donahue, in his courteous and appreciative rejoinder to my paper during this Conference. He feared he detected me defending "a canon within the canon," as if we could arbitrarily "pick and choose" what is of permanent validity within God's revelation and what is not. I admit the danger. But, I will respond fearlessly. It is not arbitrary, but a *well founded norm of exegesis*, to judge the meaning and relevance of the biblical text by what we now solidly know to be true, even if it was not known at the time the Bible was written. This holds not only of creation's six days and Joshua's sun-on-hold, but especially today of slavery, war, ecology, and feminism. I cannot go quite so far as Elisabeth Schüssler Fiorenza seemed to in telling us that the point where our exegesis must begin is *the point where we are now:* starting from what we right now know to be true and urgent, we must go back and find out not *whether* but *how* the Bible tells us that very thing. In such an approach I greatly fear the spectre of eisegesis, or of pan-biblicism (*Not* everything true or useful for us is in the Bible!). On the other hand, I fully grant to Elisabeth, and this is my answer to Jack Donahue, that God's meaning cannot have been something incompatible with what we now, from other sources, solidly know to be true. It follows also that God's *possible* or probable meaning *may* have been what would be required to be compatible with information which we now possess, not with certitude, but with the kind of high probability on which we ultimately must rely for most of the big concerns of daily life.

7. The Postbiblical Half of Evolution: My Co-Incarnate Body

Turning now to the second area suggested to me by my assigned topic, "Postbiblical horizon," we will take up some aspects of modern science. You have already heard both my own and other presentations of Darwin and evolution and their relation to the centuries *before* the Bible. But, now we will be concerned with the horizons opened out by the measurement of the brain-pan, the running-down of the universe, and the prospects which science itself seems to open out for a believer like Teilhard de Chardin.

Teilhard claims that, from the moment in which there was developed within the animal kingdom a brain sufficiently large and complex to serve the needs of those activities which are called "spiritual," the whole of evolution took a different turn. With man, instead of continuing to subdivide into multiple species, it turned in upon itself, knitting our whole planet into a vast network of interrelations and heading towards an ever greater predictable unity.

The breadth or depth of Teilhard's knowledge of theology or even of science has rightly been questioned. But, his truly great achievement was to have taken the elementary content of ultramodern science textbooks and *integrated* them with Christianity into a pattern of the future. His pattern is entirely Christocentric, but his Christ is seen chiefly as postbiblical, the future end-point of the whole evolutionary process.

Moreover, for Teilhard the Incarnation is foremost, and rightly I think, the hypostatic union between God and the whole of human or even thereby material nature *through* the one man Jesus, rather than with that one man in segregation from the rest of matter and humanity.

To take one example: the body of each one of us (including Jesus) is not a static island, but is a swirling pond of molecules which at every instant whizzingly interchange with molecular elements in other bodies outside ours, under the influence of gravitational and other laws, whereby our body and its interchanges are at each moment under influences from the farthest star, while *we* meanwhile are influencing *it* too.

Among those laws is included entropy, or the second law of thermodynamics, which means that in every operation a portion of the material and/or energy in the universe is dispersed as heat, and no longer available for any useful purpose. In popular terms, this means the universe is "running down"; and precisely to cope with that anomaly, some few scientists postulate an ongoing input of new material or energy, which they unashamedly call continuing creation.

Teilhard had a better idea. We see only the outer face of matter, but on that outer face we read plainly that the more complex becomes the structure of any living thing, the more it somehow transcends itself or performs entirely new *types* of operation: plants *grow,* animals *move,* men *think*—in measurably direct proportion to the increased complexity of their molecular structure. "Continuing quantitative increase results in qualitative change."

Teilhard cautiously skirts the question of how the *soul* differs from the visible face of matter, or how it comes immediately from God, not only in the first man, but in every single fetus that is to be born. Fools rush in where angels fear to trend, so I made that precise point the goal of my book, *Teilhard and the creation of the soul.* Fortunately, I was able to lean heavily on the *Dictonnaire de Théologie Catholique.*

The operation by which man gets a soul or by which a dog or plant gets a vital principle (equally called "soul" by Aquinas and a millennial Catholic tradition) is by a *concursus* between God and the parent-beings, which is really identical in the human and infra-human cases. It is called "immediate creation" only in the case of human production in order to accentuate the greater *worth* of the thing produced.[60]

To this I would add, with Teilhard, the soul is not really a *thing* which is produced; man is not a body plus a soul, but a "soul-éd body," an intellectually vivified body, a *corpus animatum; one* thing.[61] What we call the soul is for Teilhard the "inner face," that unseen aspect of the body itself which makes it *transcend* its measurable units of materiality.

And where does entropy come in? Not only with man, but in decreasing degree in *all* the lower material forms; that *inner face*, transcending the measurable factors, accounts for the fact that the universe is thriving and growing despite the law of entropy which rightly says that its visible and purely material face is constantly running down.

Furthermore, for Teilhard, the phenomena of complexification show that our universe is tending somewhere. The tendency of evolution from the start was to *proliferate*. When life appeared, it immediately proliferated, not only into new cells, but into numberless new species. But, the change from animal to man brought something new into the system. From that moment (admittedly rather late, five minutes before midnight!) man has never evolved into any other species.

For what seemed like a long time, between two hundred thousand and two million years, man huddled in little cradle areas over the globe, struggling just to keep alive and in existence. Only within the past few hundred years, unmeasurable seconds before midnight, man expanded rapidly and filled the whole surface of the globe. (Teilhard curiously never reckoned with the fact that before his hundredth birthday we would have got to the moon and even further.)

The terrestrial globe had now become too dense for man turned in upon himself. To avoid self destructive conflicts, a new "critical-threshold" change was needed. The whole of mankind is tending toward unification; a nerve system of communications is gradually uniting the whole planet into a sort of single being. As science or philosophy this insight is too vulnerable; but, theology has already furnished the viable model of the Body of Christ. Not *mystical* Body; Paul never called it that; he calls it "Pleroma," the completeness, the completion.

The most obvious flaw in Teilhard's methodology is his presentation of the Omega Point, the goal toward which all creation is tending in this new humanity unified in Christ. A whole book has been written on this by the sympathetic Protestant, Crespy.[62] Sometimes Teilhard says the goal is God, "all things are yours, and you are Christ's, and Christ is God's" (1 Cor 3:23); but God, of course, is *outside* the evolutionary pattern, not part of it. Usually it seems intended that *Christ* is the Omega Point, not so much the past Jesus of Nazareth, but the head of unified humanity at its end point; Christ truly is a part of evolution; his body shared or shares in the whizzing interchange of atoms and the play of gravity; his Incarnation was in a true sense the union of God with mankind itself and all material reality.

Nevertheless, apparently under prodding from those theological censors who in the end never allowed *The Phenomenon of Man* to be published anyway, Teilhard gives sometimes a formal and explicit description of Omega Point in a line pointing to Christ and God, but distinct and outside both of them.

Teilhard's theology has been further criticized for including so little about sin, not enough to compensate a youthful effort of his to explain original sin as an inseparable component of the evolutionary process itself.

The cult of Teilhard is falling off. At its peak on the verge of the Vatican Council in the sixties, it may be regarded as chiefly a vote against censorship or clericalism; I doubt whether many of the collegians whom you saw with a book of Teilhard tucked under their arm really read and understood him. Yet, very many able theologians still feel that his vision has contributed something magnificent to the postbiblical horizon. He was not able to document it, to seek allies among other scholars or (precisely because of censorship) draw conclusions from adverse criticisms.

In a way his beautiful outline, to which I heartily subscribe and of which I sketched fragments above, is poetry rather than science or philosophy. It contains very much of both, like all good poetry; but, it combines them with leaps of lyric insight which, with the data at present available, we cannot *quite* reduce to proof texts. But, could the prophets of Israel? or even Saint Paul? Let us take leave of Teilhard as a prophet of the future, of that vividly opening horizon posterior to a Bible which he seldom quoted.

8. The World Whose Revelation Is Not "Our" Bible

Our final postbiblical horizon is Ecumenism. I mean rather an anti-chauvinism which goes far beyond Protestants and Catholics sharing communion or doctrinal synods. Ecumenism in itself means "worldliness," not exactly secularism, though that too has had its theological role. But, *oikouméné* implies rather openness to the whole world, to the needs and values of all people everywhere. It includes the Third World and the blacks whose status is only now being so radically altered with little or no help from what the Bible has to say about slavery. It includes the liberation of women, not into a unisex status of partly male roles alongside continuing deference to femininity, but liberation to be fully and with dignity all that a woman and only a woman can be.

Ecumenism includes, at least as the logical prolongation of its demands, a respect and concern for Jewish believers and Jewish atheists, for Muhammad and Buddha and Confucius, even for Ian Paisley and Khomeini, at least insofar as they have *convictions* differing from our own.

These examples may suggest that the term ecumenism should be replaced by "theological pluralism." Such a synonym rightly implies that our change in outlook must begin at home, within our Catholic fold. The Dominicans and Jesuits, and other religious, have now become the best of friends and strong allies on some urgent issues; we have come a long way from the beard-plucking disputations on grace in the seventeenth century, or the exegetical barriers between Jerusalem and Rome early in the twentieth. But, there is still lots of room for true brotherly respect for theological tenets and life styles, approved by the Church in the various diocesan and lay groupings. We are being pushed towards that by the success of the more usually so-called Ecumenical Movement.

Not that this movement foresees any dazzling short range successes. Two major essentials have already been attained; first, conciliar acknowledgment that Luther and Barth rightly claimed God's revelation to stand above the Church, constantly calling it to self reform; second, humble visits of the Pope with the Orthodox patriarchs and with Canterbury and other brothers, authorization of dialogue with Lutherans and everybody on the most untouchable dogmatic themes, establishment of prestigious Vatican secretariates.

However, it has emerged that a major highly valued result of the discussions is a justly proud and unyielding awareness of the separate heritages which the various Christians are not and *must* not be prepared to abandon for the sake of unity. The Ecumenical Movement must proceed on the stipulation that it aims to unite *treasured values* into some form of visible cooperation, not to unite Christians so indifferent to their own particular Christianity that they are prepared to auction it off for higher places in a newly dawning Inter-Hierarchy. Where precisely we are to go on from the Catholic-Lutheran "agreement to disagree" on Eucharist and priesthood, or from similar documents on papacy and Mariology and celibacy, it is not easy at this moment to foresee. But, the gains which have already been made are considerable and irreversible. Our own Church no longer regards Ecumenism as our willingness to take the prodigals back whenever they are ready; Protestants, in turn, seldom use "Whore of Babylon" terminology to express their misgiving about Catholic policies differing from their own.

The richness of our human knowledge about God, whether by revelation or in the pre and postbiblical horizons, is so vast that both within our Church and in humble brotherliness with other Christians we must leave open the inevitability of controverted issues. We must hope for their solution, not by dogmatic fulminations nor by quiet mutual ignoring, but by prayer and confidence in the Spirit of God who "with unutterable groanings" (Rom 8:26) is sharing in our struggle. And, this norm which has been achieved in relation to the Orthodox and Protestants must go on to be applied to the beliefs of all men, as the postconciliar Church quickly saw.

The question has been raised, I think by Cardinal Daniélou, whether we may think it probable or possible that God has given a genuine revelation to "outsiders" in sacred books, like those of Buddha or Confucius. The Qor'an certainly contains revelation in the sense that it embodies lengthy or important items of both Old and New Testaments; Catholics, therefore, already held that a well formed Muslim possessed a knowledge of revealed truth sufficient for salvific faith. But, the question is, rather, whether the Qor'an as a specific compilation, or other books *not* drawing directly from the Bible, may be due to that *special* cooperation of God which we call authorship or inspiration.

Why should we concern outselves with such a question? How could it have any effect other than to *weaken* our confidence in our own revealed books and our zeal to transmit them to outsiders? The answer within a certain trend of loyal Catholics seems to be that precisely in the interest of gaining a fair hearing of our own Church's message we must divest it finally of the last trappings of colonialism and imperialism under which it so long sailed. There is no question of our abandoning or softpedaling Christ as the brother and savior of every man in the world; only perhaps a readiness to investigate how the "cosmic" Christ or "divine mediator" has been made known under other names in religions which, on the whole, have helped men toward God.

An intensely postbiblical horizon would indeed be constituted by the admission of sacred books, truly inspired by God and containing a real revelation of his, not just borrowed from the Bible. The question would seem to be as legitimate and discussable as the well known one of whether there could have been genuinely inspired books like Third Corinthians which somehow went astray from the canon of the Bible. Doubtless, there will be no ready answer to the question of "genuine (supernatural) extra-biblical revelation," but merely reflecting upon it may help us to revise some of our attitudes and procedures.

9. Conclusion

Let me say briefly in conclusion that I have found a considerable broadening of my own horizons in attempting to come to grips with the *prebiblical* and the *postbiblical,* as prescribed for my participation in this symposium. Admittedly the topics which I chose as pre or postbiblical have involved the Bible itself and some of the most vital controversies of its interpretation.

The needed research has not only deepened but *revised* what I had thought to be my solid information on topics to which I have devoted a lifetime of study. You would have felt pity to see how many times I had to scurry down to the library, whisk through volumes like a rat in a maze, and sometimes finally tone down my statement because I could not find the exact citation which would warrant it.

Yet, even among the declarations which survived, I believe you will have found some boldness, or perhaps even flippancy. Partly the reason for this is it seemed a duty to remain within the "shock value" framework prescribed by the title itself. The boldness needs to be regretted only if it offended any sincere convictions, not if it awoke or stimulated to a vivid new way of looking at tired old truth. In any case, this was a position paper intended to provoke discussion and lively divergence of opinion. To the extent that this result ensues, the organizers and I will feel rewarded and thanked.

NOTES

[1] Max Seckler, *Im Spannungsfeld von Wissenschaft und Kirche; Theologie als schöpferische Auslegung der Wirklichkeit* (Freiburg: Herder, 1980).

[2] A. L. Oppenheim, "Nabonidus," *Interpreter's Dictionary of the Bible* (1967): 3,494.

[3] Albert Houtin, *La question biblique chez les catholiques de France dans le 19ᵉ siècle* (Paris: Nourry, 1902), p. 15.

[4] R. North, "Akhenaten secularized?," *Biblica* 58 (1977): 246-58.

[5] Seton Lloyd, *Foundations in the Dust, the Story of Mesopotamian Exploration*[2] (London: Thames & Hudson, 1980); André Parrot, *Archéologie mésopotamienne I. Les étapes* (Paris: A. Michel, 1946); Barthel Hrouda, *Vorderasien I. Mesopotamien, Babylonien, Iran und Anatolien* (Munich: Beck, 1971).

[6] William F. Albright, *The Archaeology of Palestine* (Harmondsworth: Pelican, [1]1949; 1960 revision), p. 57. Much earlier dates are recently proposed: Robert J. Wenke, *Patterns in prehistory: mankind's first three million years* (New York: Oxford University Press, 1980).

[7] Jacques Cauvin, *Religions néolithiques de Syrie-Palestine: documents* (Centre de Recherches d'Écologie et de Préhistoire 1; Paris: Maisonneuve, 1972); my review in *Orientalia* 44 (1975): 449; Julien Ries, "Les expressions intellectuelles et religieuses de l'homme préhistorique," *Revue Théologique de Louvain* 11 (1980): 83-95; 86-88, Les expressions rituelles et religieuses des peuples sans écriture; 88-91, Art rupestre et religion; Joaquín González Echegaray, "Algunos temas bíblicos de antes de la Biblia: los comienzos del Neolítico en Palestina," in Rafael Aguirre, ed., *Escritos de Biblia y Oriente* (Jerusalem/Salamanca, 1981), pp. 317-28, on fecundation-rites, firstling-sacrifice, sanctuaries, cult of dead.

[8] Tommaso Vinaty, "Riabilitazione di Galileo? Osservazioni e riflessioni su un discorso di Giovanni Paolo II [Einstein centenary discourse to Pontifical Academy of Sciences, Nov. 10, 1979]," *Angelicum* 57 (1980): 213-56; *Ephemerides Theologicae Lovanienses* 57 (1981): 211: "On October 24, 1980,

Msgr. Poupard announced that the Holy See was going to undertake an appeal of the Galileo case according to the express wish of Pope John Paul II, Nov. 10, 1979"; Walter Brandmüller, "Le cas Galilée: vérité et légende — Origine et conséquences," *Ateismo e dialogo* 15 (Vatican 1980): 127-39; English summary, 139; cf. 149-56 by I. Campbell.

[9] Documentation on Lamarck, Mendel, and Dobzhansky in R. North, *Teilhard and the Creation of the Soul* (Milwaukee: Bruce, 1977), pp. 65-76; D. Stefan Peters, "Altruistisches Verhalten im Lichte moderner Selektionstheorien" and other contributions to the 1979 Eichstätt Science-Theology colloquium, in Philipp Kaiser, ed., *Evolutionstheorie und ethische Fragestellungen* (Regensburg: Pustet, 1981), pp. 163-88; the article on Old Testament Creationism is by Rudolf Mosis, pp. 189-229.

[10] Charles C. Gillispie, *Genesis and Geology* (Cambridge: Harvard, 1951); author distinct from the more recent Neal C. Gillespie, *Charles Darwin and the Problem of Creation* (Chicago: University, 1979).

[11] Herbert Wendt, *In Search of Adam* (Boston: Houghton Mifflin, 1956); see also Max Begouën, *Quelques souvenirs sur le mouvement des idées transformistes dans les milieux catholiques* (Paris: Bloud & Gay, 1945); and Harry W. Paul, *The Edge of Contingency: French Catholic Reaction to Scientific Change from Darwin to Duhem* (Gainesville: University of Florida, 1979). On the 1982 court rejection of Arkansas Board of Education requiring schools to teach "both pro and con" of evolution, see Francis J. Flaherty, "The creationism controversy: the social stakes," *Commonweal* 109 (1982), pp. 555-9.

[12] See more recently Rahner's "[Naturwissenschaft . . .] Grenzüberschreitungen von Seiten der Theologie," *Stimmen der Zeit* 199 (1981): 511s.

[13] George P. Klubertanz, "The Influence of Evolutionary Theory upon American Thought," *Gregorianum* 32 (1951): 583.

[14] G. Vandebroek and L. Renwart, "L'encyclique *Humani Generis* et les sciences naturelles," *Nouvelle Revue Théologique* 73 (1951): 351; more warily Gustave Weigel, "Gleanings from the commentaries on *Humani Generis,*" *Theological Studies* 12 (1951): 546; my 24 (1963): 577-601, and *Continuum* 2 (1963): 329-42.

[15] R. North, "Pannenberg's Historicizing Exegesis," *Heythrop Journal* 12 (1971): 377-400.

[16] Luis Alonso-Schökel, "Motivos sapienciales y de alianza en Gn 2-3," *Biblica* 43 (1962): 295-315; "Sapiential and Covenant Themes in Genesis 2-3," *Theology Digest* 13 (1965): 3-9 [D. J. McCarthy, ed., *Modern Biblical Studies, an Anthology from Theology Digest* (Milwaukee: Bruce, 1967), pp. 49-61; James L. Crenshaw, ed., *Studies in Ancient Israelite Wisdom* (Library of Biblical Studies; New York: Ktav, 1976), pp. 468-80].

[17] André-M. Dubarle, *Les Sages d'Israël (Lectio Divina* 1; Paris: Cerf, 1946), p. 21; see N. M. Loss, "La dottrina antropologica di Gn 1-11 'postfazione,'" in Giuseppe Di Gennaro, ed., *L'antropologia biblica* (Studio Aquilano; Naples: Dehoniane, 1981, pp. 141-206.

[18] It has been suggested that I cite here Giovanni Magnani, *La crisi della metapsicologia freudiana* (Rome: Studium, 1981), and advert to recent critiques of the once-classic Margaret Mead, *Coming of Age in Samoa* (New York: Morrow, 1961 = 1928).

[19] Max Weber, *Ancient Judaism* [*Das antike Judentum* (Tübingen: 1921)], trans. H. Gerth and D. Martindale (New York: (Glencoe) Free Press, 1967 =

1952); for his analysis of bureaucracy, see *From Max Weber: Essays in Sociology*, tr., ed., H. Gerth, C. Mills (New York: Oxford University Press, 1972 = 1946), pp. 196-244.

[20] E. Shmueli, "The 'Pariah-People' and its 'Charismatic Leadership': a reevaluation of Max Weber's *Ancient Judaism,*" *Proceedings of the American Academy of Jewish Research* 36 (1968): 167-247; F. Parente, "Max Weber e la storia dell'antico Israele," (and four other seminar papers), *Annali della Scuola Normale di Pisa* 3 (1978): 1365-1396; M. Sekine, "Rationality in OT Religion: a study of M. Weber, *Das antike Judentum,*" *Japanese essays in OT* (Tokyo: Shinchi Shobo, 1979); R. North, "Social Dynamics from Saul to Jehu," *Biblical Theology Bulletin* 12 (1982): 110.

[21] Émile Durkheim, *Les formes élémentaires de la vie religieuse* (Paris: Presses Universitaires de France, 1968); Gerald D. McCarthy, "The elementary form [*sic*! but on Durkheim] of the religious life," *Scottish Journal of Religious Studies* 3 (1982): 87-105. On William James, *The Varieties of Religious Experience* (Gifford Lectures, 1901-2; New York: Longmans, 1903), see Henry S. Levinson, *The Religious Investigations of William James* (Studies in Religion; Chapel Hill: NC Univ., 1981). Not to be overlooked is Henri Bergson, *Les deux sources de la morale et de la religion* (Paris: Alcan, ³1932).

[22] James Frazer, *Folklore in the Old Testament* (London: Macmillan, 1919); *The Golden Bough*³ (London: Macmillan, 1911-1922).

[23] Emma Brunner-Traut, "Die Geburtsgeschichte der Evangelien im Lichte ägyptologischer Forschungen," *Zeitschrift für Religions und Geistesgeschichte* 12 (1960): 97-111, citing E. Norden, *Die Geburt des Kindes, Geschichte einer religiösen Idee* (Leipzig: 1924), and M. Dibelius, "Jungfrauensohn und Krippenkind," Heidelberg University *Sitzungsberichte* 1931s/4.

[24] Hopefully in *Catholic Biblical Quarterly* 47 (1985). R. Girard, *La violence et le Sacré* (Paris: Grasset, 1979 = 1972), p. 273, accepts and carries forward W. Robertson Smith on the Sinai-camel sacrifice without advertence to critical rejection of the Nilus account in Migne *PG* 79,589-693; see J. Henninger in *Dictionnaire de la Bible, Supplément* (1958), 6,475, and *Anthropos* 50 (1955): 81-148. Girard treats his view of sacrifice more directly, but in a rather tortuous dialogue form with J.-M. Oughourlian and G. Lefort, in *Des choses cachées depuis la fondation du monde* (Paris: Grasset, 1978); now much more readably in *Le bouc émissaire* (Paris: Grasset, 1982). Available in English is only *Violence and the Sacred*, trans. P. Gregory, reviewed by N. Smart in *Religious Studies Review* 6 (1980): 173-7.

[25] Sylwester Pajak, *Urrelegion und Uroffenbarung bei Schmidt* (Institutum Verbi Divini, Studien 20: St. Augustin, 1978).

[26] Othmar Keel, ed., *Monotheismus im alten Israel und seiner Umwelt* (Biblische Beiträge 14; Fribourg: Schweizerisches Katholisches Bibelwerk, 1980); Conrad E. L'Heureux, "Searching for the origins of God" [i.e., of ideas *about* God, the unsearchable], in *Traditions in transformation, turning points in biblical faith* (Festschrift for Frank Cross), ed. B. Halpern and J. Levenson (Winona Lake, IN: Eisenbrauns, 1981), pp. 53-57; Armando Rolla, "Dio e Dèi nella Bibbia," *Asprenas* 27 (C. Scanzillo volume, 1980): 109-24.

[27] Edward Schillebeeckx, O.P., *The Eucharist* (New York: Sheed & Ward, Inc., 1968), pp. 11-86.

[28] William Van Roo, *Man the Symbolizer* (*Analecta Gregoriana* 22, Theol. A-23; Rome: Pontifical Gregorian University, 1981); Joachim Scharfenberg

and Horst Kampfer, *Mit Symbolen leben: soziologische, psychologische und religiöse Konfliktbearbeitung* (Olten: Walter, 1980); Ioan Lewis, ed., *Symbols and Sentiments; cross-cultural studies in symbolism* (London: Academic, 1978).

[29] Didier Decoin, *La Bible illustrée par des enfants* (Geneva: Calmann-Levy, 1980).

[30] Comparison with a similar mass "suicide" within the history of the Old Testament people [Josephus Flavius, *War* 7 (381)9,1]; André Paul, "De Jonestown à Massada," in *Le Fait Biblique* (*Lectio divina* 100; Paris: Cerf, 1979), pp. 105-8.

[31] Henri Cazelles, "Pentateuque," *Dictionnaire de la Bible, Supplément* (1967), 7,742; 735-858. On Rolf Rendtorff, *Das überlieferungsgeschichtliche Problem des Pentateuch* (*ZAW* Beiheft 147; Berlin/New York: de Gruyter, 1977), and related recent attacks on JEPD, see R. E. Clements and others, *Journal for the Study of the OT* 3 (1977): (2-)46-56; R. North, "Can Geography save J from Rendtorff?," *Biblica* 63 (1982): 47-55.

[32] John H. Hayes and J. Maxwell Miller, eds., *Israelite and Judaean History* (Philadelphia: Fortress, 1977), pp. 75, 177; my review in *Biblica* 59 (1978): 423-6.

[33] C.H.J. de Geus, *The Tribes of Israel, an investigation into some of the presuppositions of M. Noth's Amphictyony hypothesis* (*Studia Semitica Neerlandica* 18; Assen: Van Gorcum, 1976); Harry J. Orlinsky, "The Tribal System of Israel and Related Groups," in the A. Neuman Festschrift, *Studies and Essays* (Leiden: 1962), pp. 375-87; Roland de Vaux, "La thèse de l' 'Amphictyonie israélite,' " *Harvard Theological Review* 64 (P. Lapp memorial 1971): 415-36.

[34] George Mendenhall, *Law and Covenant in Israel and the Ancient Near East* (Pittsburgh: 1955)[= *Biblical Archaeologist* 17 (1954): 26-46, 49-76], and "Covenant," *Interpreter's Dictionary of the Bible* (1962), 1,714-723 [updated (1976), 5, 193-7 by R. Rieman]; Dennis J. McCarthy, *Treaty and Covenant*[2] (*Analecta Biblica* 21A; Rome; Pontifical Biblical Institute, 1978).

[35] A. Hulsbosch (E. Schillebeeckx, P. Schoonenberg), symposium in *Tijdschrift voor Theologie* 6 (1966): 250-73 (274-88, 289-306); my summary of the three, "Soul-Body Unity and God-Man Unity," *Theological Studies* 30 (1969): 27-60, republished [with *Continuum* 6 (1969): 63-77] as *In Search of the Human Jesus* (NY: Corpus Papers, 1970 = Alba, 1978).

[36] Edward Schillebeeckx, *Jesus, an Experiment in Christology*, trans. H. Hoskins (New York: Seabury, 1979); *Christ* (1981); *Interim Report* on both (1981).

[37] Dietrich Bonhoeffer, *Genesis 1-3, Schöpfung und Fall, Versuchung* (Munich: Kaiser, 1968); see Alberto Gallas, *Teologia* 3 (Brescia 1978): 332-57; Gerhard Ebeling, "Die 'nicht-religiöse Interpretation biblischer Begriffe,' " *Zeitschrift für Theologie und Kirche* 52 (1955): 296-360; René Marlé, "Un témoin de l'église évangélique, D. Bonhoeffer," *Recherches de Science Religieuse* 53 (1965): 44-76.

[38] R. North, "God is What we Believe in," *American Ecclesiastical Review* 158 (1968): 160-78; fuller documentation in "Secularization of and by the Gospel," in *The Christian Intellectual and the Secular World* (Catholic Commission on Intellectual and Cultural Affairs, Bulletin 12/St. Louis meeting, 1968), plus booklet of discussion, pp. 22-40.

[39] Gabriel Vahanian, *The Death of God: the Culture of Our Post-Christian Era* (New York: Braziller, 1957).

[40] Thomas J. J. Altizer, *The Gospel of Christian Atheism* (Philadelphia: Westminster, 1966); William Hamilton, *The New Essence of Christianity* (New York: Association, 1966); Altizer-Hamilton, *Radical Theology and the Death of God* (Indianapolis: Bobbs-Merrill, 1966).

[41] Harvey Cox, *The Secular City* (New York: Macmillan, 1965).

[42] Thomas E. Clarke, "Christian Secularity Finds Positive Values Outside the Institutional Church," *America*, May 29, 1965, pp. 800–803; William F. Lynch, "Toward a Theology of the Secular," *Thought* 41 (1966):349–65; R. North, "Saecularismus in revelatione biblica" [on the Dutch, H. Fiolet and A. Nijk], *Verbum Domini* 47 (1969):215–24. The evolution of "Säkular–" compounds in German is noted in *Evangelisches Kirchenlexikon* (Göttingen: Vandenhoeck, 1959), 3, 764(–776); *Religion in Geschichte und Gegenwart*³ (Tübingen: Mohr, 1961), 5, 1289; Heinz-H. Schrey, ed., *Säkularisierung* (Wege der Forschung 424; Darmstadt: Wissenschaftliche Buchgesellschaft, 1981), selections from K. Rahner, H. Cox, P. Van Buren, E. Bloch, *et al.;* bibliog. by Gisela Anders, pp. 415–35.

[43] Paul M. Van Buren, *The Secular Meaning of the Gospel based on an Analysis of its Language* (London: SCM, 1963), pp. 96; 145; *The Edges of Language, an Essay in the Logic of Religion* (New York: Macmillan, 1972). Partly renouncing his former "reductionism," Van Buren is now producing a 4 volume systematic theology, of which the first volume has appeared as *Discerning the Way: a Theology of the Jewish-Christian Reality* (New York: Seabury, 1980).

[44] R.A. Braithwaite, *An Empiricist's View of the Nature of Religious Belief* (Cambridge: University, 1955), p. 32.

[45] See G. R. Evans, *Anselm and Talking about God* (Oxford: Clarendon, 1978).

[46] Joseph A. Fitzmyer, "The Biblical Commission's Instruction on the Historical Truth of the Gospels," *Theological Studies* 25 (1964):386–402; his translation of the document, 402–8 [another in *Catholic Biblical Quarterly* 26 (1964): 305–12].

[47] Arnold J. Toynbee, *A Study of History*² (London: Oxford, 1935), 1, 212n.

[48] Renée Bloch, "Midrash," *Dictionnaire de la Bible, Supplément* (1957), 5, 1263–1281; G. Addison Wright, "The Literary Genre Midrash," *Catholic Biblical Quarterly* 28 (1966):105–38, 417–57.

[49] Raymond E. Brown, *The Sensus Plenior of Sacred Scripture* (Baltimore: St. Marys, 1955); "The *Sensus Plenior* in the Last Ten Years," *CBQ* 25 (1963):262–85.

[50] James M. Robinson, "Scripture and Theological Method: a Protestant Study in *Sensus Plenior,*" *CBQ* 27 (1965):6–27.

[51] Bruce Vawter, "The Fuller Sense: some considerations," *CBQ* 26 (1964):85–96.

[52] J.-M. Beaude, *L'accomplissement des Écritures: pour une histoire critique des systèmes de représentation du sens chrétien* (*Cogitatio Fidei* 104; Paris: Cerf, 1980), p. 174; long summary by Louis Walter, *Esprit et Vie* 91 (1981):541–3; Beaude praises the approach of Paul Beauchamp, *L'un et l'autre Testament, essai de lecture* (*Parole de Dieu;* Paris: Seuil, 1976).

⁵³ Román Sánchez Chamoso, "Una hermenéutica para la relectura actualizadora de la tradición cristiana; los criterios hermenéuticos de E. Schillebeeckx," *Salmanticensis* 25 (1978):361-442.

⁵⁴ A "return" to the fuller sense is the bottom line of the "crisis of biblicism" analyzed by Jean Delorme, "What makes exegetes run? (Qu'est-ce qui fait courir les exégètes?)," *Lumière et Vie* 29,150 (1980):77-90.

⁵⁵ Bernard J.F. Lonergan, *Insight, a Study of Human Understanding* (London: Longmans, 1957), pp. 562-94, "The truth of interpretation."

⁵⁶ Henri de Lubac, *Exégèse Médiévale, les quatre sens de l'Écriture* (*Théologie* 41f:59; Paris, Aubier, 1959-64); some comment on exegetes in vol. 1,1, pp. 34-36, and vol. 2,1, p. 11.

⁵⁷ Claus Westermann, ed., *Essays on Old Testament Hermeneutics*, trans. K. Crim (Richmond: Knox, 1966 = 1963). Note Douglas A. Knight, "Old Testament Ethics," *Christian Century* 99 (1982):55-59: The student of the Bible must distinguish sharply between description ["What *did* it mean?"] and hermeneutics ["What *does* it mean?"].

⁵⁸ M.-J. Lagrange, "Pascal et les prophéties messianiques," *Revue Biblique* 15 (1906):536 (C. Pesch enumerates 24 points:533-560); Ludovicus Lercher, *De vera religione* (Institutiones Theologiae Dogmaticae 1; Innsbruck: Rauch, 1927), pp. 221-33.

⁵⁹ Luis Alonso Schökel, "Hermeneutics in the Light of Language and Literature," *Catholic Biblical Quarterly* 25 (1963):371-86.

⁶⁰ R. North, *Teilhard and the Creation of the Soul* (Milwaukee: Bruce, 1967), pp. 258, 250, citing V. Frins, "Concours divin," *Dictionnaire de Théologie Catholique* (1923), 3,782.

⁶¹ This oneness was the point of departure of Hulsbosch in the symposium of note 35 above, and thus of the Christology of Schillebeeckx there, though he regrets such reliance on the "ephemeral" Teilhard.

⁶² Georges Crespy, *La pensée théologique de Teilhard de Chardin* (Paris: Éditions Universitaires, 1961), p. 61; so Émile Rideau, *Pensée de Teilhard* (Paris: Seuil, 1964), p. 327; my *Teilhard*, p. 106.

The Function and Role of Jesus the Christ

Peter Schineller, S.J.

One must stand in awe before the assigned topic—the function and role of Jesus the Christ. One consolation, however, is that it addresses the center, Jesus Christ, the one whose name we bear. And, if this essay sheds one small bit of light, gives one meager insight into this unfathomable mystery, then it is worth its while. More modest than the letter to the Ephesians, we can hope that this presentation will shed some small light on "the breadth and length and height and depth of Christ's love" (Eph. 3:18).

My presentation takes the form of fourteen summary statements or theses and a conclusion. Each of the statements will be expanded and grounded. The first five theses are methodological, and the sixth to fourteenth focus more on content. I consider both important, with the methodological theses giving us the means for further research into the mystery of Christ, and the content centered theses beginning to spell out the implications of Jesus Christ for Christian life today.

I say "Christian life today," for each age, indeed each person, must answer the question of Jesus to Peter, "Who do you say that I am?" This essay is my present answer to that question, and it will be successful if it leads, as it intends to, to your taking up the question and answering it for yourselves and answering it with those you minister to.

Thesis 1. Jesus came that we may have life, life in its fullness (Jn. 10:10). Our concern, therefore, is with the role and function of Jesus the Christ, not in theology or Christology, but in life.

As a priest and a theologian, I would find it much easier to stay in my area of expertise and speak of the role and function of Jesus in the Scripture, in the theology of Thomas Aquinas, the investigations of Karl Rahner; easier to address the question of the role and function of Jesus in church life, in prayer and sacraments, for example. But, that is not finally important for you or for me. It is the relation of Jesus Christ to life, in all its shapes and moods, that finally is important.

Otherwise, theology becomes an end in itself, a substitute or a screen that separates us from life. We forget to see it as it is, a theoretical construct, theory that must serve the praxis of life.

Theology, as the Second Vatican Council and as liberation theologians remind us, must be in service to humanity, whether ailing or rejoicing. Otherwise, the Marxist critique of religion (and theology) as alienating, as an opiate for the people, stands true. I am not denying or underplaying the need for scholarly, critical, historical, even scientific studies of religion, and, hence, of Christology. But, I would emphasize that such study must be oriented to life and the problems of life. I am, therefore, emphasizing the need of correlation — that is, bringing the Christian tradition to bear upon the present.[1] All theology is ultimately pastoral.

As priest, I have expertise in church matters, in explicitly religious areas, such as prayer, liturgy, sacraments. Here, too, I must be careful lest I make these aspects of life into the whole. When we say that Jesus came that we may have life, life in its fullness, we are not referring to the five percent of life which is given to explicit religious worship, but the ninety-five percent of life which is spent with family, friends, in our work and recreation. Nor should we think of the significance of Jesus for religious and priestly life which comprises one percent of the Catholic population, and overlook the ninety-nine percent who are the laity.

Areas of life which Christology must address, according to Mark Gibbs, a prominent layman, would be these: personal and family and sexual relationships; relations with one's neighbors, those known personally; one's occupation; one's leisure; one's civic and political responsibilities, and one's church duties.[2]

To ground this emphasis upon the relation of theology to life, I refer to the thought of Karl Rahner. His central book, *Foundations of Christian Faith,* is a profound reflection on Christian experience. In this sense it is theology — namely, reflection on one's faith experience which is always touched by the graceful presence of God.[3] Theology reflects upon life and leads one back into life with sharpened perception and perspective. Theology thus is important, but in a very true sense it is secondary.

More concretely, Rahner speaks of the need for a Copernican revolution in understanding the sacraments.[4] In the common view, Sunday Eucharist, for example, is seen as the high point of the week, and everything else is somewhat less sublime and significant. Confession, and the absolution of the priest, is seen as *the* moment when sins are forgiven. But, Rahner reminds us, with the tradition, that unless one approaches the sacrament of penance with at least imperfect contrition, one's sins cannot be forgiven. And, he prefers to look at Sunday Eucharist as inseparable from the week that has gone before and the week that follows — seeing that we are touching God and God is reaching out to us every day of the week; our Sunday celebration must serve to heighten this sensitivity to the presence of God in one's every-day life and activities.

As you can see, I am setting up a difficult task for myself—and one for you, too. It is to see the significance of Jesus Christ for Christian and non-Christian life. The test of a Christology is not simply whether it is found in Scripture or tradition, not whether it is approved by the teaching office of the Church, but whether it sheds light and strength on our everyday existence. Does it give meaning and a sense of direc-tion to one's frustrations and joys, one's marriage and one's child's sickness, one's hopes and failures? Can we, as theologians and ministers, explain coherently and with a solidly biblical and traditional foundation the significance of Jesus for life today? And, can we lead our parishioners and students—those we minister to—in being able to express their own Christological faith. [5] And then, even more impor-tantly, are we and those we minister to, living, putting into practice what Jesus stands for and challenges us to?

Thesis 2.   Utilization of the pastoral or hermeneutical circle will help assure that the role and function of Jesus the Christ touches human lives today.

Only in the continuous process of prayerful action and reflection in specific places and circumstances does the significance of Jesus Christ emerge. To show how this occurs, I will explain what I call the pastoral or hermeneutical circle. This circle tries to describe my work as a theologian and our common work as pastoral agents or ministers of the gospel. [6]

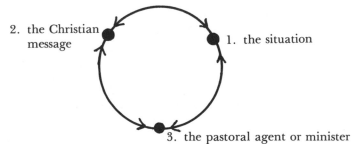

The circle has three poles: the arrows between the poles indicate that movement around the circle proceeds in both directions. The *first* pole is the situation, involving persons in a particular place. It could be an individual or a parish community or a smaller group. The *second* pole is the Christian message, the insight and input from Scripture and tradition. For the purpose of this essay, we are focussing upon Jesus Christ as the center of the Christian message. The *third* pole is the pastoral agent or minister—the resource person who tries to help mediate the Christian message to the particular situation.

An understanding of the role and function of Jesus the Christ, according to the circle, must take into account all three poles; we cannot look only to the biblical message, the gospels, or to the tradition, and from that conclude to the role of Jesus. Nor can we look only to our own parish or community situation, and analyze that situation. First, we cannot look only to the Bible. While the danger of biblical fundamentalism is especially acute in Africa, it is a danger everywhere. And, what is needed for a full Christology is not only critical, scholarly, non-fundamentalist interpretations of the Scripture, but interpretations that address the questions and issues of contemporary life. I like the image of Jean Calvin, who speaks of the Bible as spectacles, that is, helps to our vision of the world, spectacles "through which we see the world, God, life, and our neighbor."[7] Spectacles are aids, helps to our weak sight to give us clearer focus. But, rather than looking at the glasses, we look through them at our world—where God is always already present.

Secondly, we cannot expect a Christian response if we analyze the contemporary situation without the aid of the Christian message. We may find secular or humanistic solutions, but unless we bring to bear the Christian tradition upon the problem, it will remain a humanistic rather than a Christian response.

We can start at any point of the circle; for example, either with the Christian message or with our present situation. But, we must then move to the other poles—back and forth, so that the message illuminates our situation, and our situation raises questions of the biblical message. Only in the interaction among the three poles will the role and significance of Jesus the Christ emerge. In putting forth this circle, I find that I am echoing the words of a previous speaker at these conferences, Gustavo Gutierrez, who wrote in 1974:

> That is then the fundamental hermeneutical circle: from man to God and from God to man; from history to faith and from faith to history; from the human word to the Word of the Lord and from the Word of the Lord to the human word; from fraternal love to the love of the Father and from the love of the Father to fraternal love; from human justice to the holiness of God and from the holiness of God to human justice; from poor to God and from God to poor.[8]

The ministry of Jesus Christ exemplifies this circular movement as he brings God's word to bear upon the particular situation, problem, person or group he is engaged with. And we, the ministers of the gospel of Jesus Christ, must employ something of this sort if we are to bring the gospel of Jesus Christ to bear upon our situations of ministry. It is, I suggest, in the utilization of the circle that creativity emerges, that fresh insight into the mystery of Jesus Christ emerges.[9] Finally, the circle serves to remind us that we are all always on the way to becoming

Christian. We are all a community of disciples, as Avery Dulles has characterized the Church of the 1980's.[10] The full revelation of the role and significance of Jesus the Christ is always ahead of us, even as we strive now to comprehend the mystery as it impinges upon our own lives and the lives of those we minister to.

Thesis 3.   The Role and Function of Jesus the Christ will apply analogously to different contexts or situations.

The pastoral or hermeneutical circle which we have described demonstrates that all theology (and hence all Christology) is contextual. The place or situation (pole #1) makes a difference, and hence there is no one universal, univocal answer to the question of the role and significance of Jesus the Christ.

According to Feuerbach, a person thinks differently in a palace and in a hut. We could add to this, a rectory and a high rise, in India and in Rome, in Port Harcourt and in Philadelphia. We must look, therefore, to some of the factors that will affect one's Christology. Physical place has already been mentioned — the desert vs. the asphalt jungle, a village in Kenya vs. the suburbs of Chicago. Christian witness, and hence the function of Jesus the Christ, varies too, depending upon the church as a majority or a minority of the population. When Christians are ninety percent of the population, as in much of Latin America, one's theology and Christology are different from that of Asia, India where Christians comprise at most five percent of the population.[11]

The aging and the sick relate to Jesus in a way that is different from the healthy and the strong. The satisfied and the wealthy think and pray in a way that is different from those hungry and fighting for survival, as liberationist interpretations of Christianity manifest.

As we are more and more aware, one's sex also affects one's theology. We see the particular gifts, talents, insights of women who minister in parishes and who do theology. A theology of sin and a Christology explored from the feminist perspective reveal aspects of the mystery of evil and aspects of the mystery of Jesus Christ that have for too long gone unexplored.

A bishop thinks differently from a single woman, a married couple from the parish priest. We ask different questions in a rectory and in the family kitchen. Thus, the recommendations of a conference of the laity might not agree with the recommendations of a conference of bishops on such areas as family life, education, liturgy and sexuality.

In a perceptive essay written in 1963, Charles Davis described four stages of Christian theology.[12] What determined much of the nature of the theology in each of these stages was the place where theology was formulated and the status of the persons who were theologians. From bishops in the patristic era, to the monks, then to the university professors of the Middle Ages and at the time of the Reformation, to seminary professors in newly established seminaries—theology has been and remains contextual. I would add that a major shift is occurring now (as this audience attests) where theology is being shaped—in its questions and answers—by the Christian laity.

What is the significance of all this? It means that no one, no theologian, bishop, not even Jesus Christ, could come here and give you one universally valid answer on the role and significance of Jesus the Christ. As the four gospels themselves attest and as the letters of Paul to various communities demonstrate, the mystery of Jesus Christ must continually be reexpressed in new and creative ways for different contexts. [13] This, I submit, is the challenge facing us as theologians and ministers of the gospel. We have to answer the question of the role and significance of Jesus the Christ in ever new and creative ways, depending upon our situation.

But, it is also important to recall, as I do in the thesis statement, that we are speaking of analogous roles of Jesus, partially the same and partially different. Jesus remains the Christ, Son of God and Son of Mary, but how this is to be proclaimed and lived will vary. In this sense, John Macquarrie speaks of the truth of Christology as more like the truth of art than the truth of science, [14] and I would add the theologian and minister must have the creative qualities of the artist.

To return to the pastoral circle—the task of the pastoral agent or minister is to act as catalyst, helping the community or individual in their own context or situation to "give an account of the hope that is in you" (1 Pet. 3:15); that is, be ready and able to explain the role and significance of Jesus, the source of our hope—in our unique circumstances.

And, the circle reminds us that Christology remains always an unfinished process. Karl Rahner speaks eloquently of this process: "A person is always a Christian in order to become one, and this is true of what we are calling a personal relationship to Jesus Christ in faith, hope and love." [15] This relationship "is always present as something which a person still has to realize and bring to radical actualization in the living out of his whole existence throughout the whole length and breadth and depth of his life." [16]

Thesis 4.   Christian mission is not simply to *assert* the Lordship of Jesus Christ, but to *labor* to make this a reality in all spheres of human existence.

In the creed we profess belief in "one Lord, Jesus Christ." Based upon the New Testament, especially the letters of Paul, Christians confess Jesus as the Lord and center of history, the savior of all humankind. But, surely we all see and feel the large gap between this profession of faith and the actual condition of the world. Statistically,

Christians may comprise only one fifth of the world population, and no dramatic increase is foreseen. And, even Christians must give a guarded answer to the question of whether Jesus Christ is Lord over their own lives.

This gap between the actual and the ideal, I submit, is precisely the reason for Christian mission and ministry. The Lordship of Jesus cannot simply be a religious assertion, a speculative doctrine or dogma, an ontological claim. This claim becomes incredible and empty unless it is backed by and leads to action to bring about the Lordship of Jesus Christ. In this sense, the belief in the Lordship of Jesus Christ is both a gift or grace, and a task and challenge. As the German language expresses it, it is *Gabe und Aufgabe.*

One's personal belief in the universal role and function of Jesus Christ should lead us to proclaim this, not simply by words, but by actions that intend to extend his Lordship. Thus, the Christian assertion of the universality of redemption and new life in Jesus Christ functions as a goal and ideal to which we are moving, rather than as an objective fact. The Lordship of Jesus Christ is a mission statement involving our commitment to do our part to make this a reality in human history. [17]

Three thrusts of contemporary theology serve to back our thesis statement. First, liberation theology points to the oppression and injustice in so much of today's world, where mammon rather than God or Jesus Christ rules. And, based upon its belief in Jesus Christ as Redeemer, Liberator, it aims to make his liberating power present and effective where it is not yet, through a Christian faith that is linked with and committed to justice. Secondly, the theology of story is based upon the fact that a story, to be effective, must be heard and known. [18] It is not sufficient to confess or claim that Jesus is Lord of all, if this claim remains only an assertion and not an actualization. The story of God's love in Jesus Christ must be known and not simply remain present in non-Christians in an anonymous or implicit manner. As the stories of the Easter faith of the first disciples indicate, the direction of the Christian is not to stand in awe of the risen Lord, not to cling to him, but to go out and tell the good news to those who have not yet heard or believed it. Thirdly, the theology of inculturation shows that gospel, Christian values must interact in an explicit and conscious manner with all the world's cultures and traditions, and only then can we speak of a truly universal and catholic faith in Jesus Christ.

With the utilization of the pastoral circle, therefore, Christian ministry becomes the effort to make the values of Jesus Christ present in all situations and cultures. This includes the life situation of the minister him or her self; it includes the modern culture of the first world and the struggling, transitional and traditional cultures of the third world.

Thesis 5.   The effort to proclaim and establish the Lordship of Jesus Christ can be viewed as the process of inculturation or contextualization of gospel values.

Coming from two fascinating years of teaching and pastoral work in Nigeria, I must say something about inculturation. We can begin with the problem, a problem faced by every culture and people, but most acutely by those cultures less directly influenced by the Greco-Roman, Judaeo-Christian tradition — those cultures not in the mainstream of Western Christianity. Put most bluntly, how can Jesus Christ be presented or understood as the lamb of God or the good shepherd in a culture or person with little or limited experience of lambs and sheep.

Jesus lived and died almost two thousand years ago in a particular place and culture. He was male and not female. He was not married, not a soldier, not a college student or a college professor, not a homemaker. Yet, we proclaim his as the way, the truth and the life, the model and exemplar for all persons in all places and times, for mothers and fathers, old and young, teachers and students, black and white, Indonesian and European.

Inculturation is one word to describe the process by which Gospel and Christian values come to bear upon a particular culture, context or situation. Of the varied words to describe this process, such words as indigenization, localization, strategic theology, correlation, contextualization, the two most helpful seem to be inculturation and contextualization. [19] Pedro Arrupe, former General of the Jesuits, has defined inculturation as "the incarnation of Christian life and of the Christian message in a particular cultural context, in such a way that this experience not only finds expression through elements proper to the culture in question but becomes a principle that animates, directs and unifies the culture, transforming it and remaking it so as to bring about a new creation." [20]

The process of inculturation can be seen by referring again to the pastoral circle. The pastoral agent (agent of inculturation, as Arrupe calls Christian ministers) studies a particular culture or situation, and tries to bring the resources of the tradition — in our case the life, values, teaching of Jesus Christ — to bear upon that situation. As a matter of fact, Jesus Christ functions as both a model and as the content of inculturation; that is to say, just as the Word became flesh in a particular time and place, and just as Jesus went about trying to convert persons to his way of life and values, so the Christian minister today tries to bring the richness of God's love in Jesus Christ to ever new situations. Ministry is the creative task, the art, of carrying the gospel to places and persons that Jesus in his own person could not reach.

One final note. When we think of inculturation, we normally think of traditional or non-literate cultures in some distant country as the place where this takes place. As a matter of fact, in Nigeria, for example, the culture has been and is evermore being influenced by modern, technological culture or society, and in few places does the purely traditional culture remain. Thus, inculturation in Nigeria aims at a moving target, a traditional culture rapidly moving towards a more technological, mechanized society. And, even more important than inculturation into traditional societies, I would consider inculturation of gospel values into modernized societies, such as the United States. [21] Modernization refers to that new world that is emerging, and describes the profound technological, communications, economic, political, ecological shifts that are on the increase. Unless the churches can bring gospel values to bear upon this new culture, technological, modern culture, the churches will have failed in their mission. And, the failure in the first world countries will soon be followed by failure in the third world countries which are rushing to take on all the values and disvalues, all the ambiguities of modernized, technologized culture of the first world.

Thesis 6.   Jesus Christ reveals the meaning of being truly human that is achieved in the daily living of the paschal mystery or the dialectic of Christian faith.

With this thesis statement we move from the more methodological statements to content. We begin to see more concretely the shape of life that Jesus lived and what he calls us to follow and enables us to follow.

Jesus exemplifies and calls us to live the paschal mystery, or what I will call the dialectic of Christian faith. In living this mystery, one is truly human. The paschal mystery signifies the constant and recurrent movement from death to life, the dying to self and sin and living for God and one's brothers and sisters. This pattern is exemplified most clearly in the death and resurrection of Jesus, but in actuality was a recurrent pattern of his public ministry. This pattern is celebrated sacramentally in baptism and eucharist (in reality in every sacrament), but must be actualized existentially, lived personally in our daily lives and especially at the moment of death at the term of our lives.

The tradition affirms that Jesus Christ was true God and true man. I am suggesting that he reveals the true *humanum,* the true meaning of the human person in his living the paschal mystery. It is the recurrent pattern of taking up one's cross daily, of dying to self and self interest and living for others. Jesus exemplifies this during his ministry, "going about doing good" in loving service to the neighbor. This reaches its climax and full expression in his passion, suffering death and resurrection. Just as his life was for others, so his death: "greater love than this no one has than to lay down his or her life for the brothers and sisters."

Jesus thus exemplifies the daily call to self-transcendence, a call that is lived by the mother in caring for her children, the father in supporting the family through a full day's labor, and the student in engaging his or her intelligence in studies that aim at serving the human community. Each of these must overcome the inertia we all feel, the tendency to be self-centered and isolated, the desire to grasp and to serve oneself first and last. By responding to the call of the other, the mother, the father, the student transcend their own self-interest and look to the good of others. They seem to risk their own good by looking to the welfare of others. In so doing they are placing their trust in God and his gracious love, God's power and protection that will sustain them as they seem to risk their own welfare by looking first to the good of others. They are also beginning to share in the peace and joy of the Risen Lord, as they experience the gift of God's Spirit and love in their everyday lives.

In the final analysis, the mother, father, student are joining their lives to the paschal mystery of Jesus, both imitating that pattern and receiving the courage from the grace of God in Jesus Christ. As the life and teaching of Jesus undeniably affirm, it is only by passing through the cross that we can attain life. Jesus Christ is the way, as John's gospel states, and that way is the way of the cross to the life of glory. This becomes for the followers of Jesus the only way, and it becomes, therefore, the revelation of what it means to be truly human. We are, in a word, truly human, fully human only insofar as we give ourselves, surrender ourselves, transcend ourselves in faith, hope and love to the mystery of God as mediated through one's brothers and sisters, the neighbor. Only in this attitude and action of self-transcendence can we be and become our true self, the truly human that we are called to be. [22]

To summarize our argument, I can refer only to the poetic words of Joseph Sittler:

> The Christian life is here understood as a re-enactment from below on the part of men of the shape of the revelatory drama of God's holy will in Jesus Christ. . . . Suffering, death, burial, resurrection, a new life — these are actualities which plot out the arc of God's self-giving deed in Christ's descent and death and ascension; and precisely THIS SAME SHAPE OF GRACE, in its recapitulation within the life of the believer and the faithful community is the nuclear matrix which grounds and unfolds as the Christian life. [23]

Two final comments: in this continual dying and rising, in this self-transcendence in love, the Christian discovers and experiences the sustaining, protecting power of God's love. God is in fact revealed in the paschal mystery, not simply as being, or Logos, but as love which communicates itself as saving grace to the Christian. [24] The Christian, in turn, echoes this divine love, or in the words of Ricoeur, begins to live the logic of love rather than the logic of equivalency. [25] The teaching and example of Jesus, that logic of love or superabundance by which we love our enemies, forgive seven times seventy times, turn the other cheek, walk the extra mile, give to those who ask, are our daily participation in the paschal mystery of Jesus.

Finally, a few words on what I call the dialectic of Christian faith. Here I refer to the continual pattern of life, death, resurrection, a triadic pattern. By saying that the Christian life is comprised of this triadic pattern (following Jesus) we are saying that no one symbol can become the whole or entirety of Christianity. Not Incarnation, not the public life, not the passion, not the resurrection of Jesus can ever become the one single emphasis on Christian life. Rather, it is the recurrent pattern of life, death, resurrection that is the rule. Our lives are a mixture of elements, activities and passivities, joys and sorrows, dyings and risings, and any theology or Christology or spirituality that focuses on the cross to the underemphasis upon the resurrection, or vice versa, will be inadequate to the dialectic of Christian faith. By pointing to the dialectric of Christian faith, we are eventually enabled, in the words of St. Ignatius, to find God in ALL things: in our joys and sorrows, our life and death, our dying and rising.

Thesis 7.   The Role and Function of Jesus the Christ is to reveal the true God as a loving Father or parent, and not an angry, wrathful, remote deity.

In the previous statement we explained the way Jesus reveals the truly human to be a pattern of self-transcending love towards God and one's neighbor. In this thesis statement we focus upon the ultimate object of our self-transcendence, which is also the source or empowerer of self-transcendence: God.

During his public ministry Jesus did not proclaim himself but proclaimed the kingdom or rule of God. This rule consists of God's care and concern for the sinner, the poor, the blind, and, in the final analysis, is another way to speak of the grace and graciousness of God. Jesus, and the followers of Jesus, must witness to this kingdom by conduct that echoes the graciousness of God. While the Hebrew Scriptures have many beautiful ways to name God, Jesus prefers to call God his Father, and teaches his disciples to do likewise. God as Father is the creative source of life as well as the providential parent who cares for those created. The parables of Luke 15 point to this mercy and care of God. God is like the woman who searches for the lost coin, the shepherd searching for the lost sheep, and the father running to embrace the lost son and celebrating his return. These are images of the one, true God.

While Jesus teaches and exemplifies the compassion and love of the one, true God during his public ministry, all of this is tested and tried in the passion and death of Jesus. Would this God and Father remain with Jesus, uphold him and his cause? Was he truly a loving Father, or would he abandon his Son to the powers of sin, death, and evil? As we indicated in the previous statement, it is in the cross, in and through the paschal mystery, that the full revelation of the nature and love of God is given. While Jesus dies a tortuous death, one that almost causes despair as the starkness of the gospel of Mark indicates, we see that it was a death that leads to life. [26] With John we see that it was the way of the cross that is the way of glory. For God raised up Jesus, the Father gives new, glorious life to the Son, and the power of the Father's love is affirmed as power over sin, death, suffering and evil.

Based upon the teaching of Jesus and upon their experience of him as Risen Lord, the first Christians begin to express these views of the true God. Paul writes that in the power of the Spirit we have the courage and ability to call God Abba, Father. And, just as Jesus was not finally separated from the love of God through his suffering and death, so nothing in all creation can separate the Christian from the love of God in Christ Jesus (Rom 8). More succinctly, but equally faithful to the teaching and example of Jesus, John's epistle says, "God is love!" This is the true God, not a God of distance, aloof, not of wrath or anger, but of boundless love. In the words of Charles Wesley, God is pure unbounded love. In the paschal mystery, in the dialectic of Christian faith, God is revealed to be more than being, and more than logos, the God of the philosophers; he is love, agape, grace, a God who involves himself compassionately with his creation in the person of Jesus Christ. This God is Lord of the universe, and not the forces of evil. This God can be trusted.

In the early centuries of Christianity, reflection on the Scriptures and on the experience of God will lead to Christian belief in God as Triune, Father, Son and Spirit. [27] Without holding that this is explicit in either the ministry of Jesus or even in the writings of the New Testament, I do want to show briefly that it is based upon the Christ event. The proclamation of God as triune love becomes the deepest understanding and explanation of the mystery of the one, true God.

The mystery of the Trinity is a mystery of salvation and one that envelops Christian life and ministry. As God comes to us in Jesus Christ, through the power and overshadowing of the Spirit; as Jesus returns to his Father, led by the Spirit, so the Christian life follows that same pattern. As the Second Vatican Council expresses it, "united in Christ, they (Christians) are led by the Holy Spirit in their journey to the kingdom of their Father" (*Church in the Modern World*, No. 1). The daily life of the Christian is lived in light of the Triune reality—following and joined with Jesus, filled with, led by the Spirit, on the way from the Father back to the Father. So, too, Christian prayer is prayer with Jesus the Son, in the power of the Spirit, to God the Father. Properly, Christian prayer is not indiscriminately to the Father, Son or Spirit, but through and with the Son, in the power of the Spirit, to the Father, as the doxology at the end of the Eucharistic prayer proclaims.

Let me conclude with a few brief implications of belief in this one, true, Triune God. If God is Father of all *persons,* then Christians cannot be content with a family, local, tribal, sexist, or national God; if God is Father and Lord of all *time,* then we cannot exploit God's good earth to serve our present needs in such a manner that we deprive future generations of the earth's resources.

If God is the Incarnate Word, who emptied himself, then we, too, must follow that pattern and concretize, localize our love and energy. Again, the Second Vatican Council: "Prompted by the Holy Spirit, the Church must walk the same road which Christ walked; a road of poverty and obedience, of service and self-sacrifice to the death, from which death He came forth a victor by His resurrection" (*The Missionary Activity of the Church,* No. 5).

Finally, belief in the Holy Spirit gives us the assurance and power to take the necessary risks involved in a commitment of loving service to the neighbor. A power greater than our own guides and strengthens us, the power of the Spirit that enables us to follow the way of Jesus. There is no room for the weak or fainthearted, no time for despair because the Spirit, given in baptism, remains with us.

Thesis 8.   In proclaiming and living the message of the kingdom of God, Jesus shows the inseparability of the human and the divine and show Christianity as a religion of incarnation and mediation.

The last two statements maintained that Jesus Christ reveals the true *humanum* and the true *divinum.* In this statement we want to show that the divine and the human, while not identified, are inseparable. While the human is not the divine, while God is ever greater (*semper major*) in the Incarnation of Jesus Christ and in his life and teaching, we see that God is never separate from his creation.

First of all, Jesus speaks of the unity of love of God and love of neighbor. In explaining that the two great commandments are the fulfilment of the law, Jesus links them in a way that the Hebrew Scriptures do not. Love of God and love of neighbor are not two disparate activities, but rather the movement of the person to God through love of neighbor. [28] In the parable of the last judgment, Matthew 25, Jesus identifies himself with the sick, hungry, imprisoned, and makes one's love or refusal to love the sick, hungry, imprisoned the criterion of one's eternal salvation or damnation. In Luke 9:48, Jesus repeats this inseparability of himself and his Father with the least: "Whoever receives this child in my name receives me, and whoever receives me receives him who sent me." God and the human remain linked as God in Jesus Christ identifies himself with the child.

Again we see this inseparability of God and the human in the attitudes that should characterize the followers of Jesus. As Jesus is the revelation and incarnation of God in the world, so his followers continue and manifest this presence of God. The attitudes of God are shared by Jesus and by the followers of Jesus. "Be merciful as your Father is merciful." "Love one another as I have loved you." "As the Lord has forgiven you, so you must also forgive" (Col. 3:13). As God is light and in him no darkness, so Jesus is the light of the world, and his followers are challenged to be light of the world. As God is love, so in Christ the love of God appears in human form, and the Christians, filled with the Spirit of love, love one another as God has loved them. So close is the relationship of the human and the divine that we can say that wherever there is love, wherever there are peace, joy, patience, wisdom, truth—there is the Spirit of God, the fruits and gifts of the Spirit, working and active in us.

God, in his ultimate reality, is love, and the human, as God intends the human to be, is love. These meet as one in the person of Jesus, who is God's self-communication and revelation of love in his divinity, and who is the perfect receiver and responder to this love in his humanity. Thus, Karl Rahner can end his difficult but powerful book, *Foundations of Christian Faith,* with a statement on the unity between God and the world/neighbor. Based upon his Christology, Rahner shows that acts of love of neighbor are of eternal significance and validity; the love of neighbor is the concrete way in which we love God, although, with regard to the term of the love, it is never simply identical with love of God. He concludes with "the ultimate and basic axiom of Christology: in Christology man and God are not the same, but neither are they ever separate."[29]

I would like to conclude this statement on the inseparability of the divine and the human by reference to a cryptic epithet, applied to St. Ignatius Loyola. I present two translations of the Latin: "To suffer no restriction from anything however great, and yet to be contained in the tiniest of things, that is divine."[30] Or, "to be unbounded by the infinite, and yet willingly encompassed by the infinitesimal, that is divine." I take this to mean that the mark of Jesus, the mark of the true God, and the mark of the Christian (as St. Ignatius) is precisely to join together two seemingly disparate realities—the concrete and the universal, the ideal and the real, the short range and the long range, the dreamer and the pragmatist.

While we must have the greatest of plans, we must not neglect the work at hand. True love is both intensive and extensive, looking to the whole, but also focussing upon the weakest and smallest. Thus, Jesus in his ministry announced the most sweeping of all realities, the coming of God's kingdom; and he showed that it is at hand, not in generalities, but by attending to the needs of the moment, by healing Peter's mother-in-law, by blessing the smallest child, etc. In other words, the truly divine is always linked with the truly human, and we echo this divine reality; we are joined to it, empowered by it, as we turn, in love, to the least of the brothers and sisters.

Thesis 9.   Jesus the Christ reveals the depth of the ordinary and the everyday, showing the way to find God in and above all things.

Philip Murnion wrote in *America:* "I think it is fair to say that among today's Catholics there is a much sharper disjunction between their religious lives and their secular lives than once was true."[31] Whether we call it the gap between the religious and the secular, between Sunday and Monday, theology and life, the spiritual and the temporal, prayer and action, sacramental life and secular life, it seems true that many Christians live in two worlds and fail to sufficiently see the connections between the two. There is a lack of integration, and I suggest that a proper Christology, understanding of the meaning of Jesus, will help overcome that dichotomy.

By his life and teaching, Jesus points to and exemplifies the sacredness or sanctity of the ordinary. During his public ministry, he was not a priest, not part of the Jewish religious leadership. Later on, the letter to the Hebrews will speak of Jesus as high priest, but this is a theological reflection upon his life and ministry. He was not an Essene ascetic, not like John the Baptist. He was a teacher or rabbi and, in fact, might be closest to what we would call a deacon. He went about from town to town doing good, serving and teaching, eating and drinking. The occasion of a meal became an opportunity for teaching about the kingdom of God and for actualizing that kingdom through the miracle of healing, converting and forgiving. In his parables, he spoke of the family in the prodigal son, the man sowing the seed, fishing, searching for the lost coin or lost sheep. In other words, he took created realities of everyday existence and used them as a vehicle to talk of the divine reality. What we see around us every day reveals the divine, for those who have eyes to see. The parable of the last judgment in Matthew 25 shows that it is in the ordinary/extraordinary activities of love of neighbor that we find God and our eternal salvation; not orthodoxy, but orthopraxis, becomes the criterion of divine judgment.

In his prayer, Jesus constantly shows the relation of one's life with God and one's earthly commitment. His prayer concerns the choice of the apostles, gratitude for the power of God in his healing ministry, invocation of God's power to heal, and the courage to accept the will of the Father as he faces the cross. His choice of disciples and apostles turns to the ordinary rather than the religious leadership of his time. Tax collectors and fishermen become his associates. When we say with the tradition that Jesus instituted the seven sacraments, we must be careful not to identify with his ministry the carefully ritualized, parish church building sacraments as they have developed over the centuries.[32] We must recall that when the disciples of John came to Jesus looking for a sign (or sacrament) that he was the Messiah, his response was the sign of love of neighbor — the blind see, the poor have the gospel preached to them.

We see this emphasis upon the depth of the ordinary taken to its Christological conclusion in the gospel of John. There, Jesus is proclaimed as the bread of life, the way, the truth, the life, the vine, the light, the resurrection. Jesus is the prime analogate for understanding the most ordinary of created objects; there is a christic dimension to the simplest realities. The world and everything in it are not closed, but, for those who have eyes to see, it is the sign and revelation of ultimate life, divine life.

As the ministry of Jesus demonstrates, the daily experiences of meeting a friend or stranger (the Samaritan woman), greeting a child, eating a meal, sharing a cup of water, take on a graced dimension. In these experiences we touch the divine. Thus, religion can never be relegated to Sunday or to private or communal prayer before God. It must be part of one's life in the dining room, the market, the school, etc., because that is where God in Christ is found. Mark Gibbs makes this point by saying that "all orders are holy. Plumbers are as much in holy orders as the clergy, serving God and their fellows."[33] Rahner states that "when trade unionists confer, Christ is as much 'in the midst of them' as if the Rosary were being said."[34]

Emphasis upon the sacredness of the everyday and ordinary in Christology thus shows the link between redemption and creation. Schillebeeckx has spoken of Christology as "concentrated creation." That is, it reaffirms, reasserts our belief in the goodness of all creation.[35] The God whom Jesus calls Father is not the God of a new plan for a creation which has gone wrong, but, rather, in the God of Jesus, we see the supreme expression of God's eternally new being.

We might say that Jesus, through his life and teaching, offers us a new way of seeing, and, hence, living in the world. Christian faith is this way of seeing, seeing God active, laboring, providing, creating, waiting in all, in the ecstasy as well as the drudgery, in the chance encounter as well as the religious service. Christian faith is trying to see the world as Jesus saw it, and thus trying to find God in all things, and above all things.[36]

Thesis 10.   In a consumer oriented, technological society, Jesus stands for the primacy of the personal.

Consumerism stands for the attitude of aggressive grasping for more and more, the measuring of success and happiness through one's possessions. The accumulation and consumption of goods and services become a central purpose of life. Luxuries become necessities; every

good becomes a fashion; the latest is the best. It has as its object
knowledge and power, sex as well as material wealth. Consumerism
corresponds to concupiscence as defined by Tillich or Gilkey; it corresponds to that vain curiosity described by Augustine in his *Confessions.* [37]

John Kavanaugh, in his book, *Following Christ in a Consumer
Society,* contrasts the commodity or consumer form of living with the
personal. [38] In the first, value is put on things rather than persons;
knowledge becomes controlling and measuring rather than understanding and trust. In place of attitudes of respect, peace and acceptance in the personal mode, the consumerist mode fosters attitudes of
domination and manipulation. It is the contrast, in a word, between
the "having" of the consumer form of living, and the "being" of the
personal form.

Technology may be difficult to define, but it is inescapable in our
daily experience. So strong is its influence that it is now described as a
defining characteristic of our society; it is a system or even a culture.
Ellul, in his strong critique of the technological system, writes as
follows:

> Man once lived in a natural environment using technical instruments to
> get along better in it, protect himself against it and make use of it. Now
> man lives in a technological environment, and the old natural world
> supplies only his space and raw materials. [39]

In a technological society or system, the possible rather than the
necessary becomes the rule and end. We move from supplying basic
necessities to supplying luxuries. The power of the atom is geared more
towards destruction than energy. Abortion becomes a simple medical
operation. We worship the TV screen or the computer game and
ignore the neighbor, the family conversation. Ellul makes the contrast
an either/or—between the technological mode and the personal
mode. Technology aims at control and domination of one man or
machine over another, while the personal mode aims at sharing and
caring.

In this world of technology and consumerist mentality, the role and
function of Jesus the Christ is to point us to the primacy of the personal. While Jesus possessed great power over the forces of evil and
sickness, he always used these powers in the context of personal care
and faith. Clearly not neglecting the physical, he reminds us that
health of the spirit takes priority over bodily well-being. As the story of
the temptations shows, Jesus was not for the spectacular or magical,
but for the patient, slow, personal way of winning the hearts of men
and women. Many of his cures took place on the sabbath; he allowed
his disciples to pluck grain on the sabbath, and when objections arose,
he replied, "the sabbath was made for man, not man for the sabbath"
(Mark 2:27). I take this to be the priority of the personal here and now

over the encrusted traditions, over anything less than human. Just as the sabbath is made for man, so the machine of the technological age is to serve the needs of the human person, and not to become the enslaver.

Most of the ministry of Jesus consisted of personal encounters: at the well, at table, in the homes of friends or strangers, the blessing of children, the cure of the leper, the healing of the sick and the call to faith. His own life style can be characterized only by its simplicity, and he calls his followers to that same attitude. Give to those who ask, give and it will be given (Lk. 6:30, and 6:38), rather than build up one's treasury. Beware of covetousness, a man's life does not consist in the abundance of his possessions (Lk. 12:16). Seek the kingdom, for life is more than food and the body more than clothing (Lk. 12:31). These teachings of Jesus ring more true today than ever, showing us the true hierarchy of values where the kingdom is at the center.

The warnings of Jesus against the rich (the parable of Lazarus and the rich man, for example) and the words of Jesus to the rich young man, to leave all and follow, are addressed today to the Christians of the first and third world. The advice of Jesus to his followers — the little they are to take on their journey — struck me with particular force as I packed my three trunks and shipped cartons of books as I prepared to work in Nigeria.

Seek first the kingdom of God! The kingdom of God consists of a right relationship with God and right relationships with one's brothers and sisters. This is where Jesus pushes us, forces us to evaluate our priorities and our life style. Do we maintain the priority of the personal — the personal God and the neighbor? Robert Penn Warren wrote, in 1970, that "the disease of our time is the sense of being cut off from reality. Man feels that a screen has descended between him and nature, between him and other men, between him and the self."[40] Saul Bellow, in accepting the Nobel prize for literature, spoke of the need to lighten ourselves, to dump encumbrances, and, finally, to simplify.[41] We must focus on what is important and essential, rather than what is superfluous and accidental. Interpersonal values must take precedence over material, impersonal values, and character over possessions. Involved in this conversion is an abhorrence for violence and for mechanized solutions to the political and social problems of human existence.

In conclusion, let me say that I do not want to appear as reactionary, anti-technological. My concern, with that of Illich and Pope John Paul II, is that technology be directed or re-directed towards the service of humanity. The Pope asks: "Does this progress which has the human person for its author and promoter make life on earth more human in every aspect of life?"[42] Science and technology afford tremendous opportunities for the human race. The values include a sense of cooperation, a sense of the creative spirit, the need for global interdependence in utilizing resources, the countless examples of the elimination of disease. But, what the mission and ministry of Jesus remind us of is that the machine is made for the person, and the person is for God. In an age of contrasts of rich and poor, of North and South, the benefits of technology, the tools of technology must be directed more to the survival and welfare of the poor than to the increased productivity of the rich.

Thesis 11.   Jesus Christ demonstrates that God's love, and hence the Christian's, looks especially towards the weak, the poor, the marginated.

We have spoken in statements 6 and 7 of Jesus' role in revealing the truly human and the truly divine. The essence of both of these is love. In this thesis statement we wish to follow the way of Jesus and see how he specifies the direction of this love. In line with the strong voice of the prophets, such as Isaiah, Hosea and Amos, Jesus defends the rights of the poor, the weak, the marginated. His teaching and practice become the model for Christian love.

True Christian love must extend to one's enemies, one's persecutors: "For if you love those who love you, what reward have you?" (Mt. 5:46). Not those who repay one's kindness or love, but those who are unwilling or unable, such as the weak and helpless, must Christian love reach.

In the gospel of Luke, Jesus begins his public ministry by reading from the prophet Isaiah, "anointed to preach the good news to the poor, sent to proclaim release to the captive, recovering of sight to the blind, to set at liberty those who are oppressed" (Lk. 4:18). His ministry especially touches the sick, lepers, demoniacs, blind, lame, the children who are considered not worthy of the attention of the rabbi, the women who normally must remain in the background. He eats with sinners and tax collectors, with prostitutes, and says that precisely to and for these has he come! Thus, the physically, socially and morally weak and outcast become the special focus of his ministry. When asked by the disciples of John whether he is the one to come, he answers by explaining that his works of love attest to the truth of his person and mission: "Go and tell John what you have seen and heard: the blind receive their sight, the lame walk, lepers are cleansed, and the deaf hear, the dead are raised up, the poor have the good news preached to them" (Lk. 7:22).

So, too, in his teaching, the woman searches for the lost coin, the shepherd seeks the lost sheep, the father welcomes the lost son. In the gospel of Matthew, Jesus begins the sermon on the mount with God's blessing for the poor, the mourners, the persecuted. And, at the end of his ministry in Matthew, Jesus gives the parable of the last judgment where the mark of the true disciple, the mark that leads to salvation, is one's care for the hungry, the ill-clad, the prisoner, the thirsty, the sick, the stranger.

Thus, Jesus reaffirms and represents the God of the Hebrew Scripture and the New Testament as the God of the weak and the poor rather than, as one might prefer, the God of the strong and the rich. The Christian, the follower of Jesus, must echo and incarnate this viewpoint of the non-neutrality of God, with the special bias towards the poor. Jon Sobrino writes of the consciously partisan incarnation of Jesus Christ. He does not become incarnate anywhere, does not take on any sort of humanity, but takes on all that is weak and little in the flesh of history.[43] This pattern of incarnation becomes the model for the Christian movement, a movement in solidarity with the poor, as liberationist interpretations of Christianity demonstrate.

We might add that if God is the God who hears the cries of the poor, then atheism, in this perspective, is not so much disbelief in God or rejection of God; rather, it is making God into our own image, a false god who is on the side of the strong and the rich, a god who disdains the poor and weak, the victims of injustice. Such a god serves to justify our own narrowmindedness and injustice. The true God, revealed in Jesus Christ, is the God of all, letting his sun shine on the just and the unjust. Yet, as the gospel shows, he is the God with a special care and concern for the weak and the marginated.

Thesis 12.   As the mark of Jesus Christ is the sign of the cross, so the mark of the true Church of followers of Jesus Christ will be persecution.

While the gospel means good news, it does not promise us instant peace and happiness, an end to our troubles and struggles. One of the most recurrent truths of the teaching and life of Jesus (and one frequently forgotten) is that Jesus promises persecution to those who follow his way: "If they persecuted me, they will persecute you" (Jn. 15:20). During the public ministry, when Peter asked what he will get for following Jesus, Jesus replies that he will receive the hundredfold. In the gospel of Mark, which I would like to think is accurate in echoing the emphasis of Jesus upon taking up one's cross, it is added that one will also receive persecution (Mk. 10:30). So, too, the beatitudes promise persecution for those who work for justice, just as the prophets had been persecuted and just as Jesus would be.

The later writings of the New Testament echo this promise of persecution, as in 2 Tim. 3:12 ("all those who desire to live a godly life in Christ Jesus will be persecuted"). Thus, too, the letter of Peter says we should expect persecution, and rejoice in it (1 Pet. 4:12f.).

Why was Jesus persecuted? And why will his followers be persecuted? He was rejected, suffered and died because of the way he lived and because of the message he taught. He did not choose the cross for the sake of the cross, but was condemned to it through the conspiracy of religious and political leaders who wanted to do away with this troublemaker. He stirred up the people and threatened the traditions as interpreted by the religious leaders. He was considered a heretical teacher who put himself above the law, a false prophet who criticized the cult, a blasphemer who destroyed the tradition.[44] All of this resulted from his attitude of concern and solidarity with the weak and the poor, the sinner.

So, too, for the followers of Jesus. Persecution comes from living the faith, the faith linked inseparably with the concern for justice. In a sinful world, the light will continue to be rejected. So central is this message of persecution that I would consider it to be the fifth mark of the church, which is one, holy, catholic, and apostolic. Luther did speak of it in this manner, along with the preaching of the word. Perhaps more correctly than saying persecution is the fifth mark of the church, we should say that work for justice, standing with and for the poor, should be a mark of the Christian community—and this inevitably will lead to persecution.

If we are comfortable with our Christianity, it may not be a sign of grace, but a sign that we are failing to take up the cross, failing to follow Jesus on the way that leads to persecution and the cross. Only in the next world, when the kingdom of light is separated from the kingdom of darkness, will persecution cease for those who follow the path of Jesus. If the churches are not at times at odds with the political powers, that might well be a sign that we have compromised in our Christian witness. In a sinful world (which the doctrine of original sin never lets us forget) Christianity must always contain an element of counter-cultural witness, Christ against culture, in order to transform and liberate that culture.[45] Thus, the bishops of the United States, for example, in their stand on capital punishment, on the right to life, and in their debate on nuclear war, have felt and will continue to feel opposition—that opposition or persecution promised to those who stand for the values of Jesus Christ.

In many lands today, the Church is living this fifth mark of the Church, with Latin America as the prime example. The church is becoming a church of martyrs, witnesses for faith and justice. Catechists, peasants, men and women, religious and laity, priests and even an Archbishop, have suffered, even to death, for their faith. I would like to conclude with the prophetic words of Maritain, written years ago:

> Whereas a political ideal of brotherly love alone can direct the work of authentic social regeneration: and it follows that to prepare a new age for the world, martyrs to the love of neighbor may first be necessary.[46]

Thesis 13.   In Jesus Christ we receive the forgiveness of sins and, thus, are liberated from the power of evil.

The Christian doctrine of original sin has been called the most em-
pirically verifiable of all doctrines. It and its concomitant expression,
"sin of the world," give us the unwanted assurance that sin has been
with us from the beginning and will remain until the end of time. The
history of the world is a history of sin (as well as grace), and we can expect no brave new world, no utopia in which sin is removed.

Both the Apostles' and Nicene creeds affirm belief in the forgiveness
of sins, and at Eucharist we share the cup of the blood shed "for you
and for all men and women so that sins may be forgiven." Jesus Christ,
in the language of the tradition, is the Savior of the world, the
redeemer of humankind. Thus, through Jesus Christ, we believe that
the history of sin is outweighed, overbalanced by the history of forgiving grace. What we seek, what we do not deserve, what we cannot
achieve on our own, is given in and through Jesus Christ.

In the public ministry of Jesus, there are two specific occasions on
which he forgives sins: Mark 2:1-12 (and parallels) and Luke 7:36-50,
the paralytic and the woman who was a sinner. But, throughout his
ministry he offers new life and reconciliation to sinners and social outcasts by associating with them at table, in table fellowship. He brings
salvation to the house and family of Zacchaeus. His miracles push back
the forces of darkness, sickness, evil, and reveal the power and love of
God. Those who are most frequently the object of the love of Jesus are
those with little hope, the despised, the social outcasts. And Jesus,
through his words and actions, liberates them from their condition
and restores them to the human community, or even calls them to be
his disciples. In this sense he does not only reveal the forgiveness of sins
as a cleaning of the slate, but more as the reestablishment of right and
just relationships among men and women. Sin and evil are not just to
be forgiven, but to be eradicated through the coming of the kingdom
of God.[47]

The gospels speak of the extent of God's mercy and forgiveness
under the sign of Jonah. Just as Jonah was surprised, shocked, annoyed
at the boundless love of God, so the hearers of Jesus find it difficult to
believe because of their all too narrow view of the power and love of
God. By daring to call God Father, Abba, Jesus reveals that God is
turned to us in an attitude of acceptance and forgiveness, like the
father in the parable of the prodigal son. By laying down his life for his
friends, Jesus shows the extent of his own love. As Paul writes in the letter to the Romans, "It is precisely this that God proves his love for us:
that while we were still sinners, Christ died for us" (Rom. 5:6). This
text, incidentally, is singled out several times in the monumental work,
The Christ, by Schillebeeckx, as a summary of the good news of God's
forgiving love. Through his death and resurrection, Jesus reveals a way
beyond sin and death, a way that is sustained by the Father in the
resurrection. Our own way beyond sin to new life is achieved by joining
our lives to the way of Jesus, sacramentally and existentially.

Belief in the forgiveness of sins through the work of Jesus Christ does not stop there, however. It must lead to an attitude of forgiveness in imitation of the mercy and forgiveness of God. The forgiveness we receive as gift becomes a task. At times, this attitude and action of forgiveness of one's brothers and sisters (seventy times seven times) is presented as a precondition for God's forgiveness. God cannot forgive one who does not forgive his or her brother or sister (Mt. 18:23-35, Mt. 6:14f). Such reconciliation is even a precondition for true worship, as Mt. 5:23 emphasizes.

With the sacrament of reconciliation, with the penitential rite at the beginning of the Eucharistic liturgy, we might begin to take the forgiveness of God for granted, and forget that it is purchased at a great price through the passion, death and resurrection of Jesus Christ. Forgiveness is always a creative new act, an act unconditioned by the act which provokes it. In forgiveness, both the one who forgives and the one who is forgiven are freed, freed from attitudes of vengeance and freed from punishment. Forgiveness is the act of love which breaks the circle of sin, bridges the gulf of estrangement, as the father in the prodigal son who accepts back his son unconditionally, no questions asked, no apologies or explanations demanded.

So important is the article of faith on the forgiveness of sins, that Karl Barth writes powerfully:

> Every day we ought to begin, we may begin with the confession: 'I believe in the forgiveness of sins.' In the brief hour of our death we shall still have nothing else to say. [48]

As Jesus said, "I have come, not to call the righteous, but sinners." Any interpretation of the Christ event that minimizes the reality and extent of human sinfulness will, in the long run, in the test of experience, fall short and its inadequacy be made manifest.

Thesis 14.   In Jesus Christ we receive the power for liberating action and loving service.

The previous statement spoke of freedom *from* the power of sin, or a liberate*d* existence. In this statement we focus on what is inseparable from that, the positive side of freedom: freedom *for* loving service, or liberat*ing* existence and action. [49]

We are not making the claim that Jesus or the first Christians had a well developed theology of liberation, a social ethic, as we understand that today. That would be impossible for Jesus or his disciples, since both were truly human as we are and, hence, limited by time and space. But, I do claim that in the life, death and resurrection of Jesus we have the revelation and possibility of the integral liberation of humankind. This, I submit, is an important point to be made when exponents of a theology of liberation find themselves on the defensive,

needing to justify themselves and their language before more conservative and, in fact, untraditional thinkers.

Several authors, including biblical scholars, point to the significance
of Jesus the Christ for human liberation, among them Käsemann,
Mateos, Ogden, Segundo, Gutierrez and Sobrino.[50]

We begin by picking up from the previous thesis statement, the
liberating action of Jesus in healing the sick, reconciling sinners and
the marginated to the human community. By frequently performing
such liberating actions on the sabbath, Jesus was at the same time free-
ing the people from the constrictive religious leadership of the time. As
commentators suggest, significant oppression at the time of Jesus
came, not so much from the Roman occupation, as from the Jewish
religious leadership. Instead of liberating people to mature worship of
God and service to the neighbor, the emphasis was all too much on the
upholding of the tradition, the laws and regulations of the covenant in
a narrow, restrictive sense.

Thus, the healings on the sabbath serve to liberate the people from
any false religious attitude that subordinates the person to the sabbath.
When challenged by the authorities, Jesus appealed to the heart, the
common sense, the deep religious conviction of those present: "is it not
right to heal on the sabbath, to do good!" He thus shows that the ordinary believer has direct access to the truth of God, to make the judgment of what is right and wrong. Any religious leadership that under-
mines or underestimates this presence of the spirit in the hearts of the
faithful is unliberating and unworthy of following. Jesus frees his
hearers by giving them a sense of confidence in their own insight,
based upon the presence of God in their hearts.

Segundo contrasts Jesus' method of theologizing as attested to in
these cures on the sabbath with the method of the Pharisees.[51] In the
evangelical mode of Jesus, we start with and face squarely the human
situation, the signs of the times. From this stance of commitment to
alleviate human problems, we move to the theological step, the second
step. By contrast, the pharisees begin with the theology of the tradition, the certitudes from revelation, and impose them upon the present situation. "Man is made for the sabbath." They conclude that
healing on the sabbath is unlawful. The method of Jesus is the
liberating one, calling for a mature, responsible faith: "why do you not
judge for yourselves what is right?" (Lk. 12:56f). In view of what is
right in that situation, Jesus performs the healing on the sabbath.

We have spoken earlier of the role of Jesus in revealing the boundless
love of God the Father. It is this love or grace that is the possibility of
our liberating activity in human history. Rahner speaks of three key
areas of human existence where this grace of God makes a
difference.[52] It enables, first, self-transcending loving service to the
neighbor; secondly, it gives the Christian hope in the future, and

thirdly, an attitude of trust in the face of death. Thus, we are strengthened or liberated in three key relationships of human existence: towards the neighbor and community, towards the future, and towards the power of death.

The first area, one's relationship to the neighbor in loving service in imitation of Jesus, provides the basis for the struggle for justice. We will not go into detail on that here, but simply reiterate that the foundation for the works of justice must be that freedom to risk, to die to self, to be concerned about others, which comes only from the grace or love of God. Secondly, we are not paralyzed by fears of the future but, through the liberating grace of God, freed to make our contribution through our families, in our communities. Thirdly, while death remains dark and mysterious, we have hope in life after death, the hope of the risen Lord, that the same Father who raised him to new life will raise us with him.

Thus, we are able to begin to live the logic of Jesus, that faith-filled logic of giving and not counting the cost, identifying with the weak and the poor, loving one's enemies, turning the other cheek, forgiving seventy times seven, repaying evil with good. Paul presents the charter for Christian freedom in the letters to the Galatians and the Romans. In Romans 8, he shows that we are free from all that is not God — nothing can ultimately harm us because we are encompassed by the liberating love of God. No distress, no hunger, danger or persecution, "neither life nor death, neither the present nor the future, neither height nor depth nor any other creature will be able to separate us from the love of God that comes to us in Christ Jesus, our Lord" (Rom. 8:38).

Conclusion

The question Jesus asked Peter resounds through the centuries, "who do you say that I am?" Our response to that question, and the way we live out that response, determines our final destiny. There have been, and remain, a variety of responses to the question: Jesus is the Christ, Lord, Savior, Redeemer, Servant, Son of David, Good Shepherd, Judge, the way, the truth, the life. For one age, Jesus is the Pantocrator, for another, the infant in the crèche. He is the crucified one in a *theologia crucis,* the risen Lord in a *theologia gloriae.* Each of these descriptions of Jesus unveils some aspect of his role and function. And, they warn us to remain open and adaptable as we have considered this question. The mystery of the Christ event is far too rich to be captured in any one formulation. Just as God is a rock, fortress, shepherd, creator, judge, father, mother, etc., so the person and work of Jesus the Christ elude any one comprehensive definition. [53] Rather, we must employ a variety of images and frameworks to explore the treasure, the mystery of Jesus Christ which joins the human and the divine.

All the same, I am equally convinced that any one major title or aspect of the life, teaching, mission, action of Jesus Christ, if carefully and prayerfully reflected upon, will unveil the whole. Through the particular image, such as that of servant, or liberator, or the Christ, we move to the universal. If we touch the depths of any particular image, we will also move out and begin to see the whole, the whole which involves the human condition in its sinful and graced aspects, in its individual and communitarian dimensions, in its present challenges and moving to an unknown future, [54] what I call the dialectic of Christian faith.

The role and function of Jesus varied in accord with particular encounters during his public ministry. But, in each and every situation, he revealed and mediated the divine truth and love. His word and action varied, depending upon whether he addressed a child, a leper, a Pharisee, Pilate, his disciples. But, in each encounter he was the Christ of God, Jesus of Nazareth.

The ministry of Jesus, in this sense, becomes a pattern for our own creative ministry. The challenge of ministry — whether teaching, preaching, counseling, etc. — is to take from the rich treasures of the Scripture and tradition the word, the image that is called for in the particular situation we are involved in. In other words, we return to the pastoral or hermeneutical circle, and now consider the employment of that circle as an art. Rather than a laboratory research project, rather than even a contemplative exercise in the monastery, Christian ministry is better considered the art (divinely inspired) of bringing the riches of Jesus Christ to bear upon a particular situation of our own lives or of our ministry.

Two examples of such creativity in theology would be the monumental work of Schillebeeckx, *Jesus* and *The Christ. The Christ,* for example, is a retrieval of the Christian doctrine of grace as a way to interpret and understand the role and significance of Jesus Christ. The richness of this study comes not only from the depth of biblical scholarship, but also from the range of contemporary issues, such as suffering and oppression, which form the background and context of the study. A second example would be the creative interpretation of the Christ event in liberation theology, such as that of Sobrino and Boff. Here, it is their context of poverty and oppression that challenges traditional Christology. From that context they mine the biblical and postbiblical tradition to present an image of Christ that mediates life and salvation to their concrete situations. Both Schillebeeckx and Sobrino/Boff are examples of the employment of the hermeneutical circle, with Schillebeeckx placing greater emphasis upon the pole of the Christian message, and Sobrino/Boff, greater emphasis upon the context. But, the creativity emerges precisely in the correlation of the message and the situation, in both cases.

I have said that almost any particular incident of the life of Jesus, if fully examined, will unveil the whole; or, any particular image or title of Jesus will reveal the whole of Christianity. I would like to conclude with one particular image from the gospels, apt for today or every day. For me, it is a poignant and powerful way to try to sum up the role and function of Jesus the Christ. It is the image of the father in the story of the prodigal son, the father running with arms outstretched, slightly undignified, rushing to meet his son whom he has seen in the distance, returning home. This, I submit, is a true impression of the image of God/grace/love/Father/Mother, an image which liberates and inspires. This is an image we can rely upon and turn to in our need; it is bed rock reality which we can and must believe in, if we dare call ourselves Christians. One final enrichment of the picture of the father comes from a 16th century woodcut.[55] It is an etching of the jubilant faces of the father and the son as they are at the point of reunion. Their arms are extended, but they are not yet embracing. But, if you look carefully at the etching, you can see that the shadow of the father, in the background, already embraces, touches and covers the shadow of the son returning home. The boundless love of the father actually never left the son, and we, too, have the courage to believe with Paul that nothing can separate us from the love of God in Christ Jesus.

NOTES

[1] Paul Tillich develops the method of correlation in his *Systematic Theology*, I (Chicago: University of Chicago Press, 1961), pp. 59-66. David Tracy, in his *Blessed Rage for Order* (New York: Seabury, 1975), develops and criticizes this method of theology in his revisionist mode of theology.

[2] See Mark Gibbs, *God's Lively People* (Philadelphia: Westminster, 1971), pp. 106, 140-46. An Anglican layman, I find his writing most helpful; other books of his include *God's Frozen People* (London: Collins Press, 1964), and *Christians with Secular Power* (Philadelphia: Fortress, 1981).

[3] Karl Rahner, *Foundations of Christian Faith* (New York: Seabury, 1978). See, for example, pp. 8-14 on general method, and pp. 294-5, where he speaks of experience in Christology. For a way into this difficult book of Rahner, see *A World of Grace, An Introduction to the Themes and Foundations of Karl Rahner's Theology*, ed. Leo J. O'Donovan (New York: Seabury, 1980). The essay of William V. Dych, "Theology in a New Key," is most pertinent here.

[4] Karl Rahner speaks of this Copernican Revolution in at least two places: first, "Considerations on the Active Role of the Person in the Sacramental Event," *Theological Investigations* XIV (New York: Seabury, 1976), pp. 161-84; and secondly, *Meditations on the Sacraments* (New York: Seabury, 1977), especially the Introduction.

[5] I take this to be a major point and thrust of Schubert Ogden, *The Point of Christology* (New York: Harper and Row, 1982). I have been challenged by and learned much from his existential-historical approach to Jesus Christ.

[6] On the pastoral circle, see my essay, "A Method for Christian Ministry," *Emmanuel*, March 1981, pp. 137-44. Also, James D. Whitehead and Evelyn Eaton Whitehead, *Method in Ministry* (New York: Seabury, 1981), for a rich and detailed presentation of the various attitudes and inputs into a contemporary theology for ministry.

[7] See *Institutes of the Christian Religion*, Bk. I, Ch. VI, 1; and I, XIV, 1. A more complete study of the pastoral circle would have to address the difficult questions of the relative weight of the Scriptures, their authority in relation to the magisterium of the Church, the relative weight of tradition and the various ways in which the human and social sciences function, as well as the weight and significance of one's own experience as a minister or theologian.

[8] Gustavo Gutierrez, "Faith as Freedom: Solidarity with the Alienated and Confidence in the Future," *Horizons* (Spring, 1975):25-60. For further reflection on the hermeneutical circle, see J. Segundo, *The Liberation of Theology* (Maryknoll, N.Y.: Orbis Books, 1976).

[9] I take Liberation Theology and Christology as developed in liberation theology as verifying this claim. Further works in Christology, by Segundo, for example, are expected.

[10] Avery Dulles, "Imaging the Church for the 1980's," *Catholic Mind* 79 (1981):8-26. Every Christian, from the newly baptized to the aging, from Pope to child, remains a disciple, following Jesus and continually learning more of the mystery of God's love in Jesus Christ.

[11] See Denis Murphy, "A Church in the Minority," *America*, August 25, 1979, pp. 74-76, where he develops this point from his perspective in Asia, from the Christian Philippines, but near the almost totally non-Christian surrounding nations.

[12] Charles Davis, "Theology in Seminary Confinement," *The Downside Review* (1963): 307-16. As seminaries have moved to cities, to ecumenical clusters, and as laymen and laywomen and sisters have become students in seminaries or theological centers, shifts in the nature of theology also result, as anyone teaching in such a seminary can attest. In addition, we are aware of the various stages of faith and moral development through the writings of Fowler and Kohlberg. This again points to the complexity of the pole #1 which we term the situation or context.

[13] Joseph Fitzmyer speaks of this pluralism in his *Christological Catechism* (New York: Paulist Press, 1982). Recent Scripture scholarship makes us aware of this pluralism as we see the authors of the New Testament as creative theologians, exemplifying the pastoral circle as they write for specific communities facing specific questions.

[14] John Macquarrie, "Truth in Christology," in *God Incarnate, Story and Belief,* ed. A.E. Harvey (London: SPCK, 1981), pp. 24-33.

[15] Rahner, *Foundations of Christian Faith*, p. 306.

[16] *Ibid.,* pp. 306-07.

[17] On the Lordship of Christ and the tasks involved in proclaiming and living this, see *Above Every Name, The Lordship of Christ and Social Systems,* ed. Thomas E. Clarke (New York: Paulist, 1980). The reader will note that in this essay I am not entering into the most difficult question of the uniqueness and

universality of the work of Jesus Christ. Reflections on that question can be found in my essay, "Christ and Church: A Spectrum of Views," *Theological Studies* 37 (1976); 545-66, and in the more recent writings of Lucien Richard and Paul Knitter. I am saying that whatever the more theoretical considerations may lead to, we have the mission and challenge of offering the possibility of belief in Jesus Christ to all men and women.

[18] There is a growing body of literature on theology as story. For an overall view, with excellent summaries and bibliography, see John Navone, S.J., *The Jesus Story: Our Life as Story in Christ* (Collegeville, Minnesota: Liturgical Press, 1979). See also David Tracy, *The Analogical Imagination* (New York: Crossroads, 1981), where he explores the literary, classic dimensions of the Scripture based upon philosophical and literary hermeneutics.

[19] I explore some of these terms in an unpublished essay on the Church and Modernization. I rely upon the unpublished manuscript of Robert Schreiter, *Constructing Local Theologies*. Here, too, the amount of literature is rapidly growing.

[20] Pedro Arrupe, S.J., "Letter to the Whole Society on Inculturation," *Studies in the Spirituality of Jesuits* 7 (June, 1978): 2.

[21] This is developed in the unpublished paper mentioned above, under the thesis statement #2, which states, "The inculturation of Gospel values into the process of modernization is the most challenging and important place for inculturation to occur, more significant than Roman Catholic dialogue with other Christian churches, with non-Christian religions, with traditional cultures and with atheism." My experience in Nigeria serves to confirm this thesis, as I see Nigeria rushing to catch up with the First World, often uncritically. In addition, I see the Christian laity, rather than clergy or religious, as the only persons who can bring gospel values to bear upon the complex process of modernization.

[22] On the paschal mystery touching one's daily life, see my brief essay, "Living Easter," *America*, April 10, 1982, p. 276. In a profound meditation on human life before the incomprehensible mystery of God, Rahner shows that the full meaning of the human is found in one's giving, self-surrender, yes, to this mystery of God: "Thomas Aquinas on the Incomprehensibility of God," *Journal of Religion* 58 (Supplement, 1978): 107-25.

[23] Joseph Sittler, *The Structure of Christian Ethics* (Baton Rouge, Louisiana: Louisiana State University, 1958), p. 36.

[24] I am indebted to Langdon Gilkey for these reflections on the dialectic of Christian faith. See his *Reaping the Whirlwind* (New York: Seabury, 1976), pp. 310-18. He also develops this in a manuscript entitled the *Dialectics of Christian Faith*. See also Reinhold Niebuhr, "Coherence, Incoherence, and Christian Faith," in *Christian Realism and Political Problems* (New York: Scribners, 1953).

[25] Paul Ricoeur, "The Logic of Jesus, the Logic of God," *Criterion* 18 (Summer, 1979):4-6.

[26] Hans Küng, in his *On Being A Christian* (New York: Doubleday, 1976), has a powerful section on the death of Jesus, in particular pp. 339-42. Also J. Moltmann, *The Crucified God* (New York: Harper, 1974), and G. O'Collins, *The Calvary Christ* (Philadelphia: Westminster Press, 1977).

[27] I develop this view of the Trinity in "The Triune God, Luxury or Challenge?," published in Nigeria in *The Catholic Witness* (December, 1982).

[28] Karl Rahner has written powerfully and continually on this unity of Love of God and neighbor, for example, "Reflections on the Unity of the Love of Neighbor and the Love of God," in *Theological Investigations* VI (Baltimore: Helicon, 1969), and "The Church's Commission to Bring Salvation and the Humanization of the World," in *Theological Investigations* XIV (New York: Seabury, 1976).

[29] Rahner, *Foundations of Christian Faith*, p. 447.

[30] Hugo Rahner has explored the history and meaning of this epithet in *Ignatius the Theologian* (New York: Herder and Herder, 1968). Gaston Fessard also develops this in his work on the Spiritual Exercises, *La Dialectique des exercices Spirituels* (Aubier: Edition Montaigne, 1966).

[31] Philip Murnion, "A Sacramental Church," *America,* March 26, 1983, p. 228.

[32] See J. Segundo, *The Sacraments Today* (Maryknoll, NY: Orbis, 1974), who sees the sacraments as signs of a Church that is mission oriented towards serving an ailing humanity.

[33] Mark Gibbs, *God's Frozen People,* p. 17.

[34] K. Rahner, *Theology for Renewal* (New York: Sheed and Ward, 1964).

[35] *Jesus and Christ: Interim Report* (New York: Crossroads, 1981), pp. 126-28. This thesis echoes recent emphasis upon a theology and spirituality of creation. See, for example, *Western Spirituality: Historical Roots, Ecumenical Routes,* ed. Matthew Fox (Notre Dame, Indiana: Fides/Claretian, 1979).

[36] Ignatian Spirituality, rooted in the Contemplation to Attain Divine Love, in the *Spiritual Exercises* of St. Ignatius forms the background for many of my reflections in this thesis. See my monograph, "The New Approaches to Christology and Their Use in the Spiritual Exercises," *Studies in the Spirituality of Jesuits* 12 (September-November 1980): Nos. 4 and 5.

[37] See P. Tillich, *Systematic Theology* II, pp. 51-5, and Gilkey, following Tillich in his *Naming the Whirlwind* and *Reaping the Whirlwind.* See Augustine, *Confessions,* Bk 1, No. 16 and *passim.*

[38] John Kavanaugh, *Following Christ in a Consumer Society* (Maryknoll, New York: Orbis, 1982).

[39] Jacques Ellul, *The Technological System* (New York: Continuum, 1980), p. 46.

[40] Robert Penn Warren, *Chicago Sun-Times,* 6 December 1970.

[41] Saul Bellow, Address at Presentation of the Nobel Prize for Literature.

[42] Pope John Paul II, *Redemptor Hominis,* No. 15.

[43] Jon Sobrino, S.J., "A Crucified People's Faith in the Son of God," in *Jesus, Son of God?, Concilium* 153, ed. Edward Schillebeeckx and Johannes-Baptist Metz (New York: Seabury, 1982), p. 26. The theme of God's solidarity with the poor, and ours in imitation of God, is of course a major theme in liberationist interpretations of Christianity. Archbishop Oscar Romero put this at the center: "We say of that world of the poor that it is the key to understanding the Christian faith, to understand the action of the church and the political dimension of that faith and of that ecclesial action." ("The Political Dimension of Christian Love," *Commonweal,* March 26, 1982, p. 169.)

[44] See Hans Küng, *On Being a Christian,* pp. 334-39.

[45] In the background, of course, is the classic book of H. Richard Niebuhr, *Christ and Culture* (New York: Harper and Row, 1951). While I would favor, as Niebuhr does, the model of Christ transformer of culture, the dialectic of

Christian faith leads me to retain elements of the Christ against or in paradox with culture.

[46] Jacques Maritain, *Scholasticism and Politics* (New York: Doubleday, 1960), p. 29.

[47] Liberation theology emphasizes this. Not only is "malum vitandum" evil to be avoided, but even more to be eliminated, eradicated as far as possible. On the meaning and extent of human sinfulness, in addition to the writings of Reinhold Niebuhr, I find Tillich, *Systematic Theology* II, on sin as estrangement from God, self and others, powerful.

[48] Karl Barth, *Dogmatics in Outline* (New York: Harper and Row, 1959), p. 150.

[49] Schubert Ogden uses this terminology of liberated and liberating in his *The Point of Christology.*

[50] See Ernst Käsemann, *Jesus Means Freedom* (Philadelphia: Fortress Press, 1970); Juan Mateos, "The Message of Jesus," *Sojourners* (July, 1977); Jon Sobrino, *Christology at the Crossroads* (Maryknoll, New York: Orbis Books, 1978).

[51] See Juan Luis Segundo, "On a Missionary Awareness of One's Own Culture," *Studies in the International Apostolate of Jesuits* 3 (September, 1974): especially pp. 40–47.

[52] Karl Rahner, "The Quest for Approaches Leading to an Understanding of the Mystery of the God-Man Jesus," in *Theological Investigations* XIII (New York: Seabury, 1975), pp. 195–200. This is also presented in his *Foundations of Christian Faith* as a "Searching Christology," in pages 295–98.

[53] See the essay of K. Rahner, already cited, on the Incomprehensibility of God and the response to that talk by Paul Ricoeur, which reinforces Rahner's views. Ricoeur's response is in the same issue of the *Journal of Religion.*

[54] This theme of the universal manifest through the particular is expounded in David Tracy, *The Analogical Imagination* (New York: Crossroad, 1981), under the theme of the classic.

[55] I am indebted to James Luther Adams, *On Being Human Religiously* (Boston: Beacon Press, 1976), p. 99, for the reference to this woodcut. He sees it as portraying the re-creative power of love, a re-creation and, hence, a new creation.

The Revelation of God in the Gospel of Mark

John R. Donahue, S.J.

The impact of modern biblical scholarship on theology and proclamation has, by any standards, been immense—well beyond the
capacity of any individual to catalogue and synthesize. As my contribution to this volume I would like to pick one work, the Gospel of
Mark, which has been the subject of intensive study since the advent of
redaction criticism in the late fifties—a period which corresponds
roughly to the "biblical renewal" within Roman Catholicism. In the
last three decades major motifs of Mark's gospel, such as Christology,
eschatology and discipleship, have been the subject of significant
monographs.[1] Internal tensions in the community of Mark, between
advocates of a theology of glory and a theology of the cross, have been
explored, and the social setting of the work has been probed in light of
the Jewish war against Rome and the destruction of the temple (A.D.
66-70). Rather surprisingly, there has been a neglected factor in the
study of Mark's theology, a factor which Nils Dahl highlighted in a
short but significant article in 1975, where he called attention to the
lack of "any comprehensive or penetrating study of the theme 'God' in
the New Testament."[2] Since by etymology and practice theology is a
study of God and the way we speak of God, we will propose as our contribution to this year's volume some probings on the revelation of God
in the Gospel of Mark.[3]

The presentation will consist of three major sections. First, speaking
primarily as an exegete, we will offer a general description of Mark's
language about God, followed by a study of three passages in Mark
where there is a concentration of God language and which can be
described as Mark's short theological treatise (12:13-34). This first section will then conclude with some suggestions concerning the way in
which Mark's presentation of God influences his understanding of
Christology and discipleship. In the second major part of the essay, we
will concentrate on the impact of modern biblical scholarship "for
theology" by offering some proposals on the way the gospel of Mark

can be understood as "revelation," since theology has revelation as both its source and authority. Finally, we will sketch some implications of Mark's presentation of God for contemporary proclamation.

I.   The Presentation of God in Mark

The text of Mark exhibits diverse ways of speaking of God, and the term *theos,* God, is used forty-eight times, most often on the lips of Jesus and about fifty per cent of the time in "kingdom of God" sayings or in citations of the Old Testament.[4] There are four uses of "Son of God," once by Mark in the superscription to the Gospel (1:1), once in the final confession of the centurion (15:39), and twice on the lips of demons (3:11; 5:7).[5] In at least nine instances, again mainly in Old Testament quotes, *kyrios* or Lord is used of God.[6] Mark contains also circumlocutions for God which were common, especially in the diaspora Judaism of his time, such as *dynamis* (power, 14:62); "the heaven" (e.g., the authority of John, was it from heaven?, 11:32) and "the blessed one" (14:62, even though the precise phrase, "Son of the Blessed," has not been found in pre-Christian Judaism).[7] Six references to the spirit or the holy spirit (1:8,10,12; 3:29; 12:36; 13:11) suggest divine action or the presence of God, as does the use of the theological passive (e.g., 16:6, he has been raised up) and of the verb *dei,* it is necessary. Scripture is assumed to be the revelation of God; the divine power is thought to be manifest in miracles, and twice a voice from heaven declares Jesus to be a beloved son (1:11; 9:7).

As one would expect, it is Jesus who speaks most often of God and provides an initial picture of Mark's language about God. Jesus speaks of God as the creator of the human family (10:6) and of the cosmos (13:19) who will bring human history to a close (13:20) and who prepares a place for the elect (13:20,27; cf. 10:40). God alone is good (10:18), has power to do what is thought humanly to be impossible (10:27), issues commands and has a will which is to be followed (3:35; 7:8), and is a "father in heaven" who will forgive those who forgive others (11:25). If the parable of 12:1-9 is read allegorically, God is the vineyard owner who sends his "beloved son" (12:6) to collect the fruits of the vineyard, only to have him murdered by the tenants. In Mark, Jesus speaks three times of God as father (8:38; 11:25; 13:32) and once (14:36) addresses him in prayer as "Abba, father." Even though, with the exception of the voice in 1:11 and 9:7, God does not enter directly into the narrative, the reader knows (from the quotation attributed to Isaiah in 1:1, "Behold I send my messenger before my face") that God is the one who shapes the course of the life of Jesus. Jesus articulates this in the passion predictions (8:31; 9:31; 10:33-34) and in his prayer in Gethsemane (14:36). The message to the women in 16:6, "he has been raised, he is not here," is couched in the passive of divine action.

Rather surprisingly, however, in view of the presence of the Lord's prayer in other New Testament traditions, the Markan Jesus never explicitly tells his followers to address God as father. While it is true that for Mark the God of Jesus is the God of the Jewish tradition, *the way in which* the Markan Jesus speaks of God is quite different from the way he speaks in the other gospels.

A few comparisons with Matthew and Luke will illustrate Mark's distinctive language. Where Mark speaks of doing the will of God (3:35), Matthew speaks of the "will of my father in heaven" (12:50). Matthew does not hesitate to speak of God in anthropomorphic language which attributes human emotion to God. Matthew's "father in heaven" feeds the birds of the air; cares for the lilies of the field (6:26,28) and "gives good things to those who ask him" (7:11). The Matthean parables portray a God who is much closer to human history, who gives a surprising reward to those who have worked only one hour (20:9), and punishes a servant who can not act toward others with that same mercy and compassion which he has received (18:32-33). So, too, the God of Luke's Gospel is much more immediate to human history than the God of Mark. The tone is set in the hymns of the infancy narrative which are resplendent with Old Testament imagery. God is the one who out of compassion sends the morning star to give light to those who sit in darkness and in the shadow of death (1:78), who puts down the mighty, exalts the lowly, and fills the hungry with good things (1:52-53). The Lukan parables abound in images and metaphors for God which make God present to everyday human life. God is described as the shepherd (15:3), the searching woman (15:8), the forgiving father (15:20), and even the disgruntled householder aroused in the middle of a sound sleep to welcome a traveller (11:7-9). Both Matthew and Luke speak of God in a language rich in imagery and metaphor and with a sense of immediacy.

What is distinctive about Mark, then, is that the Markan Jesus speaks of God almost completely *without descriptive terms or attributes*. With the exception of 11:25, "the one who is in heaven," 12:27, "the god of the living," and 9:37, "the one who sent me," *theos* or God in Mark stands completely without modifiers, and the Markan God is notably devoid of anthropomorphisms. Neither does Mark have a sense of the immediacy of God's action in saving history that we find in Matthew and Luke. God's intervention in Mark will come mainly at the end time when the elect are gathered and the wicked punished (12:8; 13:24-30). Mark has nothing like the Q interpretation of the miracles of Jesus that through them "the kingdom of God has come upon you" (Luke 11:20 = Matt. 12:28), or the Lukan statement that "the kingdom of God is in your midst" (17:21). The final words of Jesus in Mark, "My God, My God, why have you foresaken me?" (15:34), evoke the absence of God in the mystery of the cross, and the last words of the Gospel, "they were afraid" (16:8), reinforce the numinous awe with which one should stand before the revelation of God.

Therefore, in its language about God, in its understanding of God's relation to history, and in the reaction of hearers to God's presence, Mark stresses the transcendence and mystery of God. The sobriety of God language in Mark is in contrast to the Old Testament, to much of contemporary Jewish writing, and to other parts of the New Testament. It is, however, paralleled by the tendency of Judaism in more Hellenistic environments and more influenced by Greek philosophy to move away from anthropomorphisms and to stress the transcendence of God.

The Markan way of speaking about God, therefore, provides the first building block for an initial probing of Mark's *theology*. In the following two sections, we will argue that this way of speaking about God is in accord with three pericopes which are the most directly theological in the gospel—that is, which speak of the nature and demands of God, and that Mark's way of presenting God arises out of the missionary needs of his community and also influences the way the community is to define its own faith in God and life of discipleship.

A. Mark's Short Theological Treatise (12:13–34)

While many points of entry suggest themselves as access to the importance of Mark's distinctive language about God, for a number of reasons we will turn to the three pericopes of Mark 12:13-34: the answers Jesus gives to a question on paying taxes to Caesar (12:13-17), his discussion of the resurrection (12:18-27), and his articulation of "the great Commandment" (12:28-34). This selection is not arbitrary, since in these three pericopes there is the greatest concentration of God language found in the gospel as well as the most extensive purely "theological" discourse of Jesus. As we will indicate, the passages also form a literary and thèmatic unity and come at a very significant place in the gospel and offer, therefore, a virtual little treatise "De Deo Uno" [On the One God], and provide a hermeneutical key for related issues.

Chapters eleven and twelve provide a distinct section in Mark's literary and theological structure. [8] In the previous chapters, beginning with 8:27, Jesus and his disciples are on a journey. In the preponderance of the verses, Jesus is engaged in private discourse with his disciples, telling them of the necessity of his suffering and death in Jerusalem and instructing them on the meaning of the way of discipleship as they make their "way" toward Jerusalem. Chapters eleven and twelve describe the arrival at Jerusalem and comprise almost exclusively Jesus' public debates with those hostile to him. Throughout the whole section the reader is shown just why Jerusalem will be the locale of suffering and death. At the very time Jerusalem is rejecting Jesus, Jesus is also rejecting Jerusalem, since he proclaims that the temple cult will yield to "a house of prayer for all nations" (11:17) and that the vineyard will be given to others (12:9).

Within chapters eleven-twelve, a distinct break occurs at 12:12, the conclusion of the parable of the vineyard tenants.[9] The mortal opposition to Jesus, first articulated in the gospel in 3:6 with the plan of Jewish authorities to kill Jesus, a plan which is repeated in 11:18, culminates in an abortive attempt to arrest him (12:12), after which those who have been opposing him since the cleansing of the temple leave. In 12:13 a new group of questioners appears, and the exact locale of the three following pericopes is unspecified, so the author must indicate in 12:35 that Jesus was teaching "in the temple," a return to the setting of 11:15-12:12. Not only is there a difference in questioners and location between 11:1-12:12 and 12:13-34, but there is a thematic difference. In the former part the issue could be called that of "Jesus' Messianic authority," and the questions touch on the person of Jesus and the grounding of his authority. The tone of the debates is hostile, and Jesus' answers are enigmatic, e.g., the baptism of John, was it from heaven or of human origin? (11:30), or parabolic, e.g., the vineyard workers (12:1-12). The three pericopes of 12:13-34 are more directly theological, since the issues at stake are the nature and demands of the one God, and the explicit Christological thrust recedes. In contrast to 11:11-12:12, where the authority of Jesus is continually questioned, in 12:12-34 the authority of Jesus to pronounce on difficult issues is assumed, and the questioners address Jesus in honorific language, even if it is slightly ironic.

There are further literary considerations which suggest that the three pericopes within 12:13-34 should be read as a unity.[10] Both the first and the third pericope exhibit a similar structure of debate, where a comment is added to the simple question-answer structure. Though all three pericopes address Jesus in the vocative as "teacher" (12:14, 19, 32), only the first and third mention that Jesus speaks "in truth" (*ep' alētheias*), and both of them contain complimentary ways of addressing Jesus. While the first and third pericope are more "ethical" in dealing with a way of acting consequent on belief in God—dual rendering of what is due to Caesar and to God and dual love of God and neighbor, the middle pericope on the resurrection is more theological, dealing with God as a God of the living (12:26). The structure of this subsection in Mark shows the familiar Markan pattern of threefold narration in the pattern of A,B,A'. Therefore, 12:13-34 is an independent sub-section which conveys a distinct and important theology at a very important place in the Gospel. This importance is now best seen by closer examination of the individual pericopes.

1. Paying Taxes to Caesar (12:13-17)

Before commenting in any detail on the three pericopes which comprise this section, I would like to emphasize a principle of interpretation which characterizes contemporary study of the gospels. As Louis Martyn and Raymond Brown have vividly shown in the case of John, the gospels exist on two levels.[11] On the one hand, they are stories of the past, of events which, for the reader, took place in a previous generation during the historical career of Jesus. At the same time, they are stories through which the Risen Lord continues to instruct the church. Unlike contemporary writers, the Evangelists do not clearly distinguish the level of the past from the level of present address. Also, Mark is a work forged out of the fires of persecution with the ethos of apocalyptic literature which looks to the vindication of those suffering by the imminent punishment of persecutors. In such literature, as, for example, the book of Daniel in the Old Testament and the Revelation of John in the New, those opposing the community are described as figures from the past, We would, therefore, claim that, though in 12:13-34 Jesus is in debate with the Jewish officials of his time, the Markan church is being summoned to hear the words addressed to their own time and their own situation and that this situation has actually influenced the retelling of the story. We will, thus, claim that in these three pericopes the Markan Jesus speaks to his community on the nature and demands of the one God of their Jewish heritage and indicates to them a missionary strategy as they proclaim the gospel of God to the gentiles.

The first section we will discuss, the question of the tribute to Caesar (Mark 12:13-17), is as important and controverted as almost any pericope in the gospels.[12] In form, it is a controversy where Jesus' opponents seek to "trap" him by posing a dilemma: is it right to render the tribute to Caesar or not? Jesus accepts neither alternative, but rather asks for a coin which bears Caesar's image and responds, "Render to Caesar the things of Caesar and to God the things of God." Understanding of this pericope has been obscured by quotation of the answer of Jesus almost as a slogan to justify the autonomy of the secular order, or a modified "two kingdoms" theology where God and Caesar command distinct but not overlapping allegiances. Also, the saying has become so familiar that the real issues facing the Markan community are overlooked. Though one could study the answer of Jesus in terms of the historical context of his ministry, closer analysis of the pericope will show that it is an important point of entry for Mark's presentation of God and God's demands.

Two considerations, one primarily historical and the other primarily literary and theological, enable us to assess the importance of this pericope to Mark's community.

First, Mark composed his gospel approximately forty years after the death of Jesus, most likely shortly after the horrors of the Jewish Wars of A.D. 66–70 which culminated in the destruction of Jerusalem and the temple by the armies of Titus. Seen in this light, Jesus' command to render to Caesar the things of Caesar takes on a distinct coloration. As Josephus attests, one of the things which precipitated the final and cataclysmic confrontation between Rome and the Jewish people was the ascendancy of the Zealot party with their theocratic aspirations to have no ruler but God and their desire to purify the holy land of the gentile presence. [13] Any Jewish Christian group, living in the empire during the period which led up to or followed this confrontation and which claimed allegiance to the God of Abraham, of Isaac and of Jacob (12:27), would have to come to terms with such theocratic claims. The answer of Jesus, that one must "render to God the things of God," brooks no compromise with the claims of God. However, this allegiance to God is not to be translated into theocratic ideology or political action which issues in armed conflict with the gentile Caesar. Such a view is supported by the introductory verses of this pericope where Jesus is called "no respecter of persons," a term which in biblical thought is most often used of God and which, in the New Testament, is used to justify the inclusion of the gentiles in God's saving plan. [14]

Secondly, the similarity in form and structure between the passage on the taxes to Caesar and on the great commandment (12:28–34) suggests that Mark wants us to see these two sections as complementary. Such a perspective precludes definitively an interpretation of the rendering to God and to Caesar which would allege two independent realms of life, one of which is beyond the claim of God. In the section on "The Great Commandment," twice the readers are summoned to love God with their whole hearts, minds and souls and their neighbors as themselves. The claims of God touch all aspects of life and are to be expressed through love. Therefore, the "rendering to Caesar" should be seen, not simply as some form of *détente* with evil secular power, but as a form of love of neighbor. Such a perspective is quite similar to that of Paul in Romans, chapters twelve and thirteen, where, after the exhortation to the community to a love which is genuine (12:9) and to forgiveness of enemies (12:14–20), Paul exhorts the community to obey secular authorities and to pay their taxes (13:1–7) and then immediately returns to the theme, "Owe no one anything except to love one another, for the one who loves a neighbor has fulfilled the law" (13:8). [15]

2. The Question on the Resurrection (12:18–27)

The second of the three pericopes in Mark's short treatise on God is also a controversy. Here, the opponents are the Sadducees who present

to Jesus a rather crass materialistic objection to the resurrection, citing
the Levirate law that a man must marry his brother's widow. They ask
that in the case of the death of seven brothers, who will be married to
whom at the resurrection? In presenting Jesus' response, Mark constructs an ascending response of Jesus:

vs. 24:   you do not understand Scripture nor the power of God
vs. 25:   when they rise from the dead, they neither marry nor are
          given in marriage, but are like the angels in heaven
vs. 26:   As for the dead being raised, have you not read in the book
          of Moses, I am the God of Abraham, and the God of Isaac
vs. 27:   and the God of Jacob; He is not the God of the dead, but
          of the living.

It is the final verses which provide both the greatest problem and the
key to Mark's understanding of God. In reality, the objection of the
Sadducees is answered in vs. 25, when their materialistic conceptions
of the resurrection are rejected. The further argument of vs. 26 is
somewhat subtle to modern ears. The citation of Exodus 3:6, "I am the
God of Abraham, etc.," presupposes that at the time of the appearance to Moses, the patriarchs still lived, since otherwise God could
not be their God. Also, this verse is never used elsewhere to prove the
resurrection, neither in early Christian literature nor in the Jewish
literature of the time.[16] Therefore, we would argue that Mark places
this proof from Exodus here because he wants to communicate a
distinct understanding of God and of resurrection.

What Mark does here is to have Jesus articulate a very spiritualized
concept of the resurrection which is based on the power of God and
God's fidelity to the promises made to the patriarchs. Such a view of
the resurrection is in tension with the early Christian emphasis on
bodily resurrection (cf. 1 Cor. 15:35-50). It is, however, in accord with
Mark's perspective on resurrection since he contains no appearance of
the risen Jesus and in other places in his gospel rejects materialistic interpretations of the resurrection (6:14-29). Mark's spiritualized
understanding of the resurrection is in accord with the spiritualizing
tendency of Hellenistic Christianity as it confronted more materialistic
objections to the resurrection (see 1 Cor. 15:35-38 and Acts 17:32-33).
The saying of Jesus, therefore, touches on the nature of God. God is
the living God who speaks through scripture and affirms his enduring
power over death. At the center of his theological treatise on God, the
Markan Jesus reaffirms the core of Jewish monotheism—that God is a
living God and a God of the living. This affirmation becomes an
equally firm foundation of Christian faith. Resurrection is not return
from the grave, but enduring life in the power of God. God is the one
who has power even over death.[17]

3. The Great Commandment (12:28-34)

The climax of Mark's presentation of Jesus as the one who teaches the way of God in truth (see 12:14, 32) comes when, in response to the question of the scribe as to which commandment is the first of all, Jesus expresses the core of Israel's monotheistic faith by citing the prayer, "Hear, O Israel, the Lord, our God, the Lord is one," from Deuteronomy (6:4-6) and then adds to it the command to love God with whole heart, mind and soul and the neighbor as one's self. Scholars who have studied this pericope intensely, such as Bornkamm and Berger, have argued that it took shape in an environment heavily influenced by Hellenistic Judaism. [18] Also, there is strong evidence that the second half of the pericope, in which the scribe almost in the form of a confession repeats the commandment as uttered by Jesus, is influenced by Mark's editorial activity. Especially noteworthy in this section is the stress on "intellectualistic" language, such as the addition of "with all your mind" to the command as expressed by Jesus and its repetition by the scribe. Also of significance is the statement that love of neighbor is more than burnt offerings or sacrifices. The tendency to stress ethical monotheism beyond cultic activity is characteristic of Hellenistic Judaism in its missionary activity among pagans, as is the propensity to summarize the law under major obligations to God and to neighbor. [19] Therefore, we would suggest that Mark draws here on traditions of his church which were formed in imitation of Jewish mission and apologetic preaching. In the context of Mark's Gospel, the statement of the Great Commandment concludes the last long public teaching of Jesus in Mark, since chapter thirteen is private teaching directed at four disciples. By his placing the great commandment, Mark seems to say that the preaching of the Gospel of God and the summons to repentance with which the gospel begins (1:14-15) now culminate in a theistic affirmation of faith and that the one who makes this confession is like the scribe of 12:34 who is "not far from the kingdom of God."

Not only do these pericopes present to Mark's church the core of its theology, but we would claim they are crucial to its missionary strategy. Recent studies have stressed this missionary purpose of Mark, manifest in such things as Jesus' concern to work miracles of healing and feeding on gentile territory and the culmination of the gospel in the confession of the Centurion that Jesus was a Son of God. [20] In Mark, the section 12:13-34 comes at that precise moment when, in the parable of the vineyard workers (12:1-12), Jesus indicates that the vineyard will be taken away and given to others. Mark's readers are to understand by the vineyard Israel and its heritage as cared for by God and by the "others," they themselves. The way they are to preach to others is to preach what Jesus did, the core of Jewish monotheism, faith in the living God and the presence of even the gentile Caesar in God's plan. The Markan missionary strategy here is not unlike that of Paul in Thessalonica (1 Thess. 1:9) which also builds on the heritage of Jewish monotheism. We would then claim that for Mark, prior to the specifically Christian proclamation of the cross and resurrection of Jesus, is the summons to bring people into contact with the living God who summons them to whole hearted love of both God and neighbor. Such a proclamation would also have relevance in an environment where Christians were accused of being a threat to Caesar, of atheism or disrespect of religion and of being infected with "hatred for the human race," as Tacitus, writing fifty years later, attributes to the Christians of this period. [21]

B. *Discipleship, Christology, and Mark's Theo-logy*

While we hold that the three pericopes of chapter twelve convey a distinct understanding of God oriented to the missionary needs of the Markan community, we would now like to indicate some ways in which Mark's presentation of God touches on the community's understanding of what it means to believe in the gospel and to follow Jesus; that is, on their understanding of discipleship. We will then indicate briefly the way an understanding of Mark's theology sheds light on his Christology.

Over the last decade there have been extensive studies of discipleship in Mark, so much so that for many authors it is the central theme and that the form gospel was created, not simply to communicate information about Jesus, but to depict in narrative form what it means to be involved in response to Jesus. [22] Even amid the disagreements on specific issues there is almost universal consensus that discipleship is hearing the call of Jesus to believe, repent and follow and that the disciples in the gospel provide examples of what it means to be a disciple. Most often the real meaning of discipleship is seen in the summons to "take up one's cross" (8:34) and follow Jesus in the hope that whoever loses his or her life for Jesus' sake and the sake of the gospel will save it. The historical failure of the disciples who in Mark misunderstand Jesus, abandon and finally deny him is seen as a warning against those who would, in Bonhoeffer's terms, view the gospel as "cheap grace," grace without conversion and radical discipleship. [23] In other words, discipleship is seen in the light of Christology. I would like, now, to suggest that there is another understanding of discipleship, less Christological in focus, more in line with Mark's presentation of God, but no less important to Christian theology. I will do this by giving attention to three passages in Mark: 3:31–34, the "true family" of Jesus; 8:33, Peter's rejection of the Passion prediction; and 14:36, the prayer of Jesus in Gethsemane.

1. The True Family of Jesus (3:31-34)

This passage comes at an important place in Mark's structure. After the initial presentation of Jesus as a figure mighty in word and work who heals, exorcises, and triumphs in debate over adversaries, the theme of mortal opposition to Jesus, already intimated in 2:19 and 3:6, becomes explicit. In 3:20 Jesus returns to his home, and "those around him" or his "relatives" seek to restrain him since they think he is "out of his mind." In 3:22 scribes from Jerusalem arrive and accuse Jesus of blasphemy, and in 3:31 the mother and brothers of Jesus appear outside the room where he is debating the scribes and summon him. Clearly, in this section Jesus is pictured as a figure who causes division and misunderstanding, extending even to his natural family.[24] The key verse for our purpose comes when Jesus responds to the request of his family that he cease the debate. (If, as many scholars hold, the "mother and brothers" of 3:30 are the same as "those around Jesus" in 3:20, then his natural family thinks he is out of his mind.[25]) Jesus does not respond directly to the request of his mother and brothers but says rather to the crowd:

> Here are my mother and my brothers! (3:34)
> Whoever does God's will is my brother and sister and mother (3:35).

This saying of Jesus is one which is so radical in its implications that often it is either glossed over or spiritualized. In the context of Mark, Jesus is saying that the true criterion of discipleship is neither physical relationship to him nor having responded to his call. There is a level of commitment demanded which undergirds Christology and is expressed in the doing of God's will. Also, this saying is couched in the form of one of those "universal moral directives," beginning with "whoever" and found all through Mark.[26] It is potentially, therefore, the grounding of a universalistic theology. Throughout Mark there are other cases where those who are not explicitly called to be followers of Jesus or who do not even know him do those very things which the disciples do and are praised by Jesus.[27] Prime examples would be the exorcist who is not a disciple in 9:38 about whom Jesus says, "whoever is not against us is with us," and the person who offers a disciple a drink of water "will not lose his [or her] reward" (9:41). The Markan Jesus, therefore, expresses a view of discipleship which is not rooted in either explicitly hearing or directly responding to his own summons. The foundation of such discipleship is "doing the will of God," and this brings one into a relationship with Jesus which is more intimate than that of his natural family. Mark's view of discipleship is, therefore, wider than "imitation of Christ" or even "imitation of the disciples" in the gospel. The essence of belief in the Gospel is doing the will of God, and the Markan Jesus summons people to such obedience to God rather than simply to literal imitation of his own life. Mark's understanding of God thus provides the way for a more comprehensive theology of discipleship.

2. The Misunderstanding of Peter (8:33)

The great middle section of Mark's gospel, where Jesus begins his journey to Jerusalem where he will suffer and die and during which he speaks most often of the implications of following him, begins with the confession of Peter, "You are the anointed one (Messiah, Christ)" (8:29). Jesus then follows with a prediction of his suffering, death and resurrection in Jerusalem (8:31). Immediately, then, Peter takes Jesus aside and "rebukes" him (8:32); Jesus then turns to Peter and says:

> Get behind me, Satan, because you do not think the thoughts of God, but those of men (8:33).

A number of exegetes hold that the misunderstanding of Peter arises because he is fascinated by a theology of glory which Jesus manifested in his miracles in the first part of the gospel and is unwilling to follow Jesus on the way of the cross. [28] However, the rebuke of Jesus does not confront Peter either with his wrong theology or with his cowardice. After Jesus has stated that "it is necessary" (that is, divinely willed) that he suffer and die, Peter is described as "not thinking the thoughts of God." Peter's fault (and the reason he is called "Satan") is that he does not see the Passion as a thing of God. The problem of suffering for Mark is one of *theodicy,* that God can permit or will the suffering of his beloved, and it is before this mystery that Peter falls. Therefore, in Peter Mark presents us with one whose understanding of God does not permit the scandal of the cross to enter. Again, then, it is the question of the way one thinks about God and not simply one's view of Jesus which becomes crucial for understanding Mark's theology.

3. Jesus in Gethsemane (14:32–42)

In the Garden of Gethsemane Mark's understanding of what it means to do the will of God, what it means to think the things of God, and what it means to be in the family of God, comes to vivid fulfillment in the prayer of the shaken and shattered Jesus as he stands before the mystery of a God who summons him to suffering and death. Jesus prays:

> Abba, Father, all things are possible to you.
> Take this cup from me,
> But not what I will, rather what you will (14:36).

Jesus is the one, then, who literally fulfills the conditions of 3:35, doing the will of God. Jesus is not simply a model to be followed on the way of suffering, but one who, in the midst of suffering, can (unlike Peter) accept suffering as the will of God and still address God as father. Jesus here in Gethsemane thus appears as the true disciple, not as the powerful teacher who summons others to follow him. His discipleship is confrontation with the mystery of God who appears to be pouring out his cup of wrath on the one who, at the baptism and transfiguration, is addressed as "beloved son." Jesus now speaks the language of a little child and addresses God as "Abba," thus embodying his own statement that "whoever does not receive the kingdom of God, like a little child, can not enter it" (10:15). Powerless and defenseless as the child, Jesus can still pray to God as "Abba" and use the language of love in a situation of despair.

In Gethsemane, therefore, Mark's theology or understanding of God and Christology converge. Son of God, which is the first and last title of Jesus in the gospel, can now be properly understood. Mark does not understand it in the categories of the popular religiosity of his time as a term for supernatural heroes or demigods. Much less does he think in the ontological categories of a much later period. Jesus is Son because he hears and does the will of God, because, though loved by God and chosen to proclaim the mystery of the kingdom, he struggled with finding and doing the will of God. Mark's gospel, therefore, does not widen the distance between Jesus and the believer. In calling Jesus, "Son of God," Mark's community affirms solidarity with him and their consciousness that, in doing the will of God, they are to Jesus, brothers and sisters.

II. Theology and Revelation in Mark

We have argued that the way the Markan Jesus speaks of God stresses the transcendence of God. At the same time we have seen that Jesus, whom Mark characterizes as offering a "new teaching in power" (1: 27), is the one who speaks of the way of God in truth (12:14). To affirm this is to raise the question of Mark's understanding of revelation. Though Mark never uses the technical vocabulary of revelation (apokalyptein and its cognates), there are clear indications that he sees in Jesus a unique revelation or disclosure of God. As Jack Kingsbury has most recently noted, this comes forth most dramatically in the scenes of the baptism (1:9-11) and the transfiguration (9:2-8), where Jesus is addressed as "beloved Son" (or Son of God), which highlights more than any single factor the unique filial relationship of Jesus to God.[29] For Kingsbury, the title, Son of God (see esp. 15:39), is normative for Mark in telling the reader the way God "thinks" of Jesus.[30] Other aspects of Mark support the view of Jesus as the revelation of God. The miracles show a Jesus endowed with a power normally reserved to God (e.g., 2:7, forgiving sin; 4:41, calming the waters), and they evoke that atmosphere of numinous wonder which normally accompanies a theophany (e.g., 2:12, they were all amazed and glorified God; 6:50-51, Jesus employs the divine revelational formula, "I am," and the disciples are "utterly astounded"). The exorcisms in

Mark, where Jesus emerges as the stronger one (1:7; 3:26–27), are seen as a conflict between supernatural, extra-human forces, and the demons readily acknowledge Jesus as Son of God (3:11; 5:7).[31] In fact, prior to the confession of the Centurion (15:39), designation of Jesus as Son of God is either by a heavenly voice (1:11; 9:7), or by some extra-human figure. Like the demons, the opponents of Jesus recognize that he is the unique revelation of God (2:7; 12:13) and, in the trial narrative (14:53–65) in response to whether he is the Son of the Blessed, Jesus again uses the revelational formula, "I am," but interprets Son of the Blessed in terms of the returning Son of Man.

However, to describe Jesus as the revelation of God in Mark is to leave unspecified the precise manner in which this revelation is communicated. In order to address this question, we will offer a brief survey of two major directions in the understanding of Jesus as revelation which have emerged in the last decade. They are an understanding of Christ as a "revelatory symbol," as expressed by Avery Dulles in his recent work, *Models of Revelation*, and the depiction of Jesus as "the parable of God," in the work of a number of New Testament scholars and systematic theologians.[32] Limitations of space dictate that we can offer but an inadequate overview which, we hope, will be a stimulus to a more significant engagement. What is remarkable about the works surveyed is that they are written by authors representing different methods, disciplines, and confessional backgrounds; yet, there emerges a significant unified perspective on the way Jesus the Christ can be understood as the revelation of God.

A. Christ as Revelatory Symbol

Dulles presents a panoramic survey of the models of revelation — that is, the ways in which Christianity affirms that the existence of the world and of all that is of ultimate value is due to a personal God who, though transcendent, is known by God's own testimony.[33] He proposes five ways which have dominated at different periods in the history of Christianity: revelation as (a) doctrine, (b) history, (c) inner experience, (d) dialectical presence, and (e) new awareness.[34] To these he adds a sixth which represents for him the most adequate and comprehensive position: revelation as symbolic mediation, which is particularly apt for describing biblical revelation.[35]

Dulles describes a symbol as "a sign pregnant with meaning which is evoked rather than simply stated."[36] Like Norman Perrin, he follows Philip Wheelwright in distinguishing "steno symbols" from "tensive symbols." A steno symbol is reduced to a sign and suggests a one to one correspondence. Tensive symbols are those " 'which draw life from a multiplicity of associations, subtly and for the most part subconsciously interrelated,' and which thereby derive the power to tap a vast potential of semantic energy."[37] Even when speaking simply of symbol, Dulles states that he means "tensive symbols." Dulles notes that symbols can not be restricted to the literary sphere and that "natural objects, historical persons, visible artifacts, and dreams can all be symbols," and that the relation between symbol, analogy, myth, metaphor and parable is often intertwined and complex.[38] Symbols exhibit four qualities which make them apt vehicles of revelation: (a) they give participatory, not speculative knowledge; (b) they have transforming effects; (c) they have a powerful influence on commitments and behavior; and (d) they introduce us into realms of awareness not normally available to discursive thought.[39] Here, Dulles cites Ricoeur's oft quoted phrase, "the symbol gives rise to thought."[40] Examples of such biblical symbols would be the Cross and the Kingdom of God.

The second major influence on Dulles' thought comes from theology. Drawing on Schillebeeckx's earlier description of Jesus as the sacrament of encounter with God and Rahner's understanding of "realizing symbols," he does not hesitate to call Christ "the symbol of God par excellence."[41] "Because any symbol," Dulles writes, "involves an interlocking of two levels of meaning, a 'realizing symbol' will involve two levels of reality."[42] To say that the body is a symbol of the person is to imply that the body is not simply the person, but at the same time the body must manifest the spiritual or transcendent aspect of the person. In similar fashion, Christ's humanity is really identical with himself and not a mere mask, and "this according to Christian belief is his divinity."[43] They present one single "interlocked reality."[44] The other qualities of symbol mentioned above describe the way Christ is present in the scripture and the proclamation of the church. Dulles then concludes his treatment of Christ as the symbol of God by showing the way this model of revelation relates to the other five models, and by presenting the implications of this model for a wide range of theological issues, such as the understanding of the bible, ecclesiology and eschatology.[45] At this point we will leave the richness of Dulles' proposal in order to turn to the other major proposals made in recent years.

B. *Jesus as the Parable of God*

In 1971, at the conclusion of a significant work, *A Future for the Historical Jesus,* Leander Keck drew on the then recent research on the parables, mainly by Robert Funk, and the "word event" theology of Fuchs and Ebeling, to describe Jesus as "the parable of God."[46] Until the 1960s, research on the parables had been dominated by German scholarship which argued tenaciously that every true parable had only one point of comparison and that there was no "surplus of meaning." Parables were thought to be rhetorical forms whereby Jesus presented his teaching of the Kingdom, mainly to hostile opponents, and often the picture part or the images of the parable became mere carriers for "the reality part," the kernel or core of the meaning.[47] In a landmark essay, Robert Funk had argued that parables should be seen rather as metaphors which do not explain or illustrate a subject matter but point to it in such a way that the hearer is required to become engaged in the images or the narrative in order to grasp the parable or, rather, be grasped by it.[48] Following this lead, Keck argued that parable as metaphor requires a reader or hearer to rethink reality in a whole new way, and that parables are not authenticated by discursive retelling but by the depth of life which they touch and reconstruct. Such qualities, Keck argued, are true, not only of the parables told by Jesus, but of the one who tells the parables, so that Jesus is truly the parable of God.[49]

By the mid-seventies scholars, such as John Dominic Crossan, Sallie McFague, and Edward Schillebeeckx, had all explicitly described Jesus as the Parable of God.[50] Such a description was not limited to one gospel, but based on evidence from the whole synoptic tradition, with an occasional reference to the understanding of Jesus in Paul or John.

In 1978, in an article entitled, "Jesus as the Parable of God in the Gospel of Mark," I attempted to extend this line of thought by showing that the Markan Jesus in particular can be called, "the parable of God."[51] My starting point was C.H. Dodd's classic definition of parable: "A metaphor or simile drawn from nature or common life, arresting the hearer by its vividness or strangeness, and leaving the mind in sufficient doubt about its precise application to tease it into active thought."[52] In effect, Dodd calls attention to four qualities of parable: (a) its metaphorical nature, (b) its realism, (c) its paradoxical quality ("by its vividness or strangeness"), and (d) its evocative or inviting power ("leaving the hearer . . ."). More than any other evangelist, Mark pictures Jesus as possessing these same qualities. If by metaphor is meant the referential power of language or the ability to use language from one sphere to lead into realities, then the Markan Jesus does exactly this. By his kingdom proclamation he evokes a whole series of associations of kingdom from Jewish thought, and points beyond himself to the power and activity of God at work in his teaching and ministry. The self-designation by the enigmatic Son of Man derived from Daniel 7:13-14 means that Jesus speaks of his ministry, death and return in a language which combines both lowliness and exaltation and points beyond what is seen to what is actually occurring in his life.

The realism of the Jesus in Mark has long been noted and is often softened by Matthew and Luke. Mark portrays Jesus with a series of strong emotions: pity, (1:41); anger (3:5); indignation (10:14); groans and deep sighs (1:41; 8:12); surprise at unbelief (6:6) — all of which are omitted by Matthew and Luke in their retelling of Mark. Jesus has ignorance of the one who touched him (5:31-32); of what the disciples are discussing (9:33); and of the exact time of the parousia (13:32). As Vincent Taylor remarks: "The sheer humanity of the Markan portraiture catches the eye of the most careless reader."[53]

In a gospel which has been dubbed *The Mysterious Gospel,* strangeness and paradox have long been noted.[54] The Markan Jesus evokes a reaction of surprise, wonder and awe, and the gospel ends with the dramatic phrase, "for they were afraid" (16:8). The Markan Jesus is a figure of paradox who, like a parable, challenges the way we view reality and puts our world askew. The day of the Lord's rest becomes the day of the Lord's labor (2:27-3:5, healing on the sabbath); clean is declared unclean (7:1-27); children who do not even bear the yoke of the kingdom (i.e., observe the Torah) are to enter the kingdom of God (10:13-16); the first shall be last (10:31); and the leaders in the community are to be the servants of others (10:43-44). At the very moment Jesus is being mocked as a false prophet (14:64-65), his prediction of Peter's denial is fulfilled (14:72). The women and Joseph take great pains to place in a tomb him whom no tomb will hold (15:42-16:6). As Werner Kelber has stated: "If there is one single feature which characterizes the Markan Jesus, it is contradiction or paradox," and I have stated in another context, "Irony is the rhetorical medium through which Mark conveys his message of faith."[55]

Finally, the Markan Jesus leaves the reader in sufficient doubt about his meaning to entice him or her into engagement. In the gospel narrative, this takes the form of the summons to discipleship, not only of the twelve, but of those called recently by Rhoads and Michie, "the little people" (e.g., the unknown exorcist, 9:38-41; Bartimaeus, 10:46-52; the woman who anoints Jesus for burial, 14:3-9)—all of whom do those things the chosen twelve are appointed to do, or fail to do.[56] At the beginning of the gospel, the reader is summoned to a change of heart and belief in the gospel (1:14-15), and the prophecies of Jesus which are unfulfilled in the actual narrative (1:8; 13:4-27; 14:28) involve the readers in applying the gospel to themselves. The absence of narratives of the appearance of the risen Jesus means that the gospel is open ended and parabolic. The meaning of Jesus will be answered only in the life of the believers.

This survey, inadequate as it is, would be incomplete without mention of a significant recent work, *The Oral and Written Gospel,* by Werner Kelber.[57] Drawing primarily on the brilliant research of Walter Ong, Kelber offers a full scale study of the dynamics of orality and oral tradition as well as the relation of oral speech to writing and the written tradition. Orality for Kelber suggests vitality, adaptability, and the presence of a living dialogue between people. Writing connotes fixation, distancing, and even the "death" of the oral tradition.

Parables, both in origin and function, are parade examples of orality. Even though there is often a discontinuity between the oral and written tradition, parables possess that kind of power that, when they are taken over by Mark in his gospel, they continue to shape the gospel. He writes: "The parabolic strategy of reorientation by disorientation that marks this gospel's linguistic genesis has likewise etched itself into its story line. Medium and message are connected by a compelling parabolic logic."[58] Therefore, for Kelber, the gospel of Mark may be described as a "written parable."[59] Kelber's work thus represents a culmination of a movement which began by designating *Jesus* as parable, through a description of the *Markan Jesus* as parabolic, to a hermeneutic of the whole *Gospel of Mark* as parabolic.

While, on the surface, the designations of Christ as "revelatory symbol" and of Jesus as "the parable of God" might seem in tension, there are significant convergences between symbol and parable which suggest that we are in a new phase of theological language about the relation of God and Christ. Both symbol and parable are characterized by concreteness and materiality. The symbols of God as rock and fortress (Ps. 18:9), as a mother who can not forget the child of her womb (Isa. 49:15), or as rejected suitor (Hos. 2:1-7), all lead the readers beyond themselves to God who is beyond description and comprehension. Yet, the different connotation and evocations of the different images can not be abandoned like gift wrapping, or the richness of not only the symbol but the reality symbolized is lost. So, too, the God of the parables is both searching woman (Luke 15:8-10) and forgiving father (Luke 15:11-32). Neither is adequate; neither is dispensable. The Jesus of Mark may be symbol and parable, but so, too, is the Jesus of Q (the sayings source behind Matthew and Luke), the Jesus of the pre-Pauline hymns (like Phil. 2:5-11), and the Jesus of Matthew, Luke, John, Paul, and the book of Revelation. Contemporary exegesis has stressed more than ever the plurality of the ways in which the symbol of Jesus has been expressed.

Both symbol and parable thus point beyond the vehicle or carrier of meaning to a deeper level of meaning. They participate in that quality of literature which Wimsatt has designated the "concrete universal."[60] Both symbol and parable resist a one to one correspondence, and both are effective, not simply on the intellectual level, but by their power to touch the depths of human experience and feeling. Both symbol and parable have a surplus of meaning which explains their enduring and open-ended quality, and both are effective only when the recipient becomes involved in the dynamism of the symbol or the interpretation of the parable. Thus, both appeal to the deepest level of human freedom where a person shapes his or her future by the choices made.

In terms of what we have attempted in the first major part of our presentation, the categories of parable and symbol are most apt for a contemporary representation by theology of the way the Jesus of Mark speaks of God, of his own relation to God, and the demands of God (that is, the summons to discipleship). We initially stressed the Markan emphasis on the transcendence of God and the reserved way in which Jesus speaks of God. The Markan Jesus, like the parables he utters, directs attention from and through himself to God. Mark's short theological treatise (12:13–34) provides a concrete illustration of the way Jesus speaks of God. Here, Jesus is initially addressed in categories usually reserved for God (e.g., no respecter of persons, 12:13) and, yet, points beyond himself to God as a God of the living who is to be worshipped with whole heart and soul. The interpretation of the relation of Christology and discipleship which we depicted corresponds to the self-involving quality of parable and symbol. A symbol or parable must be appropriated; Jesus as symbol or parable summons to engagement in his life and his fate. Jesus, who in the Garden begs his Father to remove the chalice of suffering and whose last words are, "My God, My God, why have you forsaken me?" (15:34), is at the same time the beloved Son (1:11; 9:7; 12:6), who is proclaimed at his death as truly the Son of God (15:39). This is a vivid illustration of the *"coincidentia oppositorum"* (the joining of opposites) which characterizes religious and symbolic speech and parabolic paradox.[61] Later theology will express this paradox in the more speculative language of two natures and one person, but this language, while interpretative of the symbol, must remain in constant dialogue with it.[62] The symbol may give rise to thought (Ricoeur), but thought must remain in constant dialogue with symbol and parable. Thus, the revelation of God in Mark offers a test case of the way in which a theology and Christology, which emerge on the basis of the literary and historical methods of exegesis, will always exist in dialogue with a more speculative mode of thought. The way from symbol to meaning and from parable to interpretation is always an open ended dialogue. The reflections on these areas which emerged with such force in the 1970s are but the seeded ground for a harvest, the first buds of which we have sketched.

III. Revelation and Proclamation in Mark

At this time I would like to speak less as a New Testament exegete, offering observations about what Mark's gospel meant to the believers of his time, and more as a Christian, reflecting on the meaning of Mark for our lives together today. I will organize my concluding reflections around the three major areas of the essay: (a) Mark's distinctive language about God, (b) its use in the missionary situation of his church, and (c) its significance for us who have been called to be "a community of disciples."

Initially, we noted that Mark speaks of God in a sober and reserved way, avoiding those anthropomorphisms which were customary in the

Jewish writings of his time and which are attested eleswhere in the New Testament. Such language emphasizes the distance and mystery of God, so it is not surprising that manifestations of God throughout the gospel are accompanied by reactions of awe, fear, wonder, and surprise.

In effect, then, we would say that Mark did not hesitate to adopt or appropriate a language about God which did not compromise the mystery of God and which was adapted to the missionary needs of his community, most likely to the gentile mission where the traditional Jewish ways of speaking about God might have been misunderstood or have become a stumbling block. We, today, in a pluralistic world, are constantly faced with a similar challenge: how to speak about God in a way which is faithful to our tradition, but sensitive to the offense or scandal this may cause. Such a challenge is especially pressing in terms of the concerns raised by women in church and society on the way the language of God, nurtured for the most part in a Near Eastern and Mediterranean patriarchal society and enshrined in centuries of liturgy and worship, can speak to them today. A decade of reflection on the use of patriarchal metaphors applied to God and attempt to construct more sex inclusive language when applied to God's action in history have shown that the task is not impossible, though no less demanding. Similar challenges face us when trying to speak a theological language sensitive to the concerns of people of a different culture (for example, people of Africa or India) and sensitive to people of a different social group or even of a stage in life (such as the youth in our own culture). The enterprise, begun by Mark when he created the genre gospel and called it "the good news of God," remains our legacy. Secondly, in respect to Mark's distinctive language, we should not underestimate the importance of the language of transcendence and mystery in contemporary theology. Much of recent Christian theology has really made God too readily available in Jesus and often devolves into a rather saccharine Jesus piety. The Jesus of Mark who speaks, not of himself, but of God, is a figure who "groans in the spirit" (8:12), confesses ignorance of the day or hour of the parousia (13:32), and dies with the cry, "My God, My God, why have you forsaken me?" (15:34). We must never forget that today many people are struggling with a problem more basic than the meaning of the life and teaching of Jesus, but with the problem of God and of belief itself. Karl Rahner has posed the challenge with his usual insight:

> It is not a few isolated tenets of faith from a host of other convictions which are in danger today, but faith itself; the ability to believe, the capacity for developing an unequivocal comprehensive and challenging belief and making it powerfully effective in our lives and throughout our lives.[63]

I would suggest that one reason which explains the intense engagement with the Gospel of Mark, not only among scholars, but among the most diverse people today, is Mark's unflinching confrontation with the mystery of God and the radicality of the gospel's summons to believe, which resonates in the most profound religious quests of the human heart.

The Missionary Dimension:

What I am about to say is implicit in what has been said. In treating Mark's short theological treatise of 12:13-34, we stressed that Mark put on the lips of Jesus teaching on three issues which would have been of vital concern to the missionaries of his church: the challenge of unconditioned loyalty to God in a non-theocratic society, where one must also render to Caesar the things of Caesar; the nature of God as a God of the living, faithful to the covenant promises, from whom even death can not cause separation; and the whole law, summed up in love of God and neighbor. These are the Markan essentials of belief for one who is "not far from the kingdom of God." The Markan missionary strategy is to speak of God and God's relevance to the most central issue of life. Again, I would suggest that the missionary enterprise of the church today must not lose sight of its basic mandate to speak to people of God—this is, after all, what theology in its etymological sense is all about—discourse about God. A modern example of engagement in such a challenge is provided by Vincent Donovan in *Christianity Rediscovered,* an account of his missionary work among the Masai people of East Africa.[64] While it is impossible to summarize this stimulating and significant work, I will call attention to one incident. Donovan recounts that there was a general feeling among the missionaries that "it would be a hundred years before the Masai are willing and ready to talk with us about God" and that the dominant missionary strategy was to provide schools, hospitals, and technical skills.[65] Donovan describes his growing dissatisfaction with these views and his desire to live among the Masai and speak to them of God. He tells of the beginning of this experiment when he first went to a Masai Kraal and told the elder of his desire to speak of God. His words speak more eloquently than mine:

> I then pointed out that we were well known among the Masai for our work in schools and hospitals, and for our interest in the Masai and their cattle. But now I no longer wanted to talk about schools and hospitals, but about God in the life of the Masai, and about the message of Christianity. Indeed it was for this very work of explaining the message of Christianity to the different peoples of Africa that I came here from long away.

> Ndangoya looked at me for a long time, and then said in a puzzled way, "If that is why you came here, why did you wait so long to tell us about it?"[66]

At their baptisms, Christians are commissioned to herald the word of God, just as Jesus' baptism was his commission to proclaim the kingdom of God. The life of Jesus, portrayed in the gospels, is the life of one who spoke of God to the most diverse kinds of audiences: learned scribes and Pharisees, laborers whom he called to be disciples, tax collectors, sinners, gentiles, and Samaritans—people who represented the religious traditions of his people as well as those whom those very traditions called outcasts. In so doing, he shocked and shattered the conventions of his society and, like the parables he uttered, caused surprise and wonder. Jesus took the language of the world of his own experience—the world of the simple rhythm of farming, of the unexpected joy in finding a treasure, and even that of somewhat shady business practices (Luke 16:1-9)—and made that world carry the message of God's mercy and love. It is incumbent on the church today to take up into its message the world of everyday experience where people live and work, suffer and die, and make it the carrier of the good news. In this sense, not only will Jesus be the parable of God, but the church itself is summoned to be a living parable of God.

Finally (and this word may be for the weary the best news I have given about Mark's good news), as a people who hears the word of God and proclaims it, like the disciples in Mark 10:29, we have acquired new "brothers, sisters, mothers, fathers and children for the sake of the gospel." We are, in terms used by John Paul II, "a community of disciples."[67] We are also a family of faith, and in this family are not simply those who explicitly followed the call of Jesus, but those, like the unknown exorcist of Mark (9:38-41), who confront the power of evil, who do the work of Jesus and are "for him," and who do the will of God and are, therefore, brothers, sisters, and mother to Jesus. Solidarity with those of the faith and those who do the will of God is to characterize the Christian today. Such a perspective provides the basis for a sense of vocation and mission which transcends denominational adherence and, hence, is catholic in the sense of universal; it also provides a way of thinking about the church, the new temple, as a house of prayer for all people (Mark 11:17). In an age when the things of Caesar threaten to consume the things of God, only a common sense of standing before the mystery of God can confront the idolatry of power. In a culture like that of the United States, where the prime cultural value is "autonomy," a sense of unhindered self determination, the call to love the neighbor as one's very own self can be heard only by those who are open to loving God with heart and mind. In the face of so much in our society which speaks of death, and confronted with the possible extinction of human life by nuclear holocaust, we must have the courage to speak of the God of Abraham, of Isaac, and of Jacob, a God of the living, whose final message, spoken before the door of death now emptied of its power, is: "Do not be alarmed; he is not here, he has been raised up" (Mark 16:6).

NOTES

[1] Some helpful surveys of recent research are H. Conzelmann, "Literaturbericht zu den Synoptischen Evangelien," *TRu* 37 (1972): 220-72; S.P. Kealy, *Mark's Gospel: A History of Its Interpretation* (New York: Paulist, 1982); H.C. Kee, "Mark's Gospel in Recent Research," in J. L. Mays, ed., *Interpreting the Gospels* (Philadelphia: Fortress, 1981), pp. 130-47 (= *Int* 34 (1978): 353-68); J. Kingsbury, "The Gospel of Mark in Current Research," *RelSRev* 5 (1979): 101-107.

[2] "The Neglected Factor in New Testament Theology," *Reflection* (Yale Divinity School) 73 (1975): 5-8.

[3] The content of the first major section of this essay has been covered with extensive exegetical detail and documentation in J. Donahue, "A Neglected Factor in the Theology of Mark," *JBL* 101 (1982): 563-94.

[4] Kingdom sayings, 1:15; 4:11; 4:26; 4:30; 9:1; 9:47; 10:14-15; 10:23-25; 12:34; 14:25; 15:43 (by the narrator); Old Testament citations, 12:23, 3 times citing Exod. 3:2; 12:30, citing Josh. 22:5; 15:34, citing Ps. 22:1; the citations of Micah 3:1 in Mark 1:1 and of Zech. 13:7 in Mark 14:27 make God the subject of the action.

[5] In 1:24 a demon calls Jesus "holy one of God."

[6] *kyrios* in explicit Old Testament citations: 12:11 = Ps. 118:23; 12:29-30 (3 times) = Deut. 6:4 − 5; 12:36 (twice) = Ps. 110:1; by the narrator citing the Old Testament, 1:3 = Isa. 40:3; 11:9 = Ps. 118:36.

[7] See R. Marcus, "Divine Names and Attributes in Hellenistic Jewish Literature," *Proceedings of the American Academy of Jewish Research*, 1931-32 (Philadelphia: Jewish Publication Society of America, 1932), pp. 43-120.

[8] The first ten chapters take place, for the most part, in Galilee and other regions north of Jerusalem and Judea, while from chapter eleven Jesus remains totally in Jerusalem. The whole Jerusalem section is structured by time references to days (e.g., 11:11, 19; 14:1, 12), giving the impression of a week spent in Jerusalem. Chapters eleven and twelve consist of a traditional group of controversies set in Jerusalem; see M. Albertz, *Die Synoptischen Streitsgespräche* (Berlin: Trowitsch und Sohn, 1921), and M. Cook, *Mark's Treatment of Jewish Leaders* (NovTSup 51; Leiden: Brill, 1978).

[9] E. Lohmeyer, *Das Evangelium des Markus* (MeyerK 1/2; 17th ed.; Göttingen: Vandenhoeck und Ruprecht, 1967), p. 249; R. Pesch, *Das Markusevangelium* (2 vols.; HTKNT 2; Freiburg/Basel/Wein: Herder, 1976-77), 2.224. Lohmeyer counts 12:13-34 as a distinct unity, and Pesch describes 12:13-34 as *Jesu messianische Lehre im Tempel*.

[10] In what follows here, I draw heavily on J. Dewey, *Markan Public Debate: Literary Technique, Concentric Structure and Theology in Mark 2:1-3:6* (SBLDS 48; Chico, CA: Scholars Press, 1980), esp. pp. 54-63; 155-67.

[11] R. Brown, *The Community of the Beloved Disciple* (New York: Paulist, 1979); L. Martyn, *History and Theology in the Fourth Gospel* (rev. ed.; Nashville: Abingdon, 1979).

[12] In addition to the treatments in the standard commentaries, see O. Cullmann, *The State in the New Testament* (New York: Scribner's, 1956), p. 20; J. M.D. Derrett, "Render to Caesar," in *Law in the New Testament* (London: Darton, Longmann and Todd, 1970), pp. 313-38; C.H. Giblin, "The 'Things of God' in the Question Concerning Tribute to Caesar (Lk 20:25; Mk 12:17; Mt 22:21)," *CBQ* 33 (1971):510-27; M. Hengel, *Christ and Power* (Philadelphia: Fortress, 1977), p. 19.

[13] For an excellent history of this period, based on the writings of Josephus, see D. Rhoads, *Israel in Revolution* (Philadelphia: Fortress, 1976).

[14] Acts 10:34; Rom. 2:11; Eph. 6:9; Col. 3:25; James 2:9. This language suggests judicial impartiality, and in Acts and Romans is used to undergird God's acceptance of the gentiles.

[15] On the relation of the church to civil authorities, see the recent study of V. Furnish, *The Moral Teaching of Paul* (Nashville: Abingdon, 1979), Chapter V.

[16] J. Wellhausen, *Das Evangelium Marci* (Berlin: Georg Reimer, 1909), p. 95. From the foundation that God was a God of the living, the Old Testament concluded that the dead were separated from God (see Ps. 6:5).

[17] E. Schweizer, *The Good News According to Mark* (Atlanta: John Knox, 1977), p. 249: "He [Jesus] points to God's power which goes beyond the limits of our imagination and to God's present promise which exceeds our power of comprehension and will therefore be stronger than death."

[18] There is a growing consensus that the double command of love took shape in an environment strongly influenced by Hellenistic wisdom, rather than in Palestinian Christianity. See K. Berger, *Die Gesetzesauslegung Jesu, Teil 1, Markus und Parallelen* (WMANT 40; Neukirchen-Vluyn: Neukirchener, 1972), pp. 11-202; G. Bornkamm, "Das Doppelgebot der Liebe," in *Neutestamentliche Studien f. R. Bultmann* (BZNW 21; Berlin: Gruyter, 1954), pp. 85-93; B. Gerhardsson, "The Hermeneutical Program in Matthew 22:37-40," in *Jews, Greeks and Christians*, Fs. W.D. Davies, ed. R. Scroggs and R. Hamerton-Kelly (Leiden: Brill, 1976), pp. 129-50; R.H. Fuller, "The Double Commandment of Love," in *Essays in the Love Command*, ed. R.H. Fuller (Philadelphia: Fortress, 1978), pp. 41-56. Fuller goes against the "Hellenistic consensus" and derives the command from the historical Jesus.

[19] Berger, *Gesetzesauslegung*, pp. 143-65.

[20] R. Pesch (*Markusevangelium*, 1.53-63) has stressed very strongly the missionary purpose of Mark, calling it a *Missionsbuch*. See also D. Senior, "The Struggle to be Universal: Mission as a Vantage Point for New Testament Investigation," forthcoming in the *CBQ*.

[21] Tacitus, *Ann.* 15:44, states that Christians were persecuted "odio generis humani." See S. Benko, "Pagan Criticism of Christianity During the First Two Centuries," in *Aufstieg und Niedergang der römischen Welt*, ed. W. Haase (Berlin/New York: Gruyter, 1980), vol. 23, 1065; P. Keresztztes, "The Imperial Roman Government and the Christian Church. I, From Nero to the Servii," *Ibid.*, 215.

[22] The major monographs on discipleship are (in chronological order): R.P. Meye, *Jesus and the Twelve: Discipleship and Revelation in Mark's Gospel*

(Grand Rapids: Eerdmans, 1968); S. Freyne, *The Twelve: Disciples and Apostles* (London: Sheed and Ward, 1968); K-G. Reploh, *Markus—Lehrer der Gemeinde* (SBM 9; Stuttgart: Katholisches Bibelwerk, 1969); G. Schmahl, *Die Zwölf im Markusevangelium* (Trier: Paulinus, 1974); K. Stock, *Die Boten aus dem Mit-Ihm Sein* (AnBib 70; Rome: Biblical Institute, 1975); E. Best, *Following Jesus: Discipleship in the Gospel of Mark* (JSNTSup 4; Sheffield: JSOT Press, 1981); J. Donahue, *The Theology and Setting of Discipleship in the Gospel of Mark* (Milwaukee: Marquette University, 1983). A very important article is R. Tannehill, "The Disciples in Mark: The Function of a Narrative Role," *JR* 57 (1977): 386-405.

[23] D. Bonhoeffer, *The Cost of Discipleship* (New York: Macmillan, 1959).

[24] On the complicated development of this pericope, see R. Pesch, *Markusevangelium*, 1. 209-25.

[25] J.D. Crossan, "Mark and the Relatives of Jesus," *NovT* 15 (1973): 81-113; W. Kelber, *The Kingdom in Mark: A New Place and a New Time* (Philadelphia: Fortress, 1974), p. 25.

[26] Q. Quesnell, *The Mind of Mark* (AnBib 38; Rome: Biblical Institute, 1969), pp. 134-38.

[27] On those in the gospel who, though not explicitly called disciples, do the same kinds of things as the disciples, see E. Schweizer, "The Portrayal of the Life of Faith in the Gospel of Mark," in Mays, *Interpreting the Gospels*, 172-73 = *Int* 32 (1978): 391-93. In the course of an interesting study of characterization in Mark, D. Rhoads and D. Michie call such people the "little people." See *Mark as Story* (Philadelphia: Fortress, 1982), pp. 129-36.

[28] The most vigorous proponent of this view is T. Weeden, *Mark: Traditions in Conflict* (Philadelphia: Fortress, 1971). In basic agreement with his view is Werner Kelber, *Kingdom in Mark*, p. 146; "The Hour of the Son of Man and the Temptation of the Disciples," in *The Passion in Mark*, ed. W. Kelber (Philadelphia: Fortress, 1976), pp. 41-60; and *Mark's Story of Jesus* (Philadelphia: Fortress, 1979), esp. 46-49.

[29] J.D. Kingsbury, *The Christology of Mark's Gospel* (Philadelphia: Fortress, 1983), p. 66.

[30] *Ibid.*, pp. 67-68.

[31] Gerd Theissen, *The Miracle Stories of the Early Christian Tradition* (Philadelphia: Fortress, 1983), p. 89: "The possessed person is the theatre of a conflict between supernatural, extra-human forces."

[32] A. Dulles, *Models of Revelation* (Garden City, NY: Doubleday, 1983). Those who describe Jesus as the parable of God will be listed below in n. 50.

[33] Dulles, *Models*, p. 3.

[34] *Ibid.*, pp. 36-114.

[35] *Ibid.*, pp. 122-54.

[36] *Ibid.*, p. 132.

[37] *Ibid.*, citing Philip Wheelwright, *Metaphor and Reality* (Bloomington: Indiana University, 1962), p. 94. Dulles also cites N. Perrin who earlier had made extensive use of the distinction between "steno" and "tensive" symbols in his *Jesus and the Language of the Kingdom* (Philadelphia: Fortress, 1976), esp. pp. 29-32.

[38] Dulles, *Models*, p. 133.

[39] *Ibid.*, pp. 136-38.

⁴⁰ *Ibid.*, p. 137; P. Ricoeur, *The Symbolism of Evil* (Boston: Beacon, 1969), p. 348.

⁴¹ Dulles, *Models*, p. 158; The works Dulles calls on here are E. Schillebeeckx, *Christ the Sacrament of the Encounter with God* (New York: Sheed and Ward, 1963), p. 18, and K. Rahner, "The Theology of Symbol," in *Theological Investigations*, vol. 4 (Baltimore: Helicon, 1966), pp. 221-52.

⁴² Dulles, *Models*, p. 159.

⁴³ *Ibid.*

⁴⁴ *Ibid.* Dulles cites here the Vatican II document, *Lumen Gentium*, art. 8.

⁴⁵ *Ibid.*, pp. 193-210; 211-27; 228-45.

⁴⁶ L. Keck, *A Future for the Historical Jesus* (Nashville: Abingdon, 1971), pp. 243-49; R. Funk, *Language, Hermeneutic and the Word of God* (New York: Harper and Row, 1966), esp. ch. 3, "Language as Event: Fuchs and Ebeling," and ch. 5, "The Parable as Metaphor."

⁴⁷ Excellent surveys of the development of research into the parables are: N. Perrin, *Jesus and the Language of the Kingdom*, pp. 89-193; W. Harrington, "The Parables in Recent Study," *BTB* 2 (1972): 219-41; J. Kingsbury, "Major Trends in Parable Interpretation," *CTM* 42 (1971): 579-96.

⁴⁸ Above, n. 46.

⁴⁹ Keck, *Future*, p. 243.

⁵⁰ J. Crossan: "Jesus proclaimed God in parables, but the primitive church proclaimed Jesus as the Parable of God" [*In Parables: The Challenge of the Historical Jesus* (New York: Harper and Row, 1973), p. xiv.]; S. McFague: ". . . we consider *Jesus as a parable of God" [Metaphorical Theology Models of God in Religious Language* (Philadelphia: Fortress, 1982), p. 48.]; this whole section of McFague's work, entitled "Metaphor, Parable and Scripture," pp. 31-66, is indispensable for engagement with the study of Jesus as parable; see also her earlier work, *Speaking in Parables: A Study in Metaphor and Theology* (Philadelphia: Fortress, 1975); E. Schillebeeckx: "Jesus is a parable and he tells parables" [*Jesus: An Experiment in Christology* (New York: Crossroads, 1979), p. 116.]. Though Schillebeeckx's work was published in Dutch in 1974, it did not become significant in the United States until its publication in English.

⁵¹ First published in *Int* 32 (1978): 369-86, reprinted in Mays, *Interpreting the Gospels*, pp. 148-67.

⁵² C.H. Dodd, *The Parables of the Kingdom* (New York: Scribner's, 1961), p. 16.

⁵³ V. Taylor, *The Gospel according to St. Mark* (London: Macmillan, 1966), p. 121.

⁵⁴ T.A. Burkill, *Mysterious Revelation: An Examination of the Philosophy of St. Mark's Gospel* (Ithaca, NY: Cornell University, 1963). In a discussion at the meeting of the Society for the Study of the New Testament at Duke University in 1976, the eminent New Testament scholar, Ernst Käsemann, said of Mark: "The mysterious gospel continues to guard its mysteries."

⁵⁵ Quote by Donahue is found in *The Passion in Mark*, p. 79; that by Kelber, *Ibid.*, p. 179.

⁵⁶ Above, n. 27.

⁵⁷ (Philadelphia: Fortress, 1983).

⁵⁸ *Ibid.*, p. 131.

⁵⁹ *Ibid.*, p. 220.

[60] W.K. Wimsatt, *Verbal Icon* (New York: Noonday Press, 1953), pp. 69-83, for a discussion of the concrete universal.

[61] Dulles, *Models*, p. 138, who is citing here M. Eliade, *Patterns in Comparative Religion* (New York: Sheed and Ward, 1958), p. 419.

[62] Dulles, *Models*, p. 159: "The classical doctrine of the 'two natures' spells out in more conceptual language the implications of the symbolic character of Christ as God's concrete revelation in the flesh."

[63] *Belief Today* (New York: Sheed and Ward, 1967), p. 68.

[64] (Maryknoll, NY: Orbis, 1982).

[65] *Ibid.*, p. 15.

[66] *Ibid.*, p. 22.

[67] John Paul II, *Redemptor Hominis*, n. 21. See the use of "community of disciples" as a model for the church in A. Dulles, *A Church to Believe In: Discipleship and the Dynamics of Freedom* (New York; Crossroad, 1982), pp. 1-18.

Index of Persons